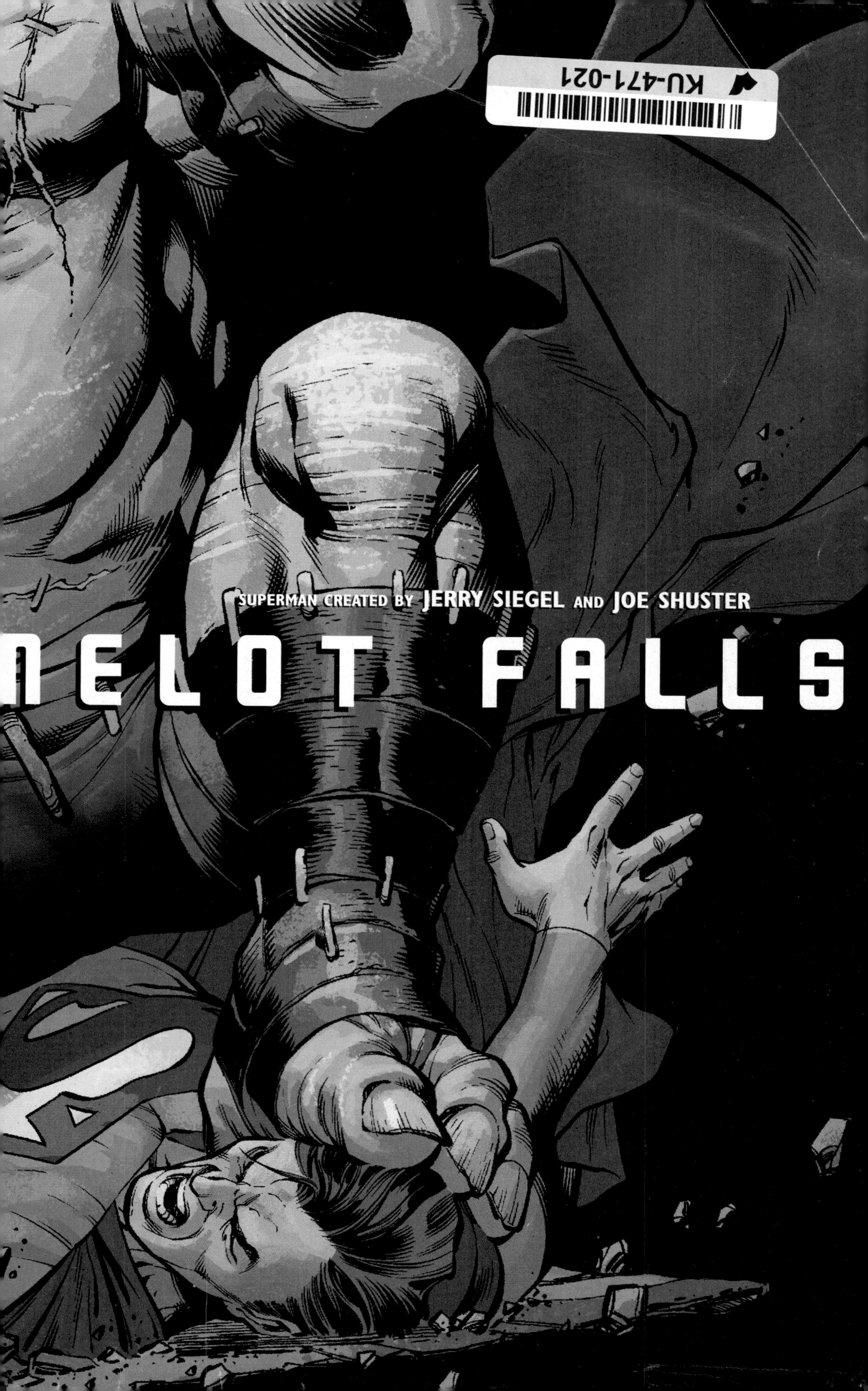
SUPERMAN CREATED BY JERRY SIEGEL AND JOE SHUSTER
NELOT FALLS

Dan DiDio
Senior VP-Executive Editor

Matt Idelson
Editor-original series

Nachie Castro
Associate editor-original series

Bob Harras
Group Editor-collected edition

Robbin Brosterman
Senior Art Director

Paul Levitz
President & Publisher

Georg Brewer
VP-Design & DC Direct Creative

Richard Bruning
Senior VP-Creative Director

Patrick Caldon
Executive VP-Finance & Operations

Chris Caramalis
VP-Finance

John Cunningham
VP-Marketing

Terri Cunningham
VP-Managing Editor

Stephanie Fierman
Senior VP-Sales & Marketing

Alison Gill
VP-Manufacturing

Hank Kanalz
VP-General Manager, WildStorm

Jim Lee
Editorial Director-WildStorm

Paula Lowitt
Senior VP-Business & Legal Affairs

MaryEllen McLaughlin
VP-Advertising & Custom Publishing

John Nee
VP-Business Development

Gregory Noveck
Senior VP-Creative Affairs

Cheryl Rubin
Senior VP-Brand Management

Jeff Trojan
VP-Business Development, DC Direct

Bob Wayne
VP-Sales

Cover illustration by Carlos Pacheco and Jesús Merino
Cover colored by Dave Stewart

SUPERMAN: Camelot Falls

Published by DC Comics.
Cover and compilation copyright © 2007 DC Comics.
All Rights Reserved.

Originally published in single magazine form in
SUPERMAN 654-658. Copyright ©2006 DC Comics.
All Rights Reserved. All characters, their distinctive like-
nesses and related elements featured in this publication
are trademarks of DC Comics. The stories, characters and
incidents featured in this publication are entirely
fictional. DC Comics does not read or accept unsolicited
submissions of ideas, stories or artwork.

DC Comics, 1700 Broadway, New York, NY 10019
A Warner Bros. Entertainment Company
Printed in Canada. First Printing.

HC ISBN: 1-4012-1204-2
HC ISBN 13: 978-1-4012-1204-9
SC ISBN: 1-4012-1205-0
SC ISBN 13: 978-1-4012-1205-6

Special thanks to Amy Calkins, Lucian Muntean
& Nataša Stanković

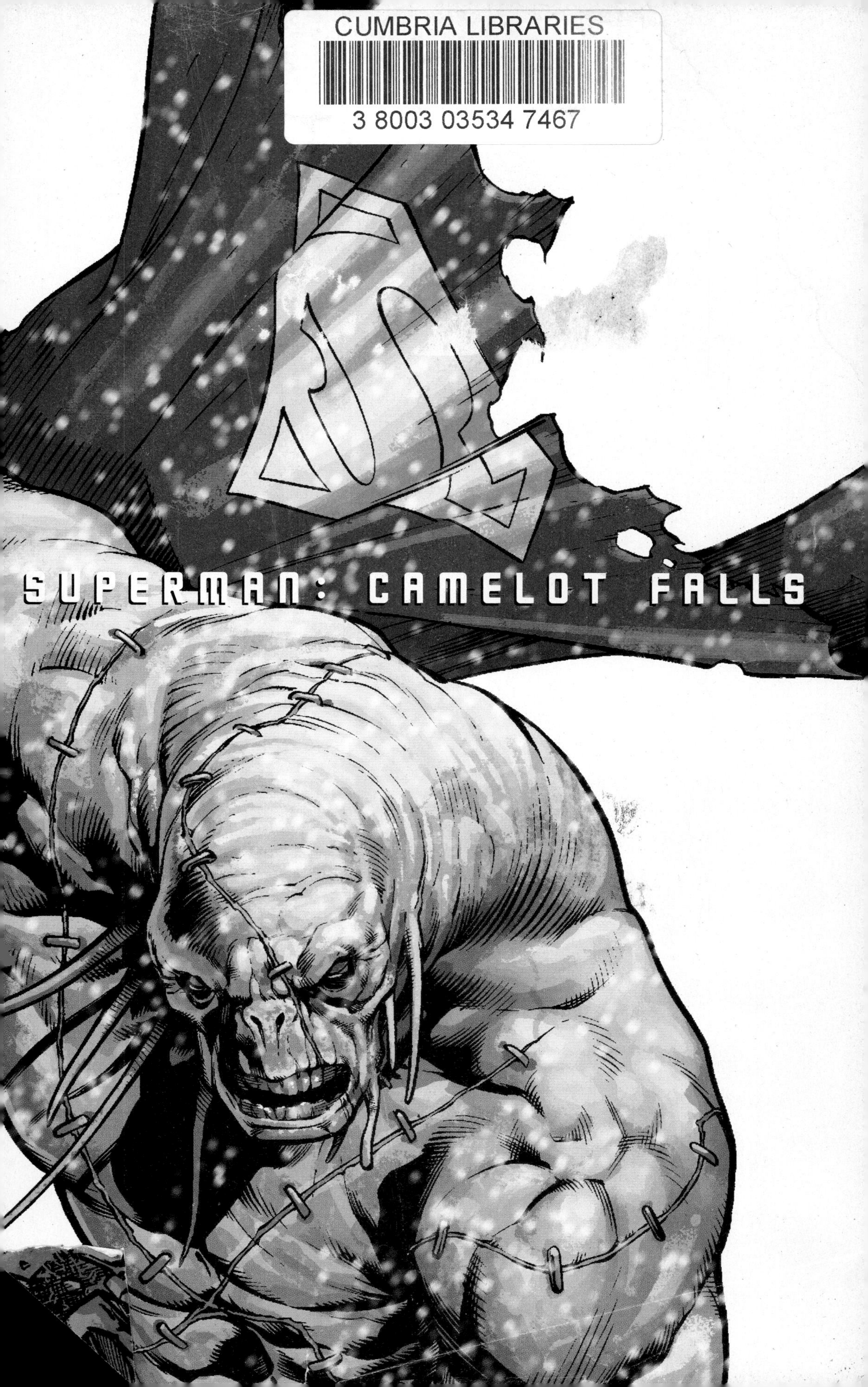
SUPERMAN: CAMELOT FALLS

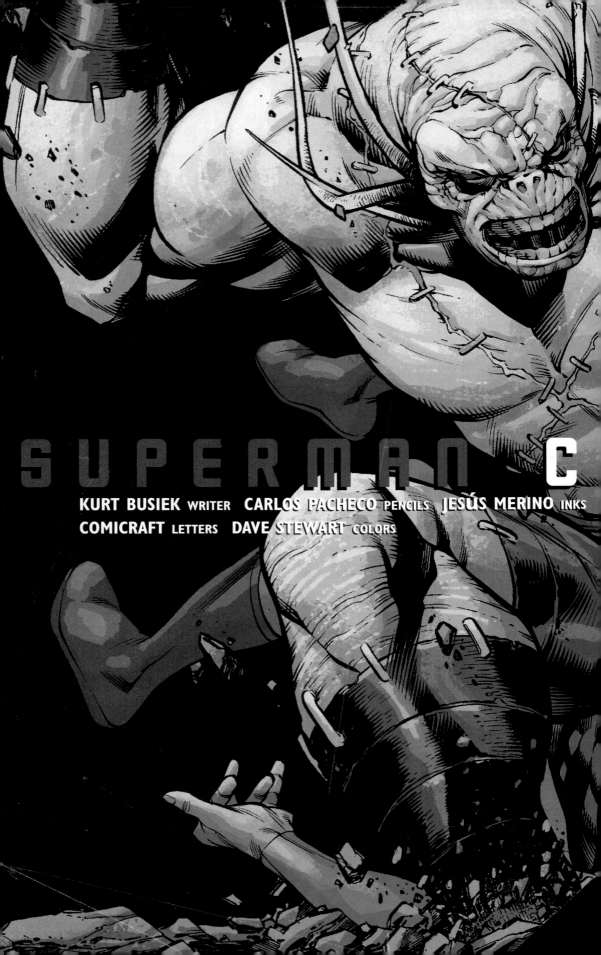

SUPERMAN C

KURT BUSIEK WRITER **CARLOS PACHECO** PENCILS **JESÚS MERINO** INKS
COMICRAFT LETTERS **DAVE STEWART** COLORS

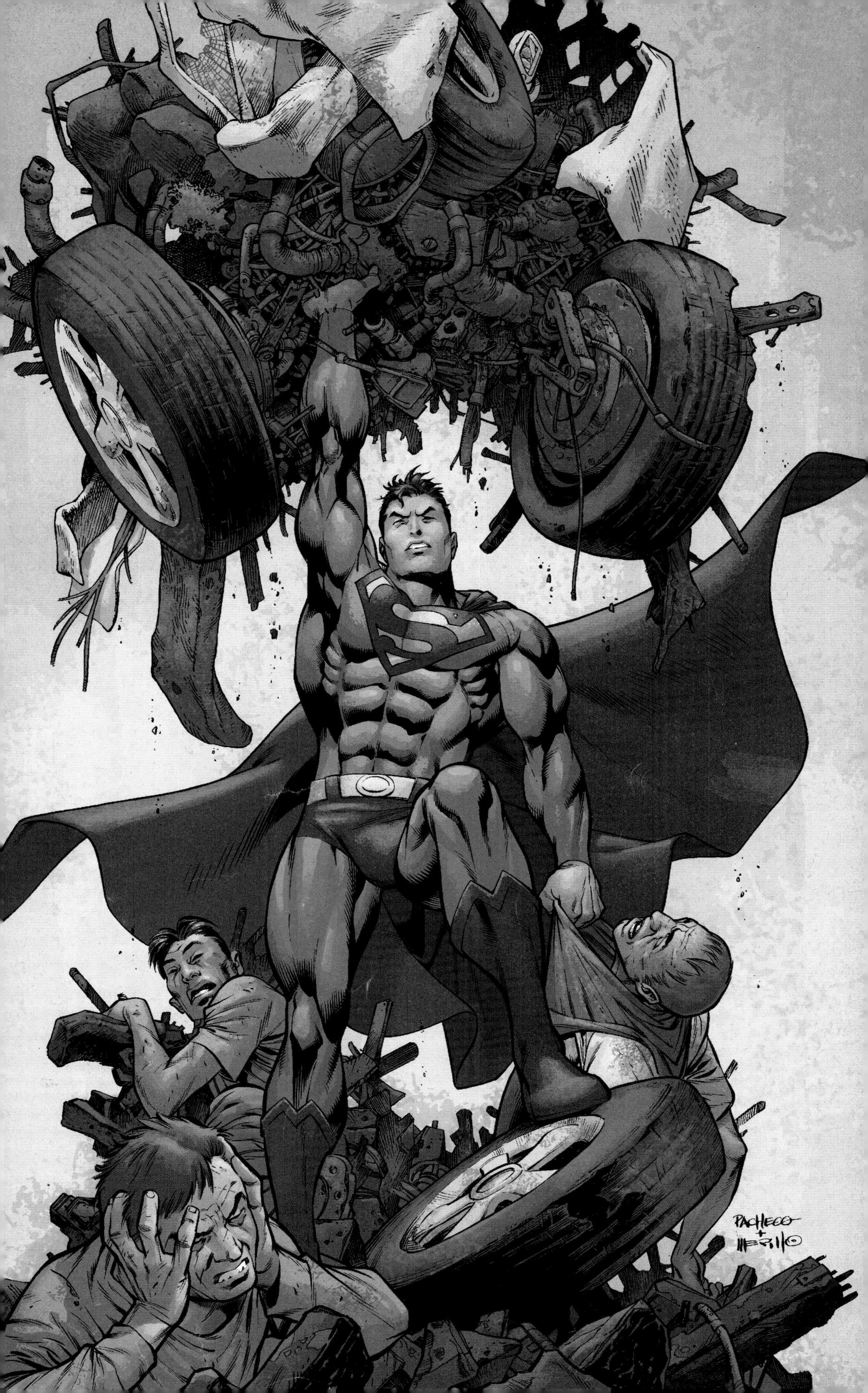
PACHECO

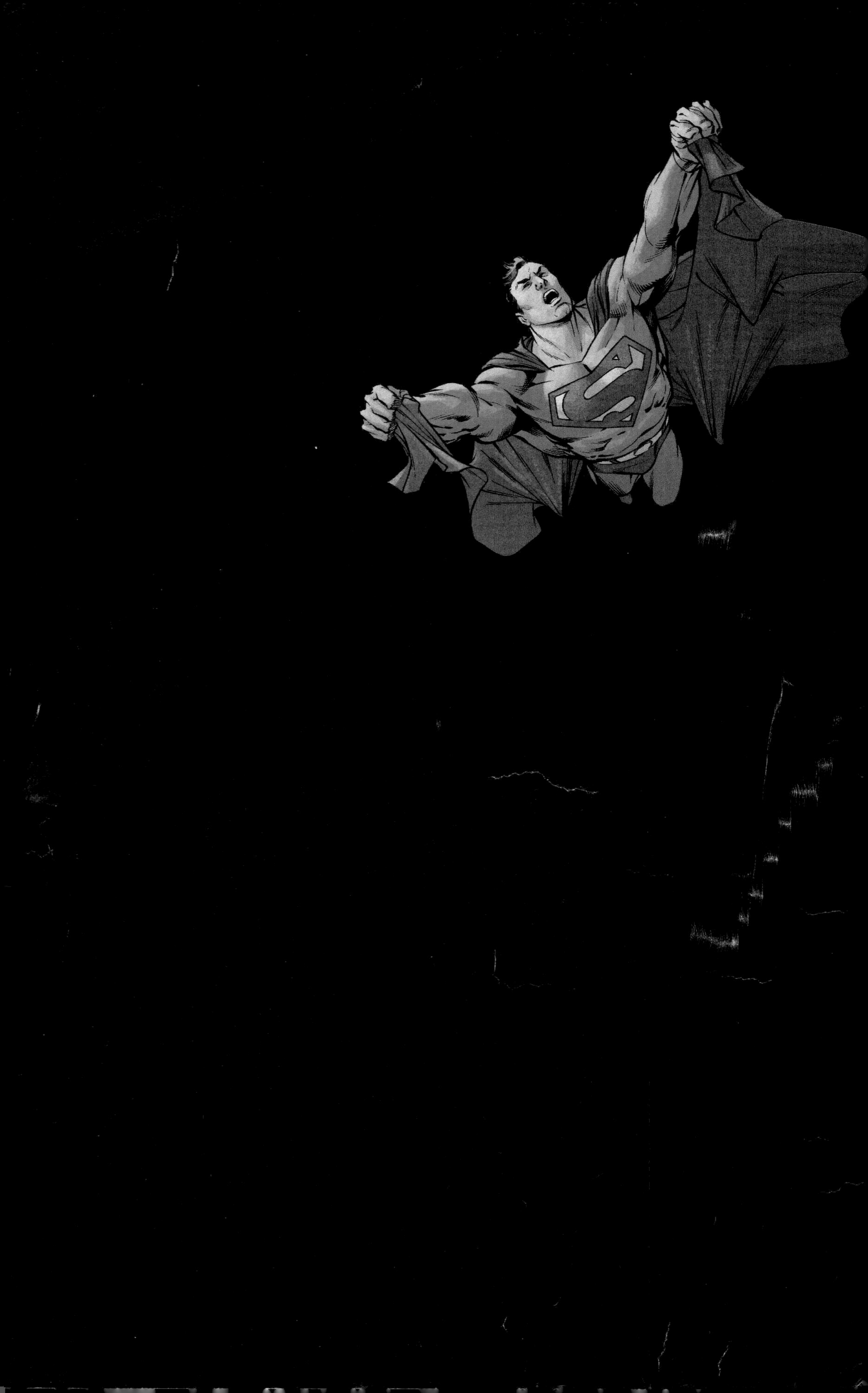

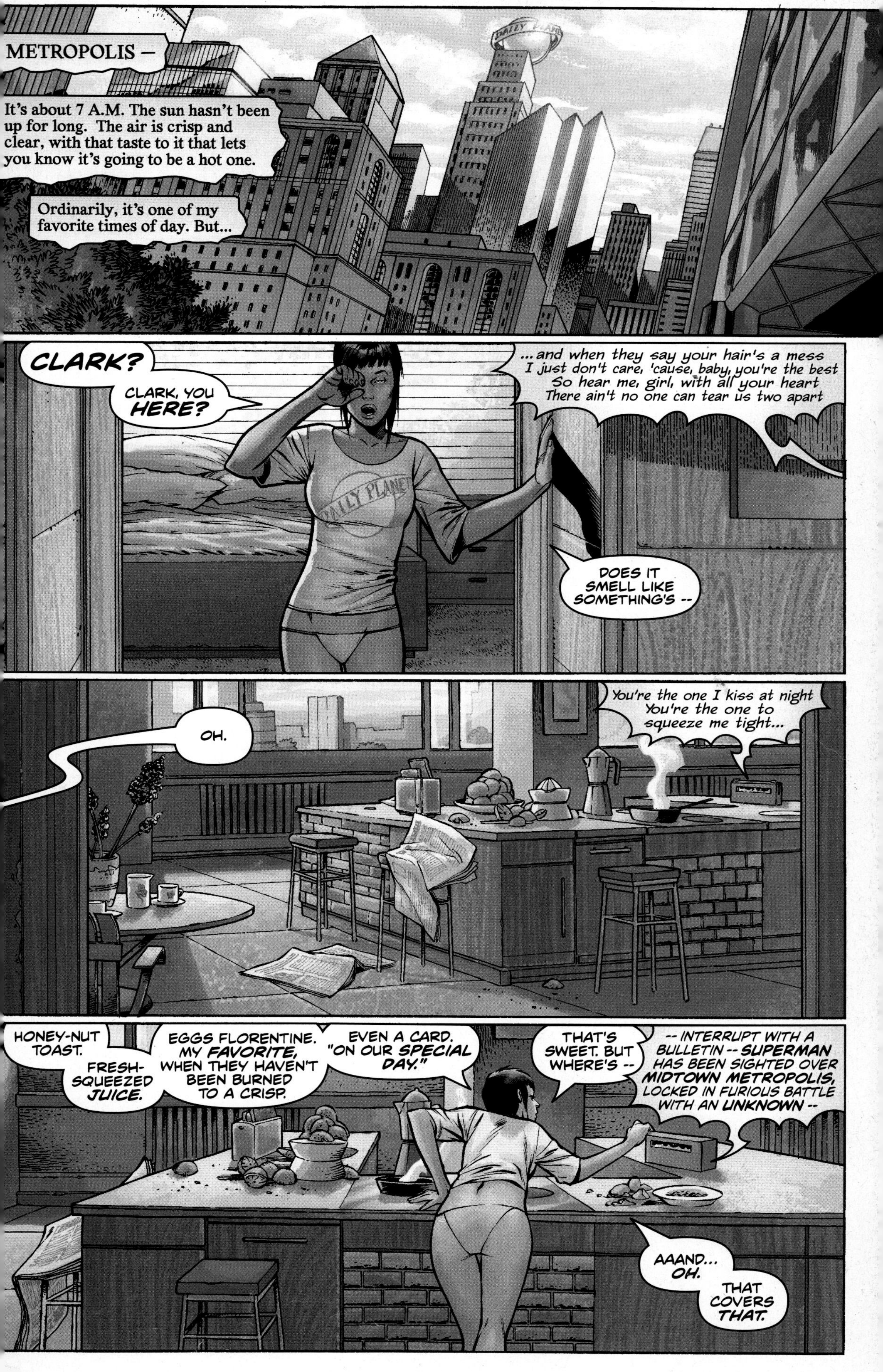
METROPOLIS —
It's about 7 A.M. The sun hasn't been up for long. The air is crisp and clear, with that taste to it that lets you know it's going to be a hot one.
Ordinarily, it's one of my favorite times of day. But...
CLARK?
CLARK, YOU HERE?
...and when they say your hair's a mess I just don't care, 'cause, baby, you're the best So hear me, girl, with all your heart There ain't no one can tear us two apart
DAILY PLANET
DOES IT SMELL LIKE SOMETHING'S --
OH.
You're the one I kiss at night You're the one to squeeze me tight...
HONEY-NUT TOAST.
FRESH-SQUEEZED JUICE.
EGGS FLORENTINE. MY FAVORITE, WHEN THEY HAVEN'T BEEN BURNED TO A CRISP.
EVEN A CARD. "ON OUR SPECIAL DAY."
THAT'S SWEET. BUT WHERE'S --
-- INTERRUPT WITH A BULLETIN -- SUPERMAN HAS BEEN SIGHTED OVER MIDTOWN METROPOLIS, LOCKED IN FURIOUS BATTLE WITH AN UNKNOWN --
AAAND... OH.
THAT COVERS THAT.

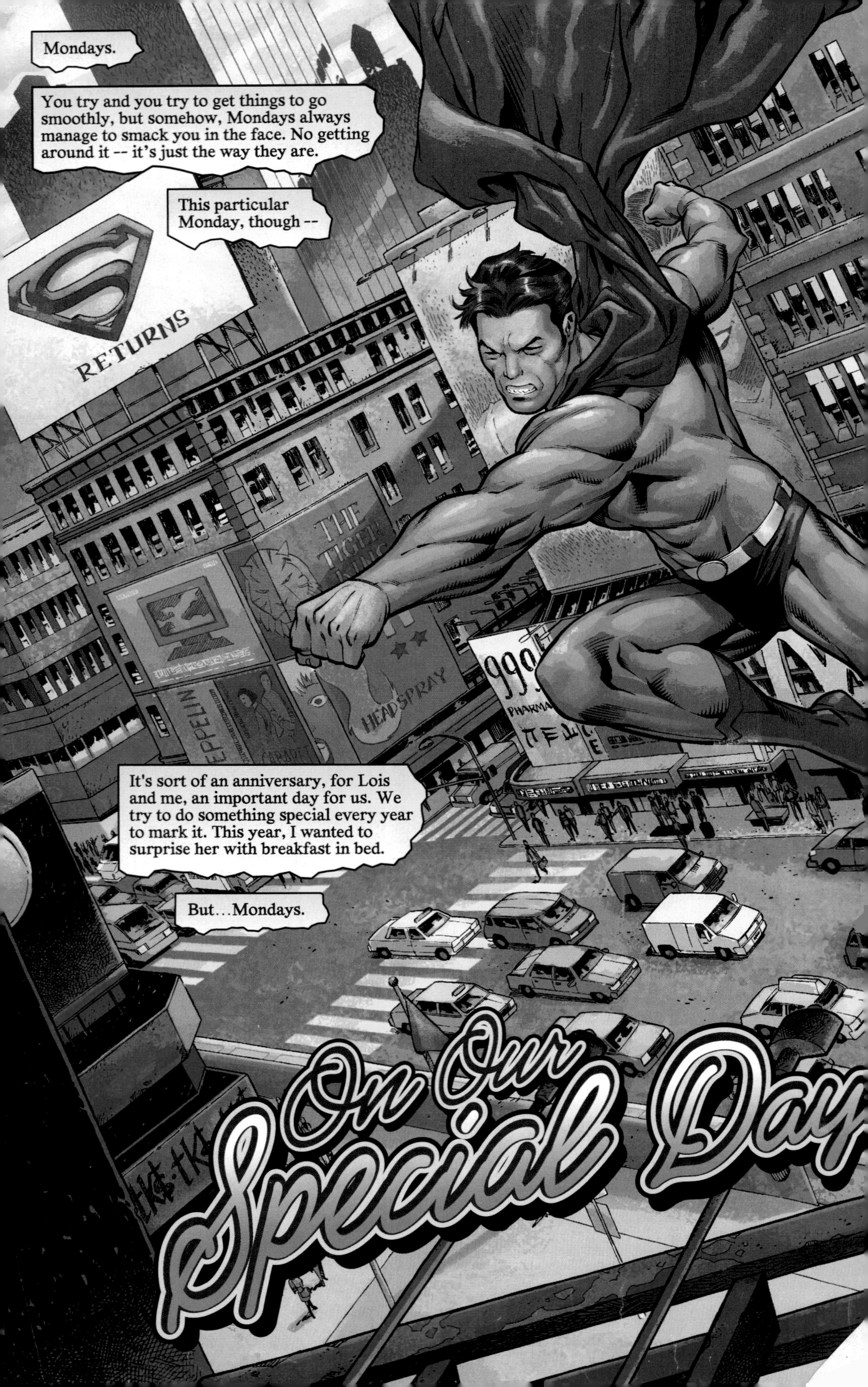
Mondays.
You try and you try to get things to go smoothly, but somehow, Mondays always manage to smack you in the face. No getting around it -- it's just the way they are.
This particular Monday, though --
SUPERMAN RETURNS
THE TIGER KING
HEADSPRAY
ZEPPELIN
PHARMA
It's sort of an anniversary, for Lois and me, an important day for us. We try to do something special every year to mark it. This year, I wanted to surprise her with breakfast in bed.
But…Mondays.
On Our Special Day

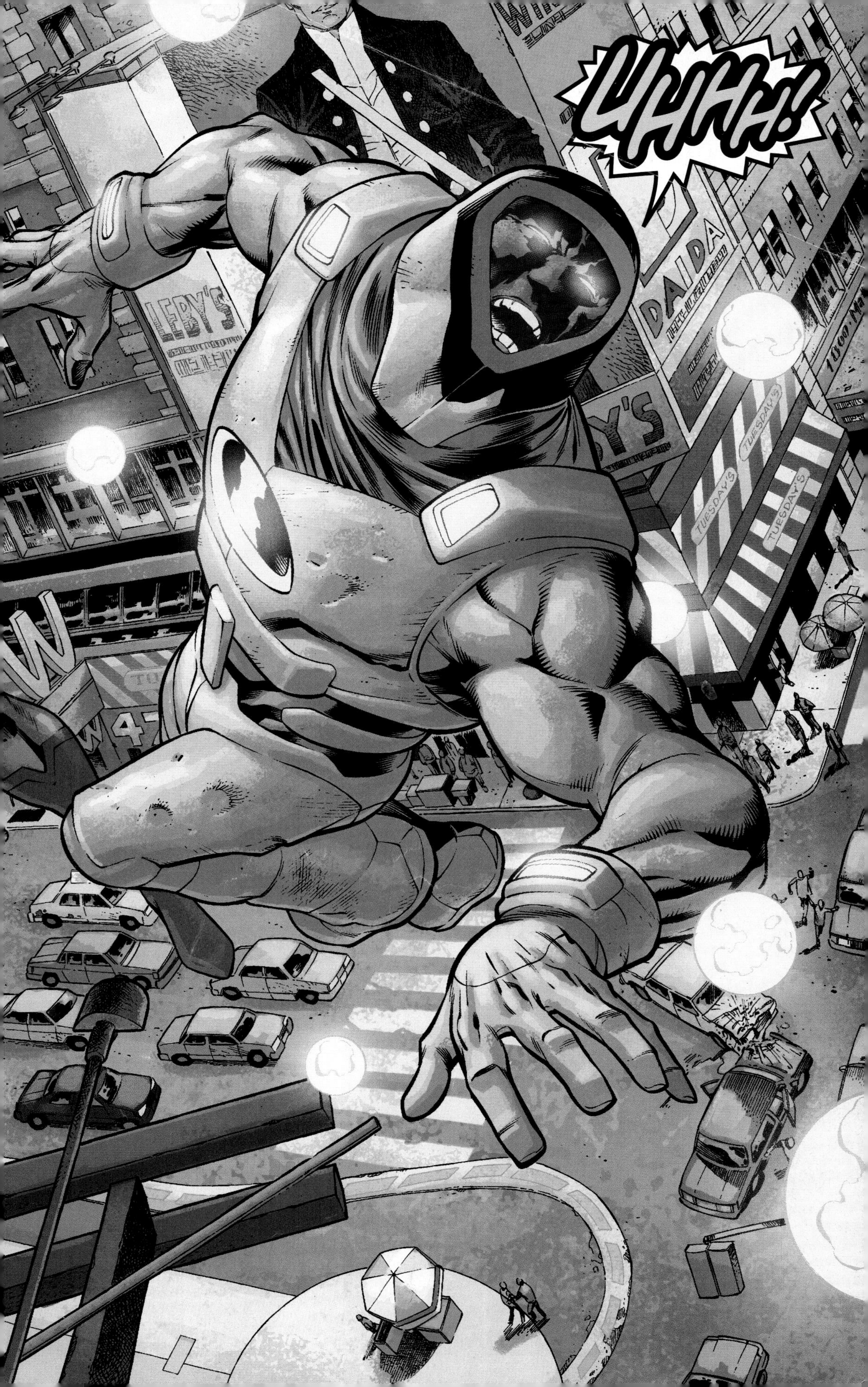
UHHH!
LEBY'S
DAIDA
TUESDAY'S
TUESDAY'S

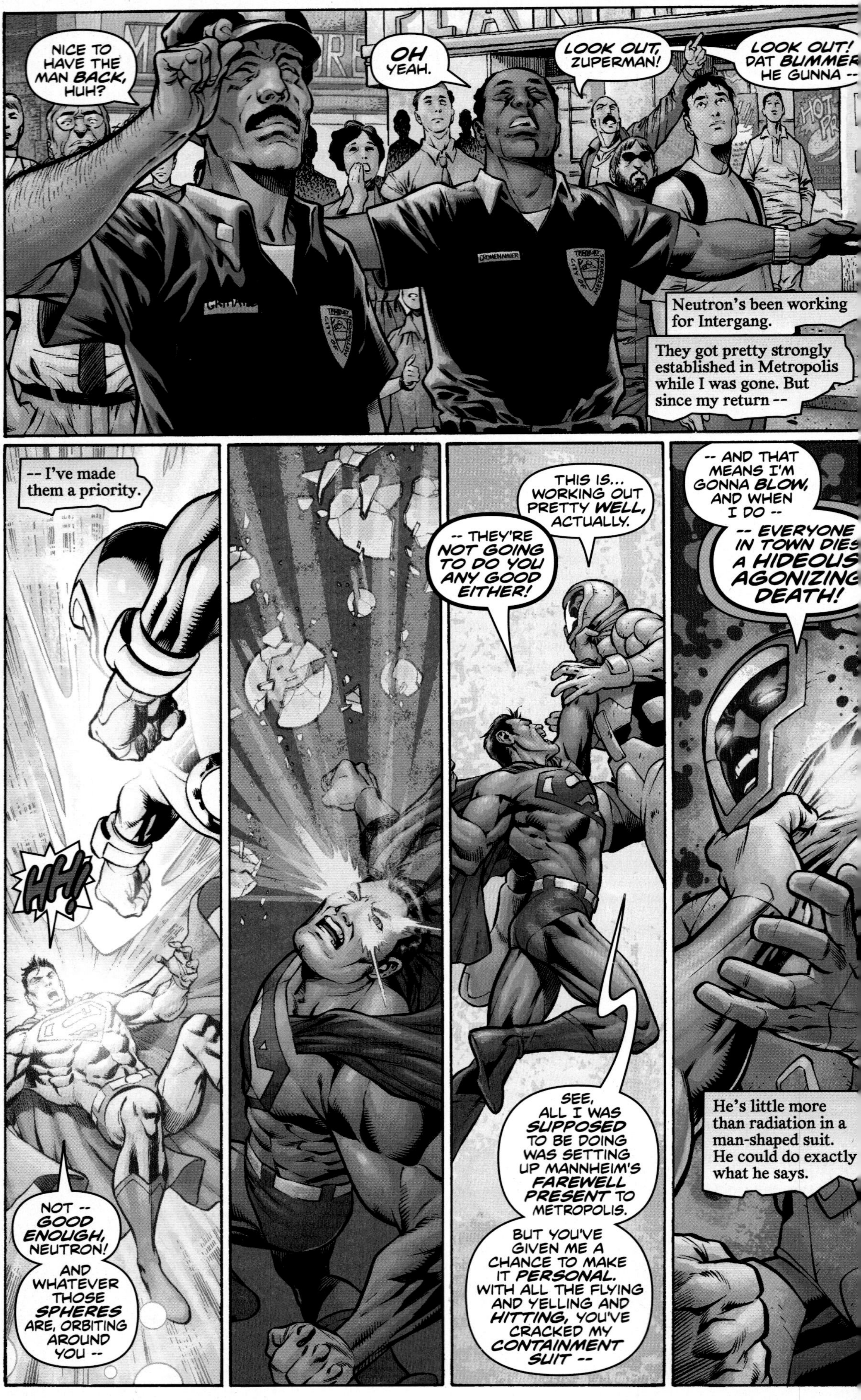
NICE TO HAVE THE MAN BACK, HUH?
OH YEAH.
LOOK OUT, ZUPERMAN!
LOOK OUT! DAT BUMMER HE GUNNA --
Neutron's been working for Intergang.
They got pretty strongly established in Metropolis while I was gone. But since my return --
-- I've made them a priority.
HH!
NOT -- GOOD ENOUGH, NEUTRON!
AND WHATEVER THOSE SPHERES ARE, ORBITING AROUND YOU --
-- THEY'RE NOT GOING TO DO YOU ANY GOOD EITHER!
THIS IS... WORKING OUT PRETTY WELL, ACTUALLY.
SEE, ALL I WAS SUPPOSED TO BE DOING WAS SETTING UP MANNHEIM'S FAREWELL PRESENT TO METROPOLIS.
BUT YOU'VE GIVEN ME A CHANCE TO MAKE IT PERSONAL. WITH ALL THE FLYING AND YELLING AND HITTING, YOU'VE CRACKED MY CONTAINMENT SUIT --
-- AND THAT MEANS I'M GONNA BLOW, AND WHEN I DO --
-- EVERYONE IN TOWN DIES A HIDEOUS AGONIZING DEATH!
He's little more than radiation in a man-shaped suit. He could do exactly what he says.

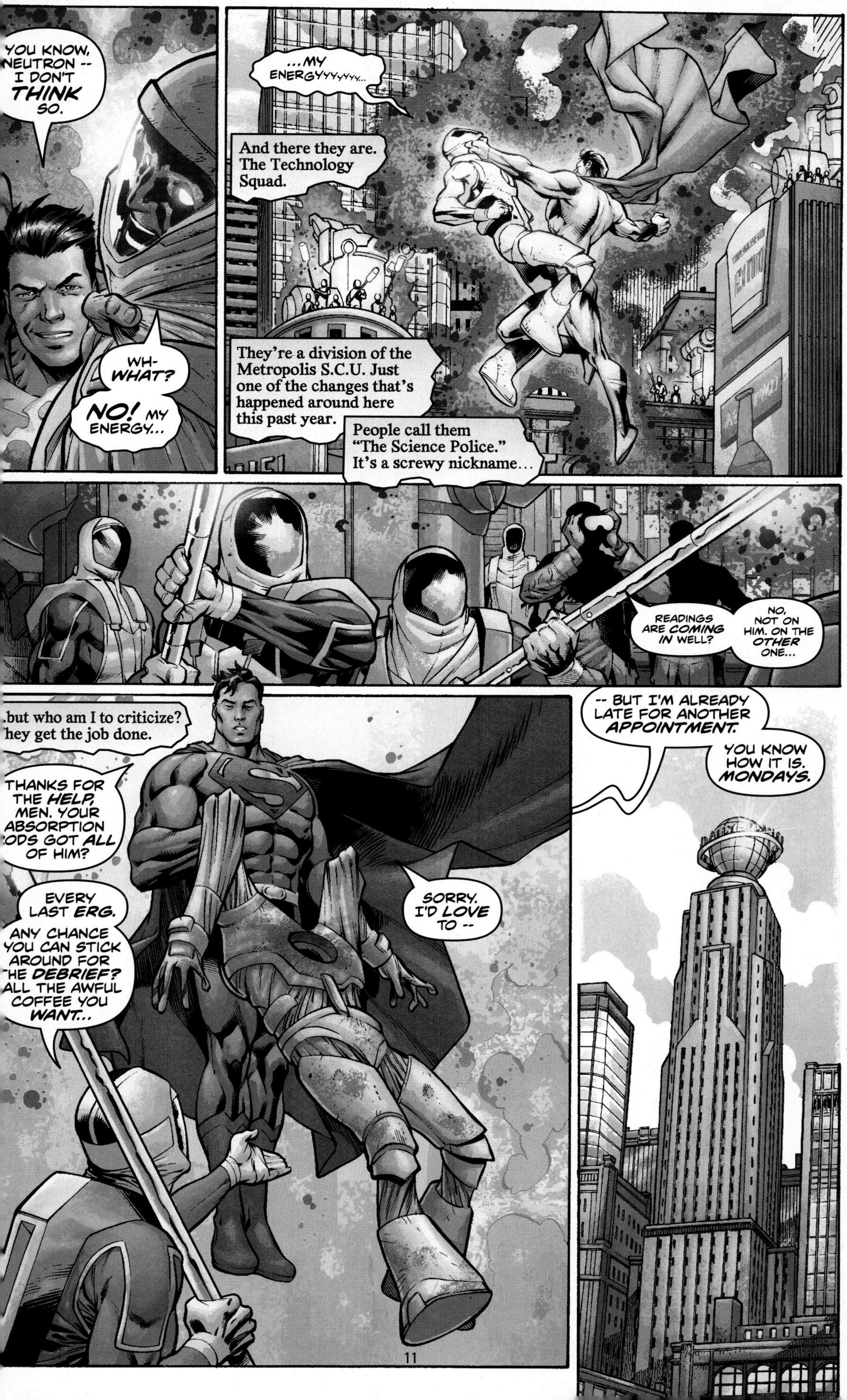
YOU KNOW, NEUTRON -- I DON'T THINK SO.
WH- WHAT?
NO! MY ENERGY...
...MY ENERGYYYYYYY...
And there they are. The Technology Squad.
They're a division of the Metropolis S.C.U. Just one of the changes that's happened around here this past year.
People call them "The Science Police." It's a screwy nickname...
READINGS ARE COMING IN WELL?
NO, NOT ON HIM. ON THE OTHER ONE...
.but who am I to criticize? hey get the job done.
THANKS FOR THE HELP, MEN. YOUR ABSORPTION RODS GOT ALL OF HIM?
EVERY LAST ERG.
ANY CHANCE YOU CAN STICK AROUND FOR THE DEBRIEF? ALL THE AWFUL COFFEE YOU WANT...
SORRY. I'D LOVE TO --
-- BUT I'M ALREADY LATE FOR ANOTHER APPOINTMENT.
YOU KNOW HOW IT IS. MONDAYS.

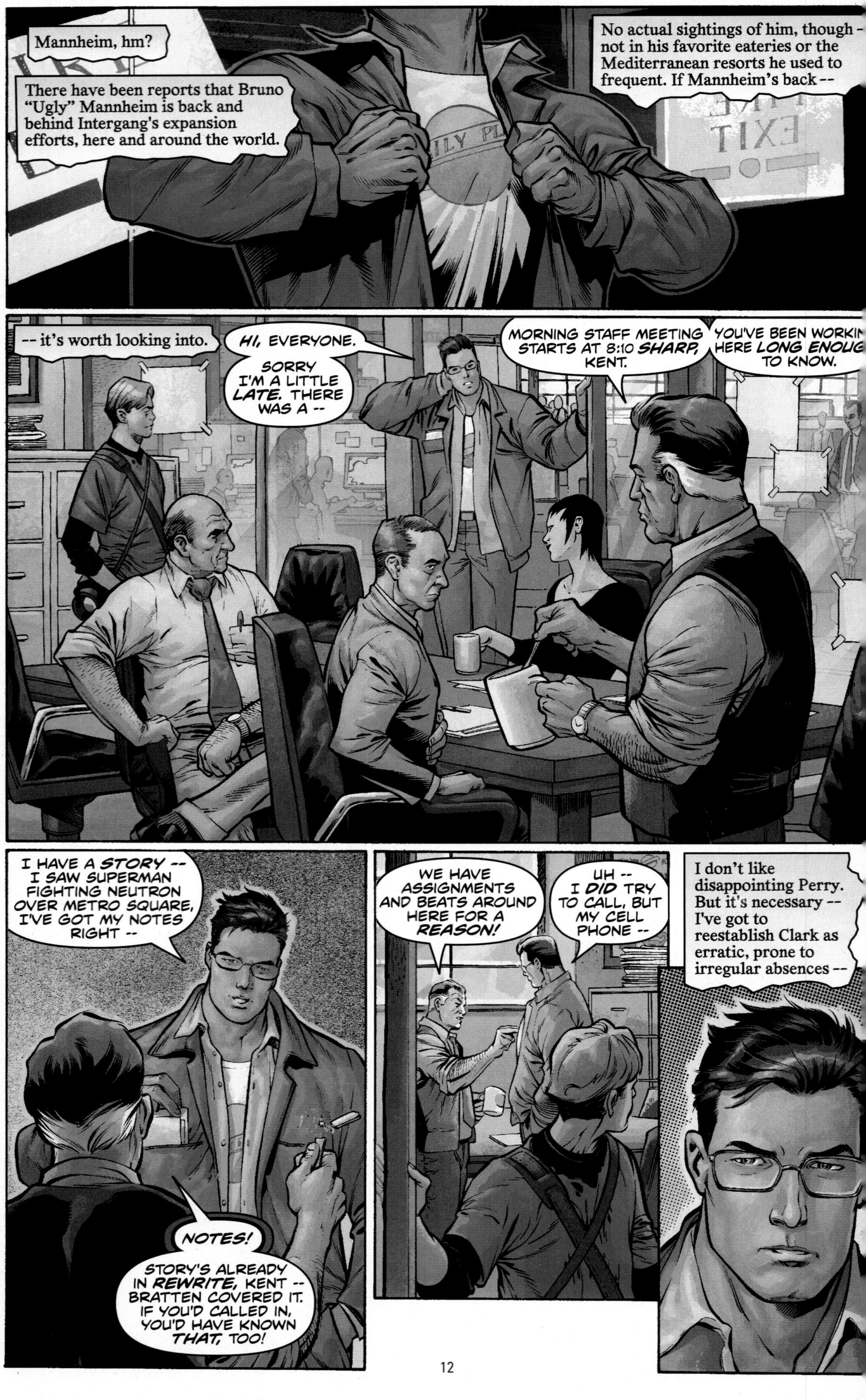

Mannheim, hm?
There have been reports that Bruno "Ugly" Mannheim is back and behind Intergang's expansion efforts, here and around the world.
No actual sightings of him, though - not in his favorite eateries or the Mediterranean resorts he used to frequent. If Mannheim's back --
-- it's worth looking into.
HI, EVERYONE.
SORRY I'M A LITTLE LATE. THERE WAS A --
MORNING STAFF MEETING STARTS AT 8:10 SHARP, KENT.
YOU'VE BEEN WORKIN HERE LONG ENOUG TO KNOW.
I HAVE A STORY -- I SAW SUPERMAN FIGHTING NEUTRON OVER METRO SQUARE, I'VE GOT MY NOTES RIGHT --
NOTES!
STORY'S ALREADY IN REWRITE, KENT -- BRATTEN COVERED IT. IF YOU'D CALLED IN, YOU'D HAVE KNOWN THAT, TOO!
WE HAVE ASSIGNMENTS AND BEATS AROUND HERE FOR A REASON!
UH -- I DID TRY TO CALL, BUT MY CELL PHONE --
I don't like disappointing Perry. But it's necessary -- I've got to reestablish Clark as erratic, prone to irregular absences --

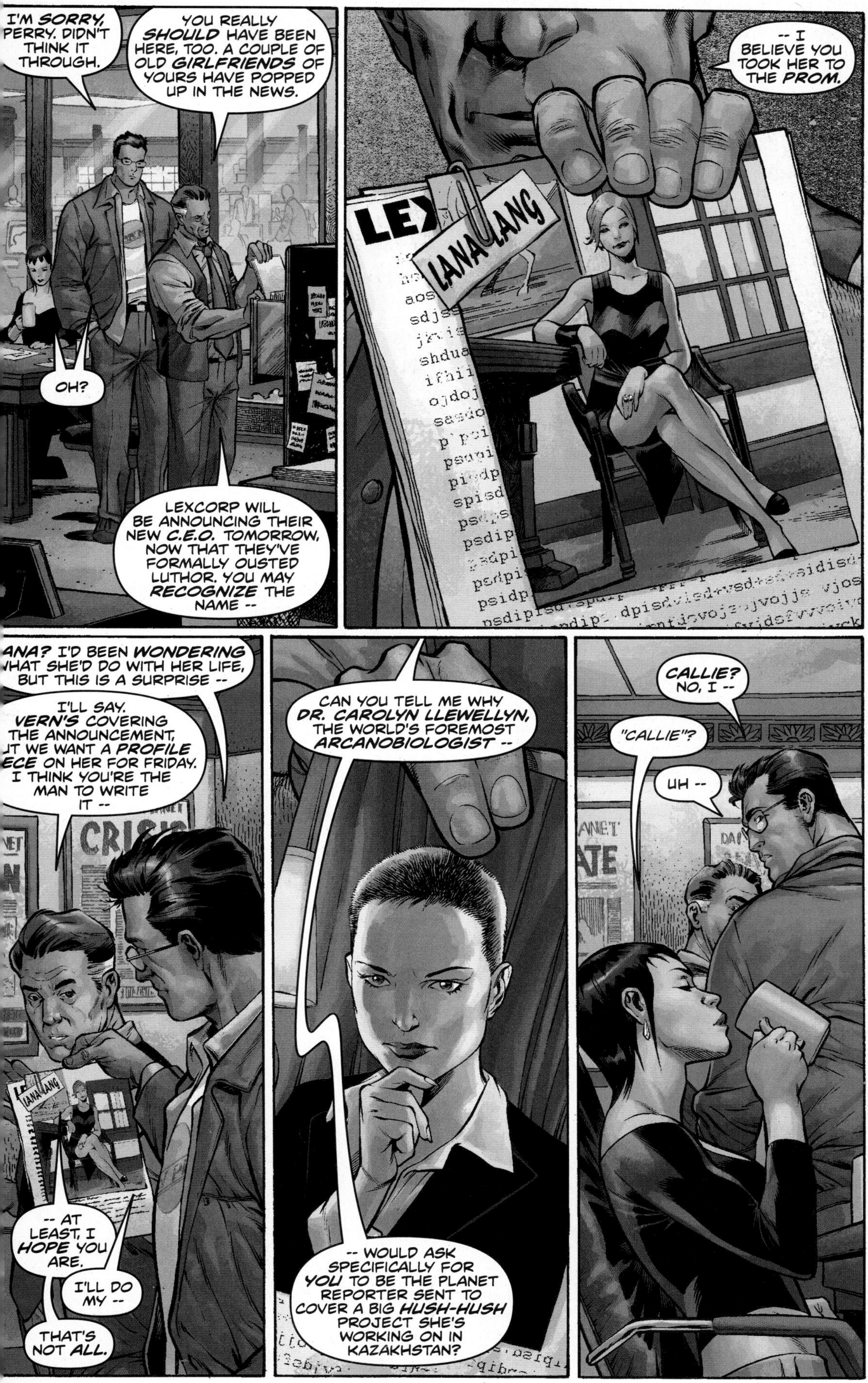
I'M SORRY, PERRY. DIDN'T THINK IT THROUGH.
YOU REALLY SHOULD HAVE BEEN HERE, TOO. A COUPLE OF OLD GIRLFRIENDS OF YOURS HAVE POPPED UP IN THE NEWS.
OH?
LEXCORP WILL BE ANNOUNCING THEIR NEW C.E.O. TOMORROW, NOW THAT THEY'VE FORMALLY OUSTED LUTHOR. YOU MAY RECOGNIZE THE NAME --
-- I BELIEVE YOU TOOK HER TO THE PROM.
LEX
LANA LANG
ANA? I'D BEEN WONDERING WHAT SHE'D DO WITH HER LIFE, BUT THIS IS A SURPRISE --
I'LL SAY. VERN'S COVERING THE ANNOUNCEMENT, UT WE WANT A PROFILE ECE ON HER FOR FRIDAY. I THINK YOU'RE THE MAN TO WRITE IT --
CRISIS
-- AT LEAST, I HOPE YOU ARE.
I'LL DO MY --
THAT'S NOT ALL.
CAN YOU TELL ME WHY DR. CAROLYN LLEWELLYN, THE WORLD'S FOREMOST ARCANOBIOLOGIST --
-- WOULD ASK SPECIFICALLY FOR YOU TO BE THE PLANET REPORTER SENT TO COVER A BIG HUSH-HUSH PROJECT SHE'S WORKING ON IN KAZAKHSTAN?
CALLIE? NO, I --
"CALLIE"?
UH --

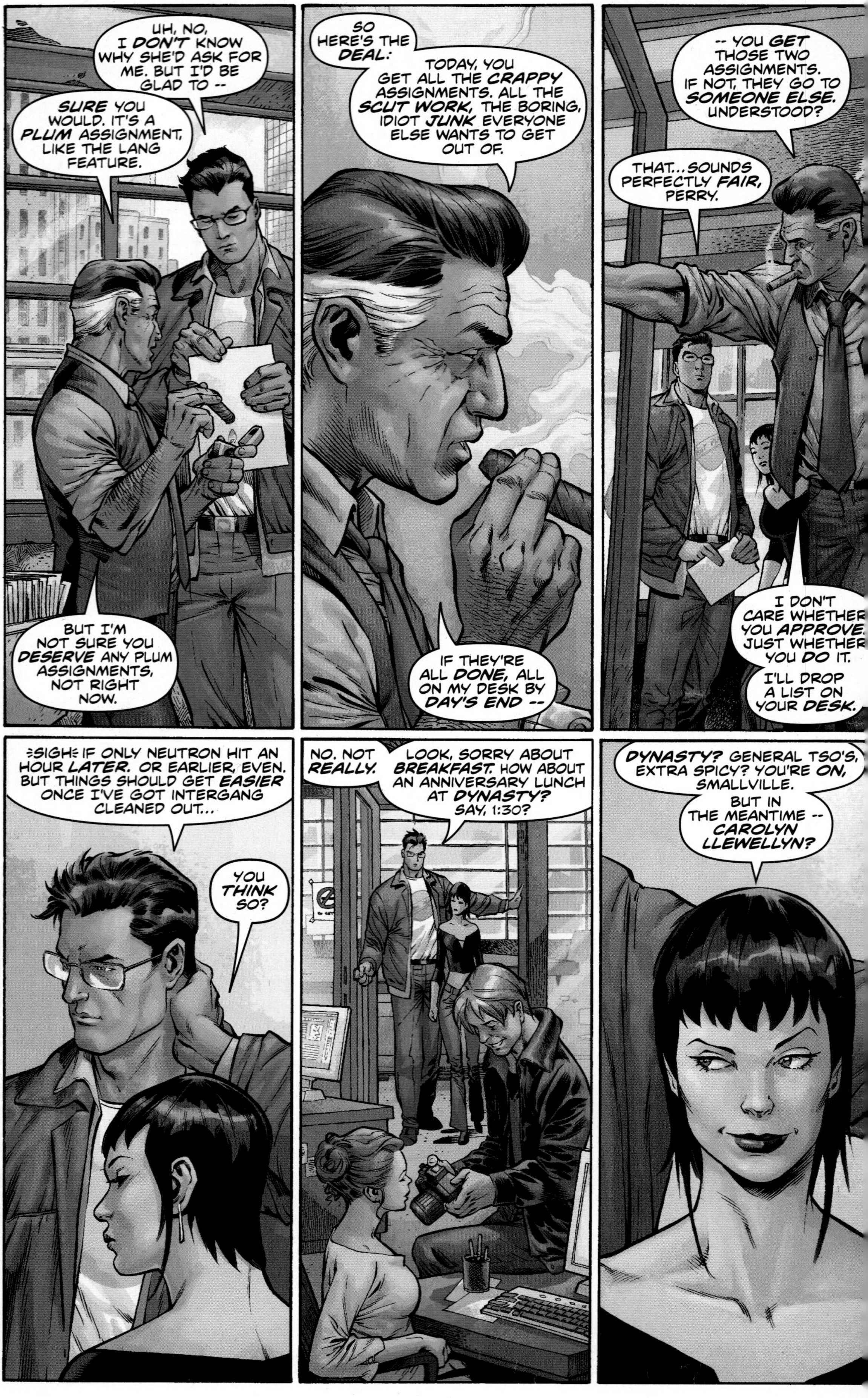
UH, NO, I *DON'T* KNOW WHY SHE'D ASK FOR ME. BUT I'D BE GLAD TO --
SURE YOU WOULD. IT'S A *PLUM* ASSIGNMENT, LIKE THE LANG FEATURE.
BUT I'M NOT SURE YOU *DESERVE* ANY PLUM ASSIGNMENTS, NOT RIGHT NOW.
SO HERE'S THE *DEAL:*
TODAY, YOU GET ALL THE *CRAPPY* ASSIGNMENTS. ALL THE *SCUT WORK,* THE BORING, IDIOT *JUNK* EVERYONE ELSE WANTS TO GET OUT OF.
IF THEY'RE ALL *DONE,* ALL ON MY DESK BY *DAY'S END* --
-- YOU *GET* THOSE TWO ASSIGNMENTS. IF NOT, THEY GO TO *SOMEONE ELSE.* UNDERSTOOD?
THAT... SOUNDS PERFECTLY *FAIR,* PERRY.
I DON'T CARE WHETHER YOU *APPROVE.* JUST WHETHER YOU *DO* IT.
I'LL DROP A LIST ON YOUR *DESK.*
=SIGH= IF ONLY NEUTRON HIT AN HOUR *LATER.* OR EARLIER, EVEN. BUT THINGS SHOULD GET *EASIER* ONCE I'VE GOT INTERGANG CLEANED OUT...
YOU *THINK* SO?
NO. NOT *REALLY.*
LOOK, SORRY ABOUT *BREAKFAST.* HOW ABOUT AN ANNIVERSARY LUNCH AT *DYNASTY?* SAY, 1:30?
DYNASTY? GENERAL TSO'S, EXTRA SPICY? YOU'RE *ON,* SMALLVILLE.
BUT IN THE MEANTIME -- *CAROLYN LLEWELLYN?*

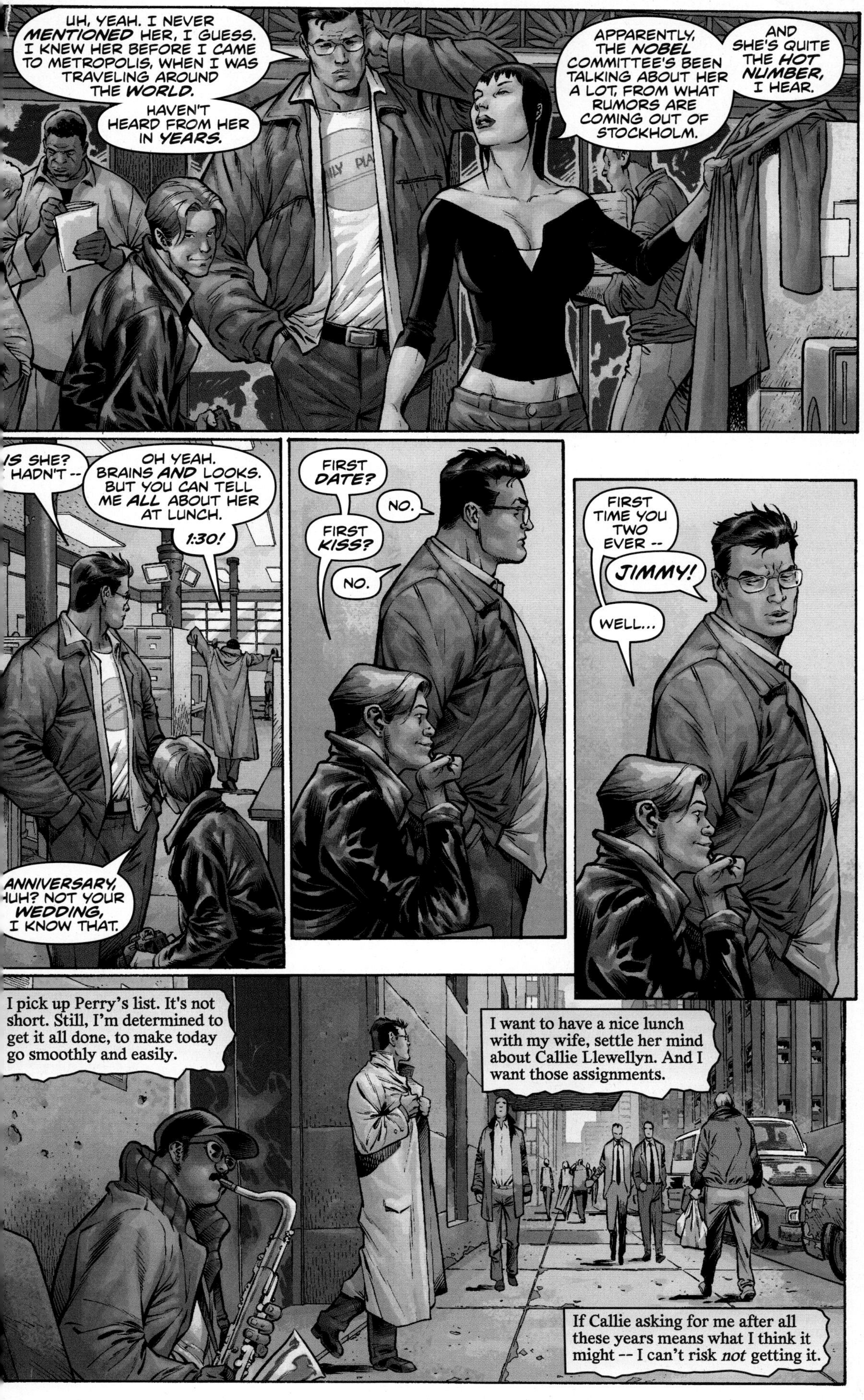
UH, YEAH. I NEVER MENTIONED HER, I GUESS. I KNEW HER BEFORE I CAME TO METROPOLIS, WHEN I WAS TRAVELING AROUND THE WORLD.
HAVEN'T HEARD FROM HER IN YEARS.
APPARENTLY, THE NOBEL COMMITTEE'S BEEN TALKING ABOUT HER A LOT, FROM WHAT RUMORS ARE COMING OUT OF STOCKHOLM.
AND SHE'S QUITE THE HOT NUMBER, I HEAR.
IS SHE? HADN'T --
OH YEAH. BRAINS AND LOOKS. BUT YOU CAN TELL ME ALL ABOUT HER AT LUNCH.
1:30!
ANNIVERSARY, HUH? NOT YOUR WEDDING, I KNOW THAT.
FIRST DATE?
NO.
FIRST KISS?
NO.
FIRST TIME YOU TWO EVER --
JIMMY!
WELL...
I pick up Perry's list. It's not short. Still, I'm determined to get it all done, to make today go smoothly and easily.
I want to have a nice lunch with my wife, settle her mind about Callie Llewellyn. And I want those assignments.
If Callie asking for me after all these years means what I think it might -- I can't risk not getting it.

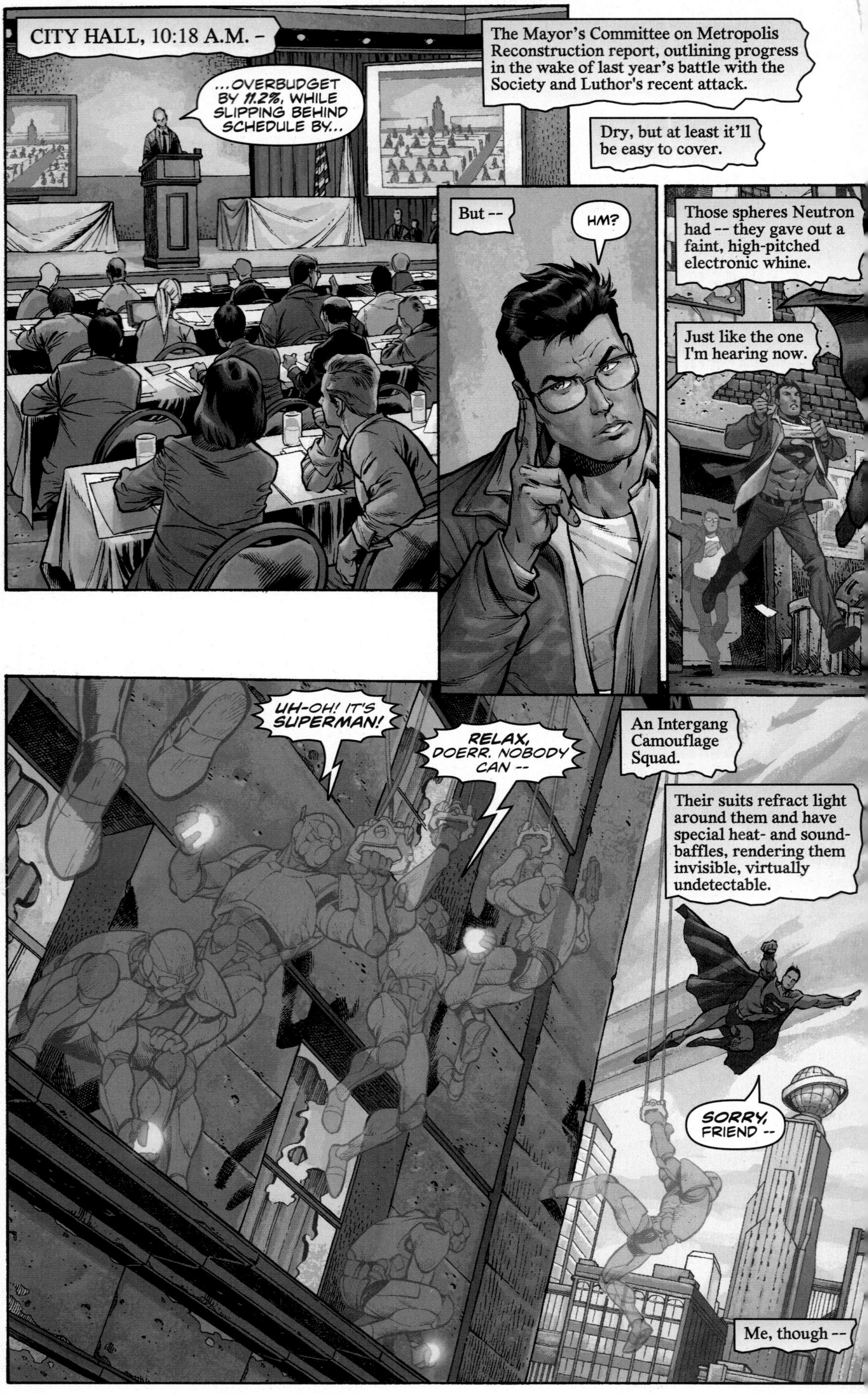
CITY HALL, 10:18 A.M. –
...OVERBUDGET BY 11.2%, WHILE SLIPPING BEHIND SCHEDULE BY...
The Mayor's Committee on Metropolis Reconstruction report, outlining progress in the wake of last year's battle with the Society and Luthor's recent attack.
Dry, but at least it'll be easy to cover.
But --
HM?
Those spheres Neutron had -- they gave out a faint, high-pitched electronic whine.
Just like the one I'm hearing now.
UH-OH! IT'S SUPERMAN!
RELAX, DOERR. NOBODY CAN --
An Intergang Camouflage Squad.
Their suits refract light around them and have special heat- and sound-baffles, rendering them invisible, virtually undetectable.
SORRY, FRIEND --
Me, though --

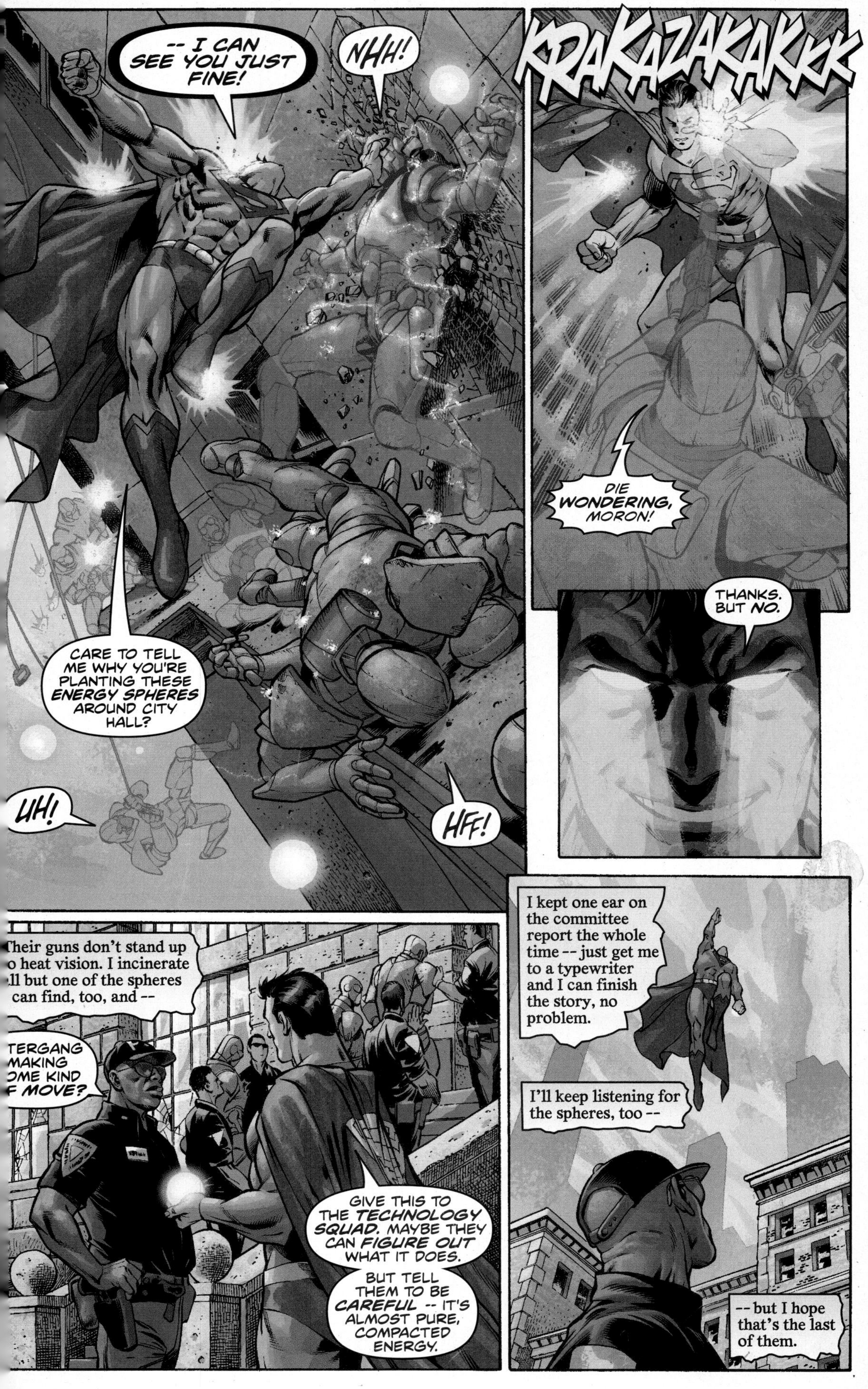
-- I CAN SEE YOU JUST FINE!
NHH!
CARE TO TELL ME WHY YOU'RE PLANTING THESE ENERGY SPHERES AROUND CITY HALL?
UH!
HFF!
KRAKAZAKAKKK
DIE WONDERING, MORON!
THANKS. BUT NO.
Their guns don't stand up o heat vision. I incinerate ll but one of the spheres can find, too, and --
TERGANG MAKING OME KIND F MOVE?
GIVE THIS TO THE TECHNOLOGY SQUAD. MAYBE THEY CAN FIGURE OUT WHAT IT DOES.
BUT TELL THEM TO BE CAREFUL -- IT'S ALMOST PURE, COMPACTED ENERGY.
I kept one ear on the committee report the whole time -- just get me to a typewriter and I can finish the story, no problem.
I'll keep listening for the spheres, too --
-- but I hope that's the last of them.

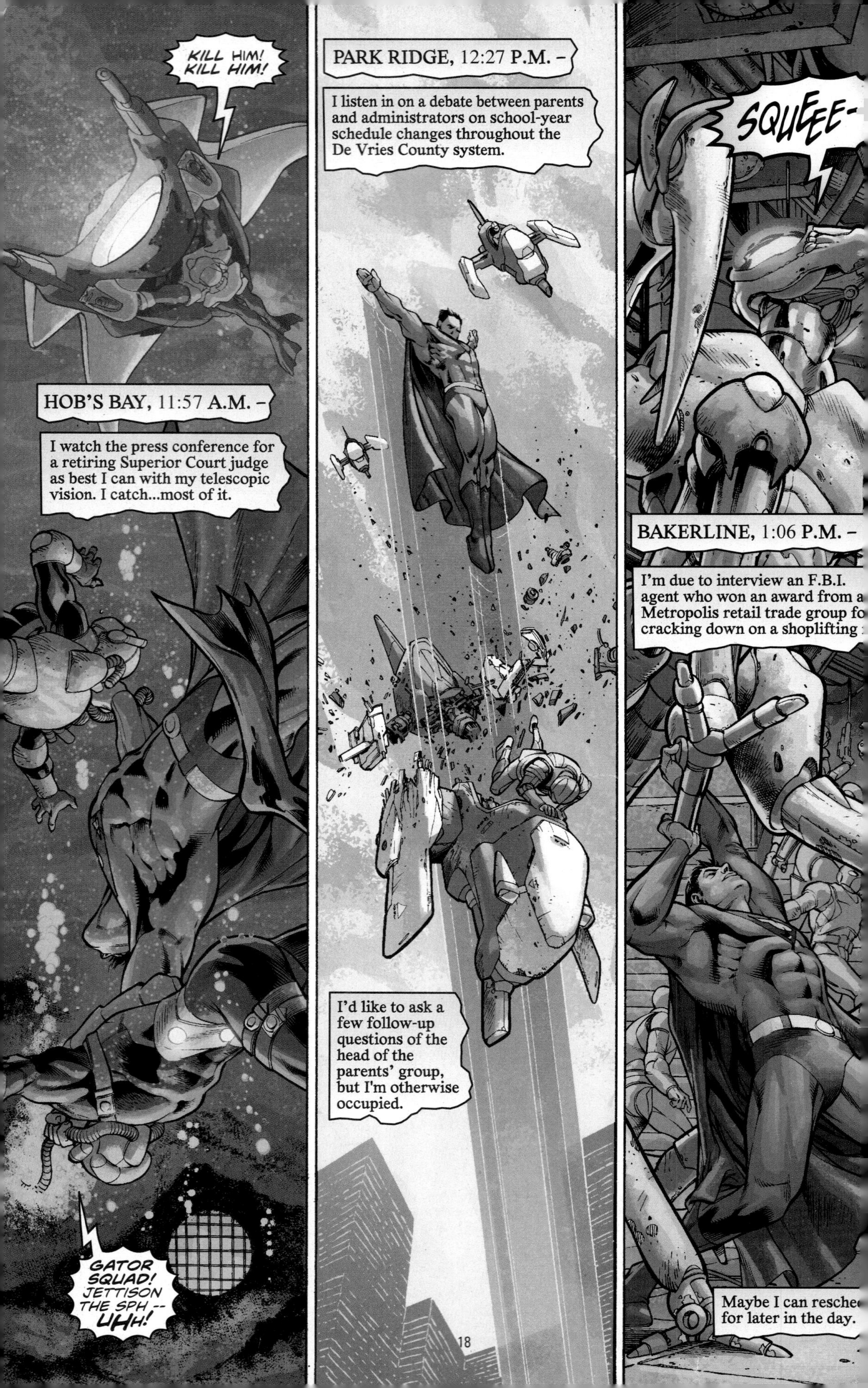
KILL HIM! KILL HIM!
HOB'S BAY, 11:57 A.M. –
I watch the press conference for a retiring Superior Court judge as best I can with my telescopic vision. I catch...most of it.
GATOR SQUAD! JETTISON THE SPH -- UHH!
PARK RIDGE, 12:27 P.M. –
I listen in on a debate between parents and administrators on school-year schedule changes throughout the De Vries County system.
I'd like to ask a few follow-up questions of the head of the parents' group, but I'm otherwise occupied.
SQUEEE-
BAKERLINE, 1:06 P.M. –
I'm due to interview an F.B.I. agent who won an award from a Metropolis retail trade group fo cracking down on a shoplifting
Maybe I can resche for later in the day.

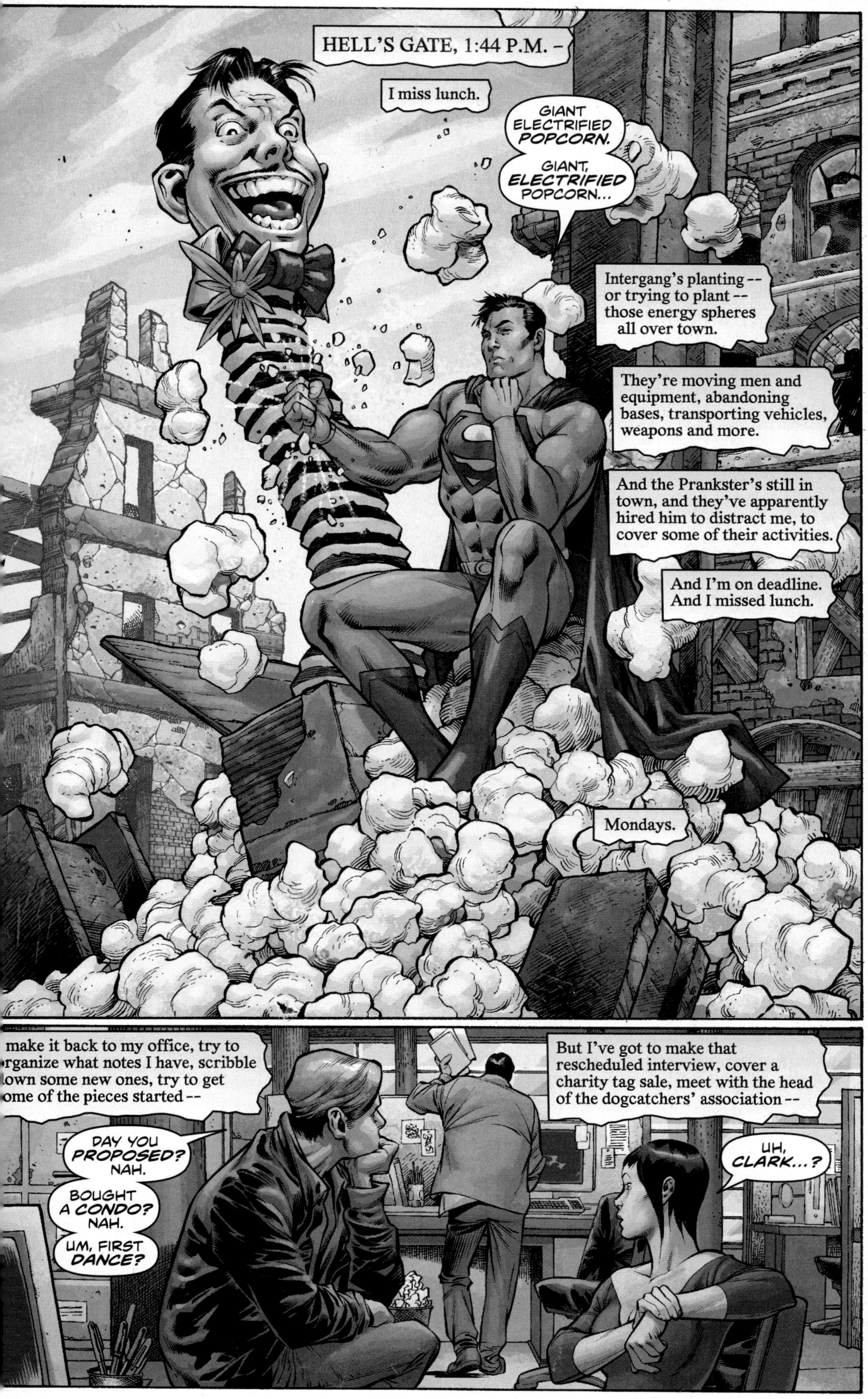
HELL'S GATE, 1:44 P.M. –
I miss lunch.
GIANT ELECTRIFIED POPCORN.
GIANT, ELECTRIFIED POPCORN...
Intergang's planting -- or trying to plant -- those energy spheres all over town.
They're moving men and equipment, abandoning bases, transporting vehicles, weapons and more.
And the Prankster's still in town, and they've apparently hired him to distract me, to cover some of their activities.
And I'm on deadline. And I missed lunch.
Mondays.
make it back to my office, try to rganize what notes I have, scribble own some new ones, try to get ome of the pieces started --
But I've got to make that rescheduled interview, cover a charity tag sale, meet with the head of the dogcatchers' association --
DAY YOU PROPOSED? NAH.
BOUGHT A CONDO? NAH.
UM, FIRST DANCE?
UH, CLARK...?

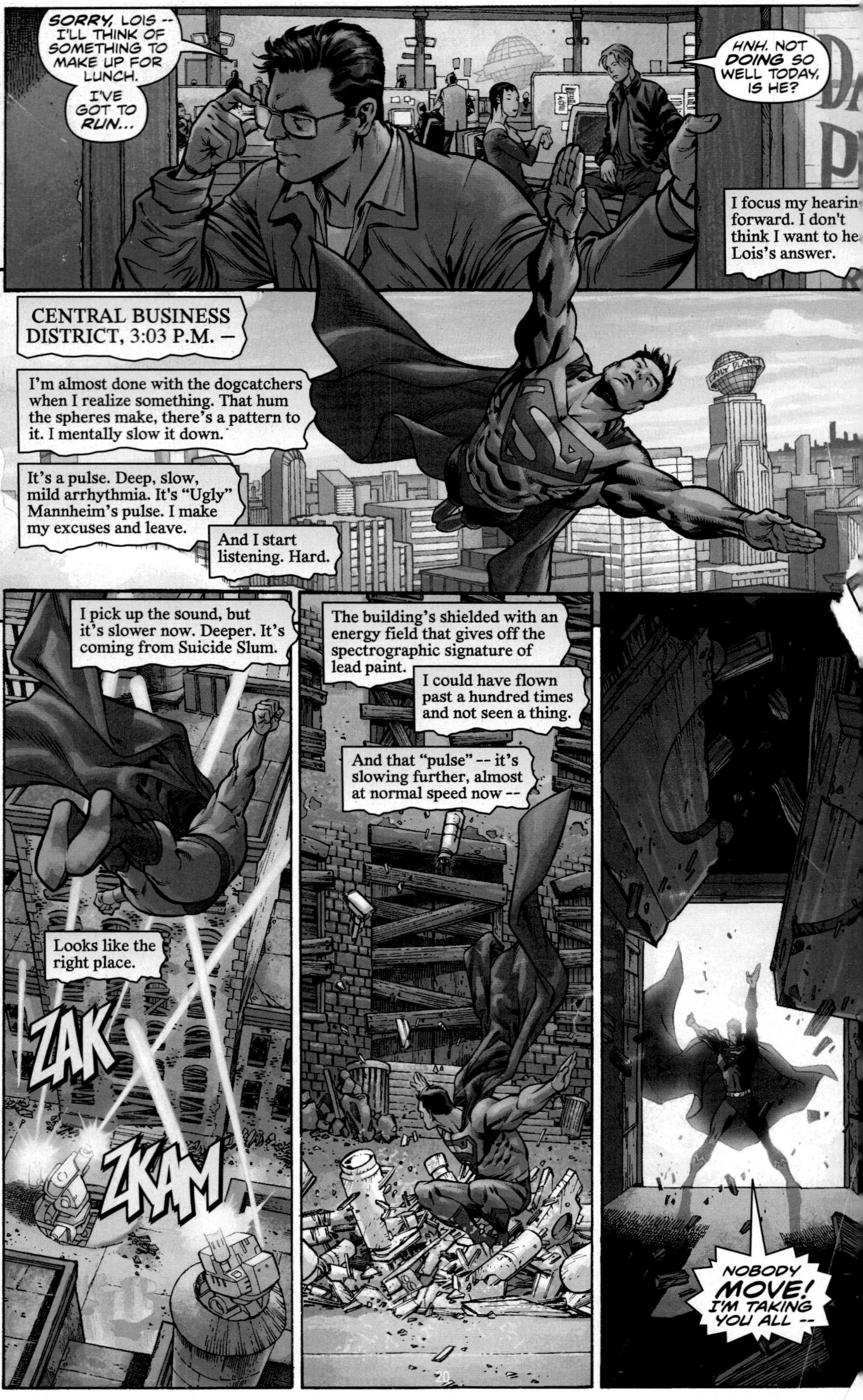

SORRY, LOIS -- I'LL THINK OF SOMETHING TO MAKE UP FOR LUNCH.
I'VE GOT TO RUN...
HNH. NOT DOING SO WELL TODAY, IS HE?
I focus my hearin forward. I don't think I want to he Lois's answer.
CENTRAL BUSINESS DISTRICT, 3:03 P.M. –
I'm almost done with the dogcatchers when I realize something. That hum the spheres make, there's a pattern to it. I mentally slow it down.
It's a pulse. Deep, slow, mild arrhythmia. It's "Ugly" Mannheim's pulse. I make my excuses and leave.
And I start listening. Hard.
I pick up the sound, but it's slower now. Deeper. It's coming from Suicide Slum.
Looks like the right place.
ZAK
ZKAM
The building's shielded with an energy field that gives off the spectrographic signature of lead paint.
I could have flown past a hundred times and not seen a thing.
And that "pulse" -- it's slowing further, almost at normal speed now --
NOBODY MOVE! I'M TAKING YOU ALL --

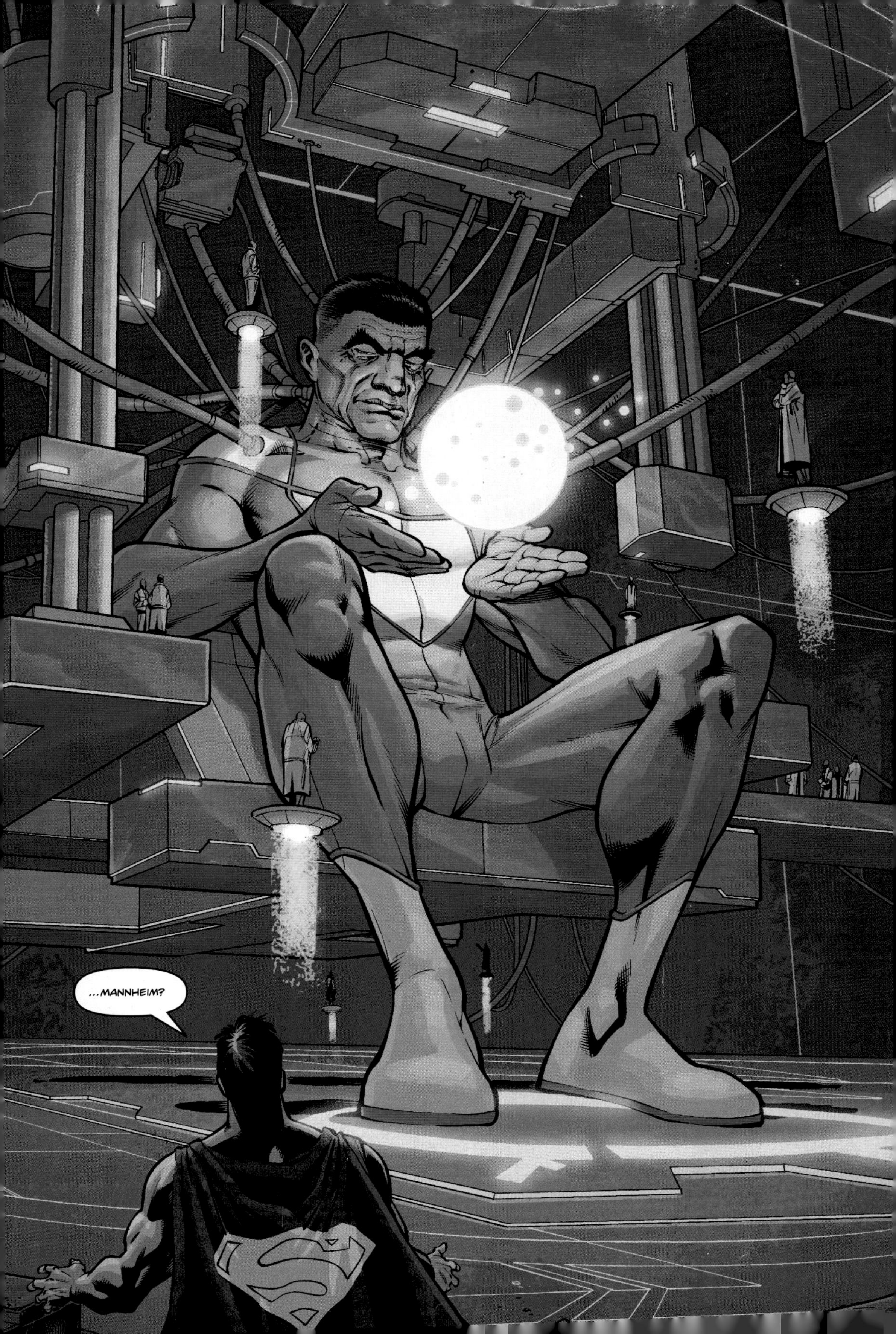
...MANNHEIM?

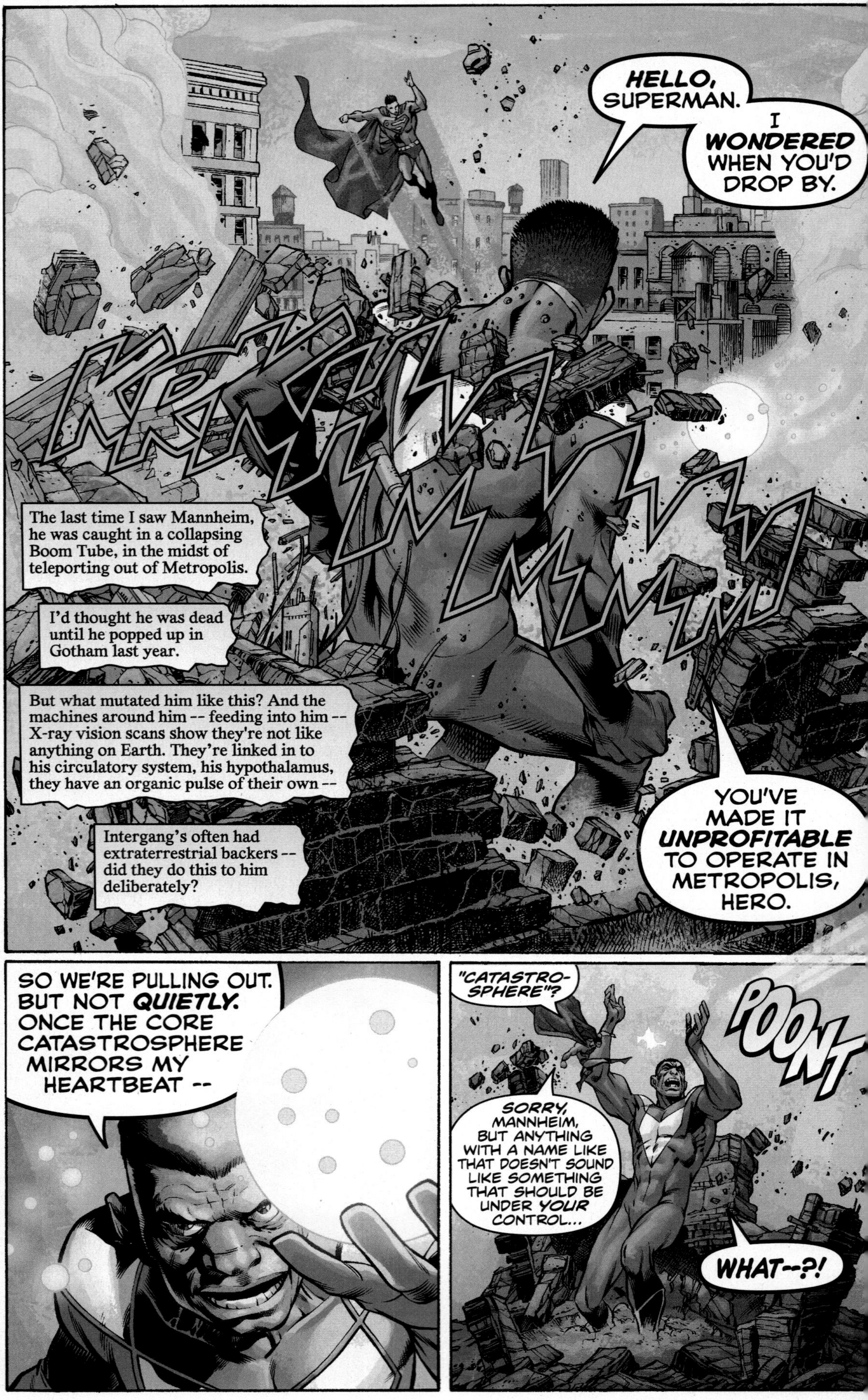
HELLO, SUPERMAN.
I WONDERED WHEN YOU'D DROP BY.
KRAKKOOM
The last time I saw Mannheim, he was caught in a collapsing Boom Tube, in the midst of teleporting out of Metropolis.
I'd thought he was dead until he popped up in Gotham last year.
But what mutated him like this? And the machines around him -- feeding into him -- X-ray vision scans show they're not like anything on Earth. They're linked in to his circulatory system, his hypothalamus, they have an organic pulse of their own --
Intergang's often had extraterrestrial backers -- did they do this to him deliberately?
YOU'VE MADE IT UNPROFITABLE TO OPERATE IN METROPOLIS, HERO.
SO WE'RE PULLING OUT. BUT NOT QUIETLY. ONCE THE CORE CATASTROSPHERE MIRRORS MY HEARTBEAT --
"CATASTROSPHERE"?
POONT
SORRY, MANNHEIM, BUT ANYTHING WITH A NAME LIKE THAT DOESN'T SOUND LIKE SOMETHING THAT SHOULD BE UNDER YOUR CONTROL...
WHAT--?!

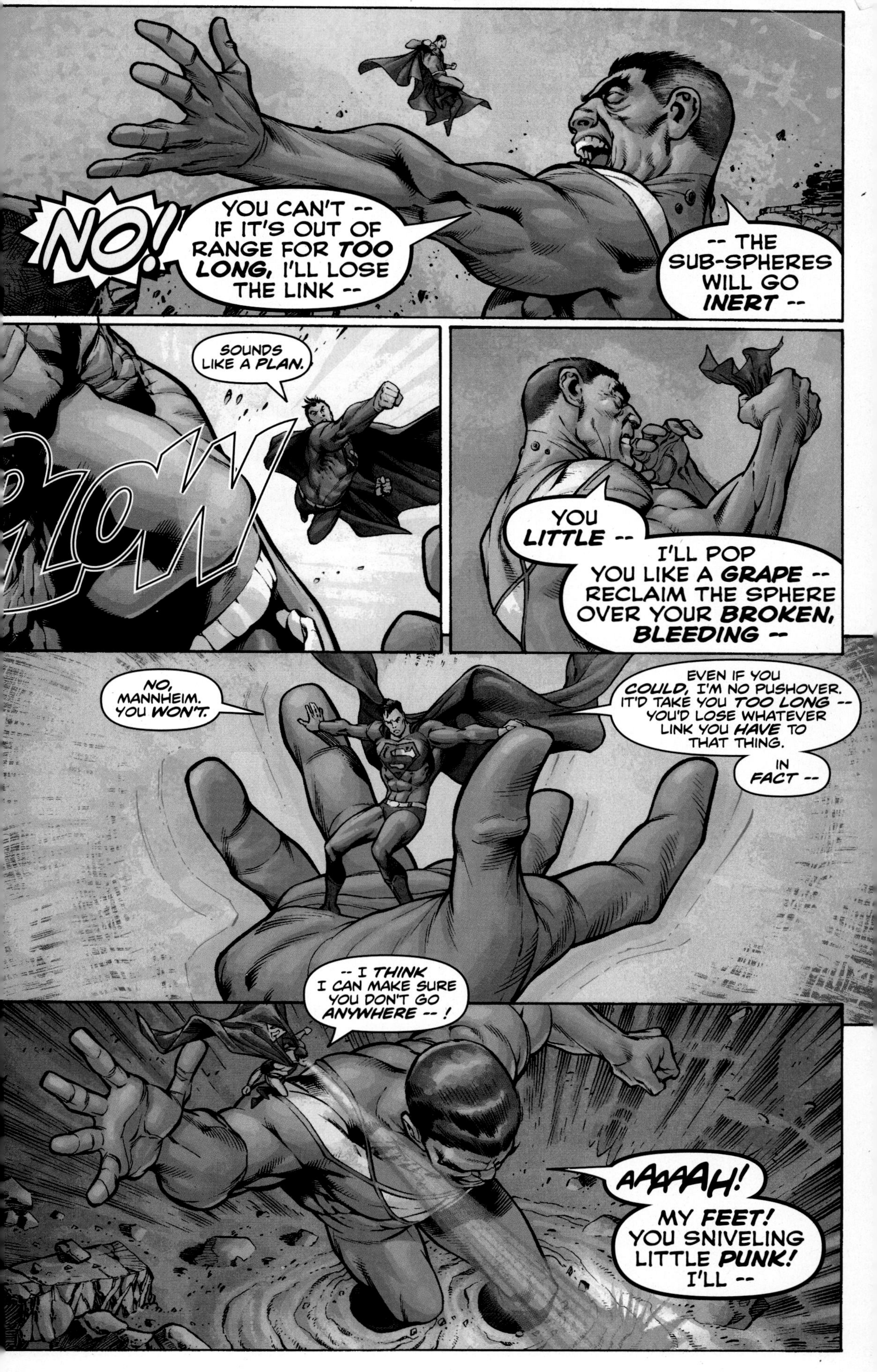
NO!
YOU CAN'T -- IF IT'S OUT OF RANGE FOR TOO LONG, I'LL LOSE THE LINK --
-- THE SUB-SPHERES WILL GO INERT --
SOUNDS LIKE A PLAN.
POW
YOU LITTLE --
I'LL POP YOU LIKE A GRAPE -- RECLAIM THE SPHERE OVER YOUR BROKEN, BLEEDING --
NO, MANNHEIM. YOU WON'T.
EVEN IF YOU COULD, I'M NO PUSHOVER. IT'D TAKE YOU TOO LONG -- YOU'D LOSE WHATEVER LINK YOU HAVE TO THAT THING.
IN FACT --
-- I THINK I CAN MAKE SURE YOU DON'T GO ANYWHERE -- !
AAAAAH!
MY FEET! YOU SNIVELING LITTLE PUNK! I'LL --

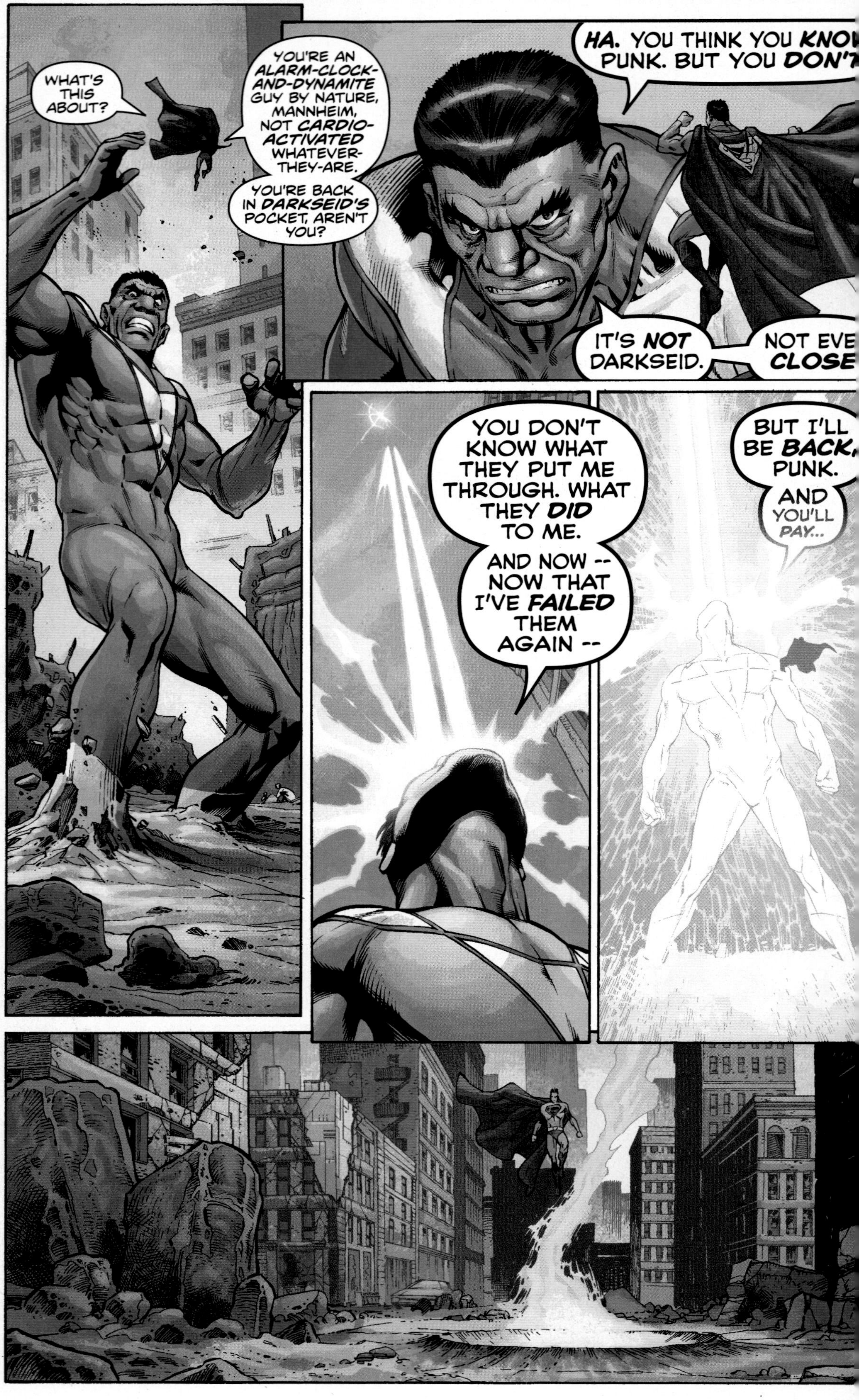
WHAT'S THIS ABOUT?
YOU'RE AN ALARM-CLOCK-AND-DYNAMITE GUY BY NATURE, MANNHEIM, NOT CARDIO-ACTIVATED WHATEVER-THEY-ARE.
YOU'RE BACK IN DARKSEID'S POCKET, AREN'T YOU?
HA. YOU THINK YOU KNO PUNK. BUT YOU DON'T
IT'S NOT DARKSEID.
NOT EVE CLOSE
YOU DON'T KNOW WHAT THEY PUT ME THROUGH. WHAT THEY DID TO ME.
AND NOW -- NOW THAT I'VE FAILED THEM AGAIN --
BUT I'LL BE BACK, PUNK.
AND YOU'LL PAY...

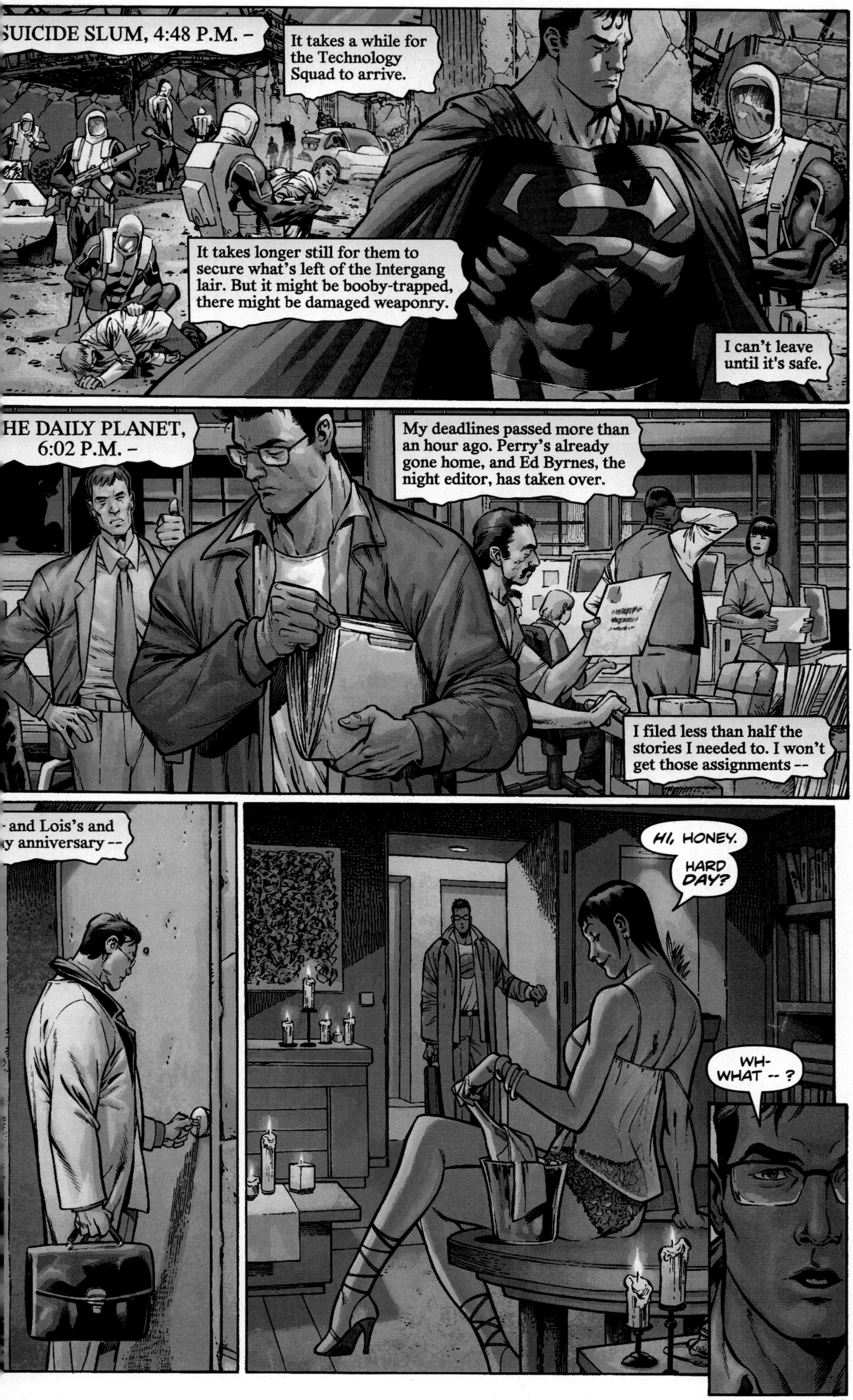
SUICIDE SLUM, 4:48 P.M. –
It takes a while for the Technology Squad to arrive.
It takes longer still for them to secure what's left of the Intergang lair. But it might be booby-trapped, there might be damaged weaponry.
I can't leave until it's safe.
HE DAILY PLANET, 6:02 P.M. –
My deadlines passed more than an hour ago. Perry's already gone home, and Ed Byrnes, the night editor, has taken over.
I filed less than half the stories I needed to. I won't get those assignments --
- and Lois's and
y anniversary --
HI, HONEY.
HARD DAY?
WH- WHAT -- ?

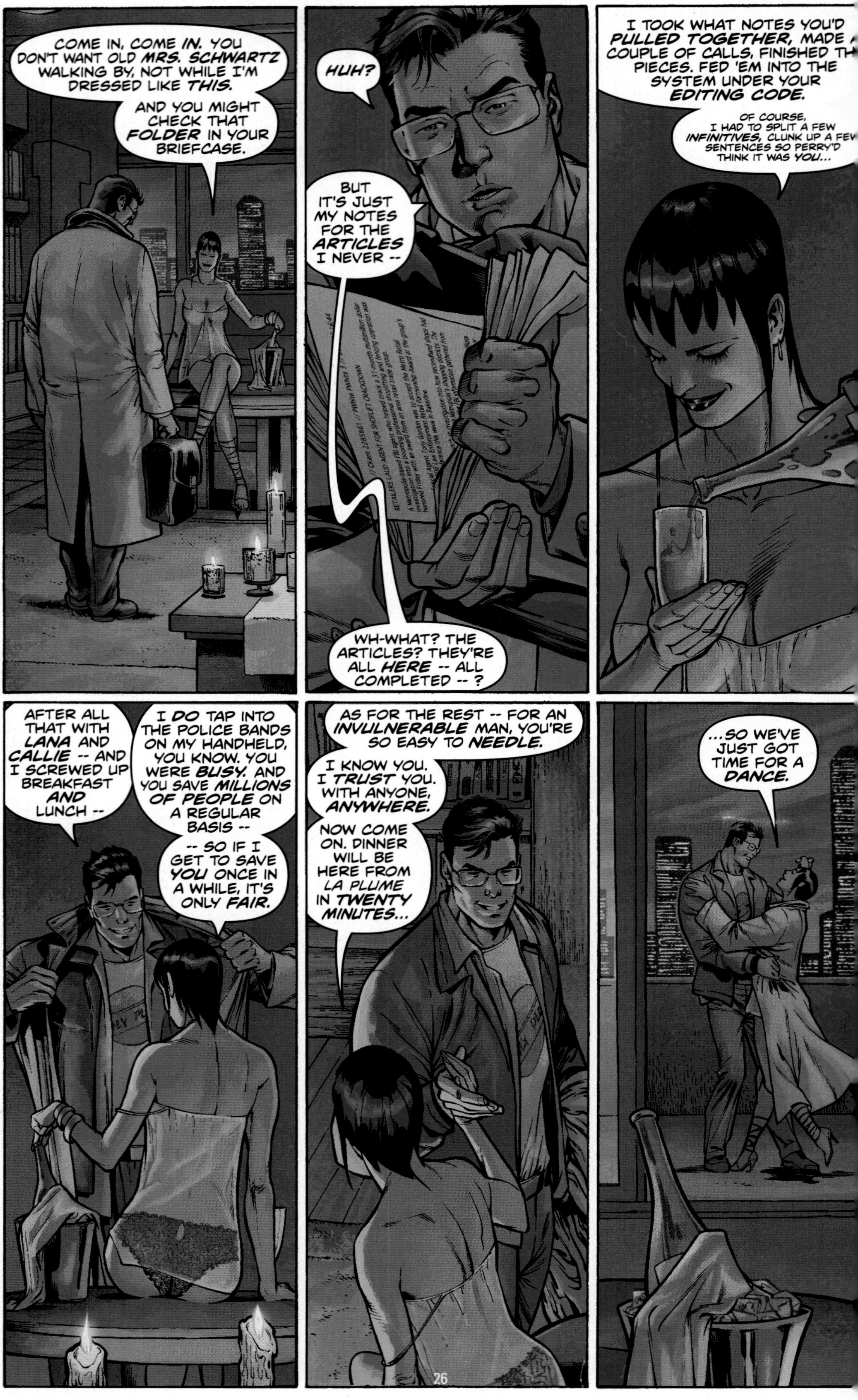
COME IN, COME IN. YOU DON'T WANT OLD MRS. SCHWARTZ WALKING BY, NOT WHILE I'M DRESSED LIKE THIS.
AND YOU MIGHT CHECK THAT FOLDER IN YOUR BRIEFCASE.
HUH?
BUT IT'S JUST MY NOTES FOR THE ARTICLES I NEVER --
WH-WHAT? THE ARTICLES? THEY'RE ALL HERE -- ALL COMPLETED -- ?
I TOOK WHAT NOTES YOU'D PULLED TOGETHER, MADE A COUPLE OF CALLS, FINISHED TH PIECES. FED 'EM INTO THE SYSTEM UNDER YOUR EDITING CODE.
OF COURSE, I HAD TO SPLIT A FEW INFINITIVES, CLUNK UP A FEW SENTENCES SO PERRY'D THINK IT WAS YOU...
AFTER ALL THAT WITH LANA AND CALLIE -- AND I SCREWED UP BREAKFAST AND LUNCH --
I DO TAP INTO THE POLICE BANDS ON MY HANDHELD, YOU KNOW. YOU WERE BUSY. AND YOU SAVE MILLIONS OF PEOPLE ON A REGULAR BASIS --
-- SO IF I GET TO SAVE YOU ONCE IN A WHILE, IT'S ONLY FAIR.
AS FOR THE REST -- FOR AN INVULNERABLE MAN, YOU'RE SO EASY TO NEEDLE.
I KNOW YOU. I TRUST YOU. WITH ANYONE, ANYWHERE.
NOW COME ON. DINNER WILL BE HERE FROM LA PLUME IN TWENTY MINUTES...
...SO WE'VE JUST GOT TIME FOR A DANCE.

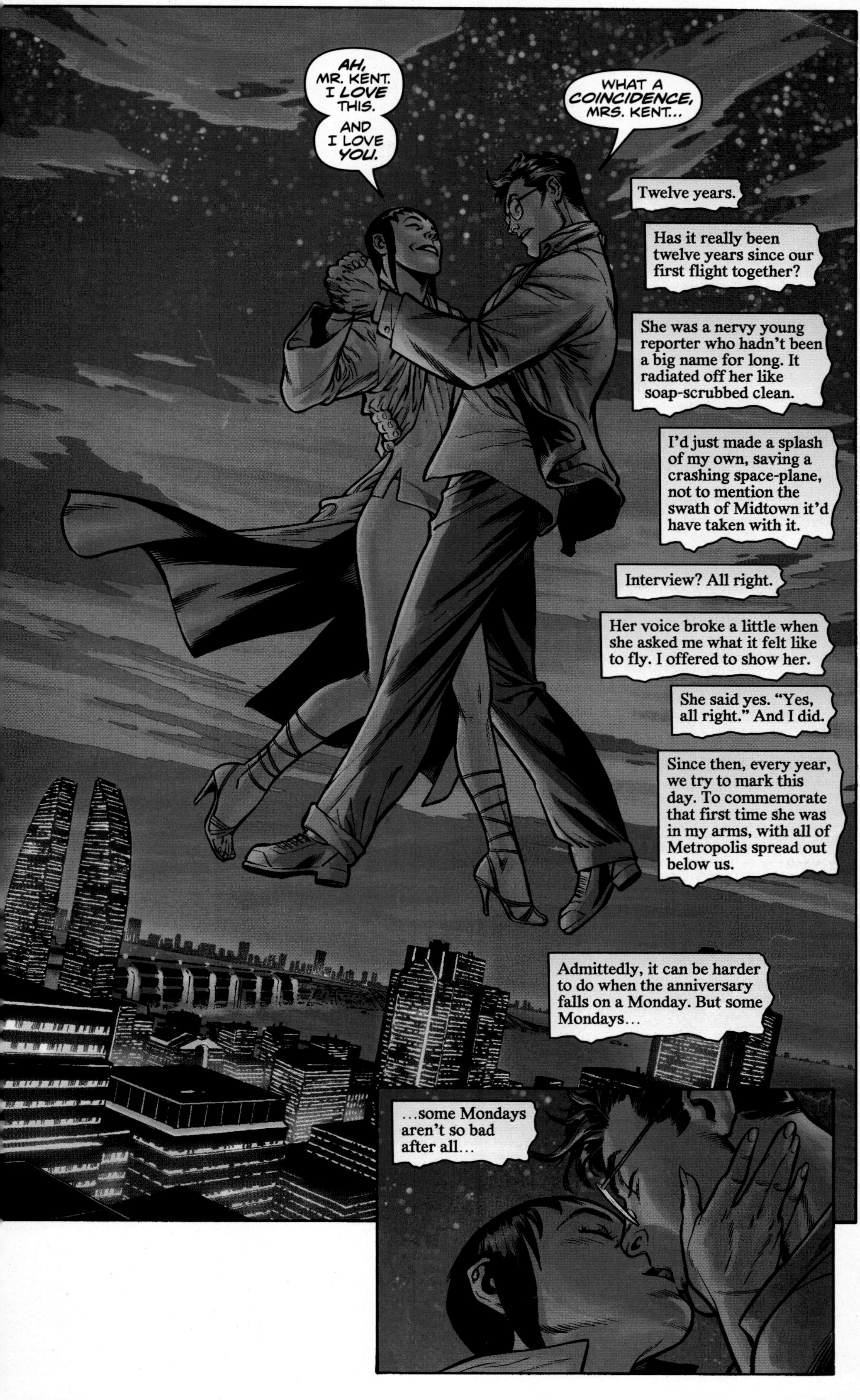
AH, MR. KENT. I LOVE THIS.
AND I LOVE YOU.
WHAT A COINCIDENCE, MRS. KENT...
Twelve years.
Has it really been twelve years since our first flight together?
She was a nervy young reporter who hadn't been a big name for long. It radiated off her like soap-scrubbed clean.
I'd just made a splash of my own, saving a crashing space-plane, not to mention the swath of Midtown it'd have taken with it.
Interview? All right.
Her voice broke a little when she asked me what it felt like to fly. I offered to show her.
She said yes. "Yes, all right." And I did.
Since then, every year, we try to mark this day. To commemorate that first time she was in my arms, with all of Metropolis spread out below us.
Admittedly, it can be harder to do when the anniversary falls on a Monday. But some Mondays...
...some Mondays aren't so bad after all...

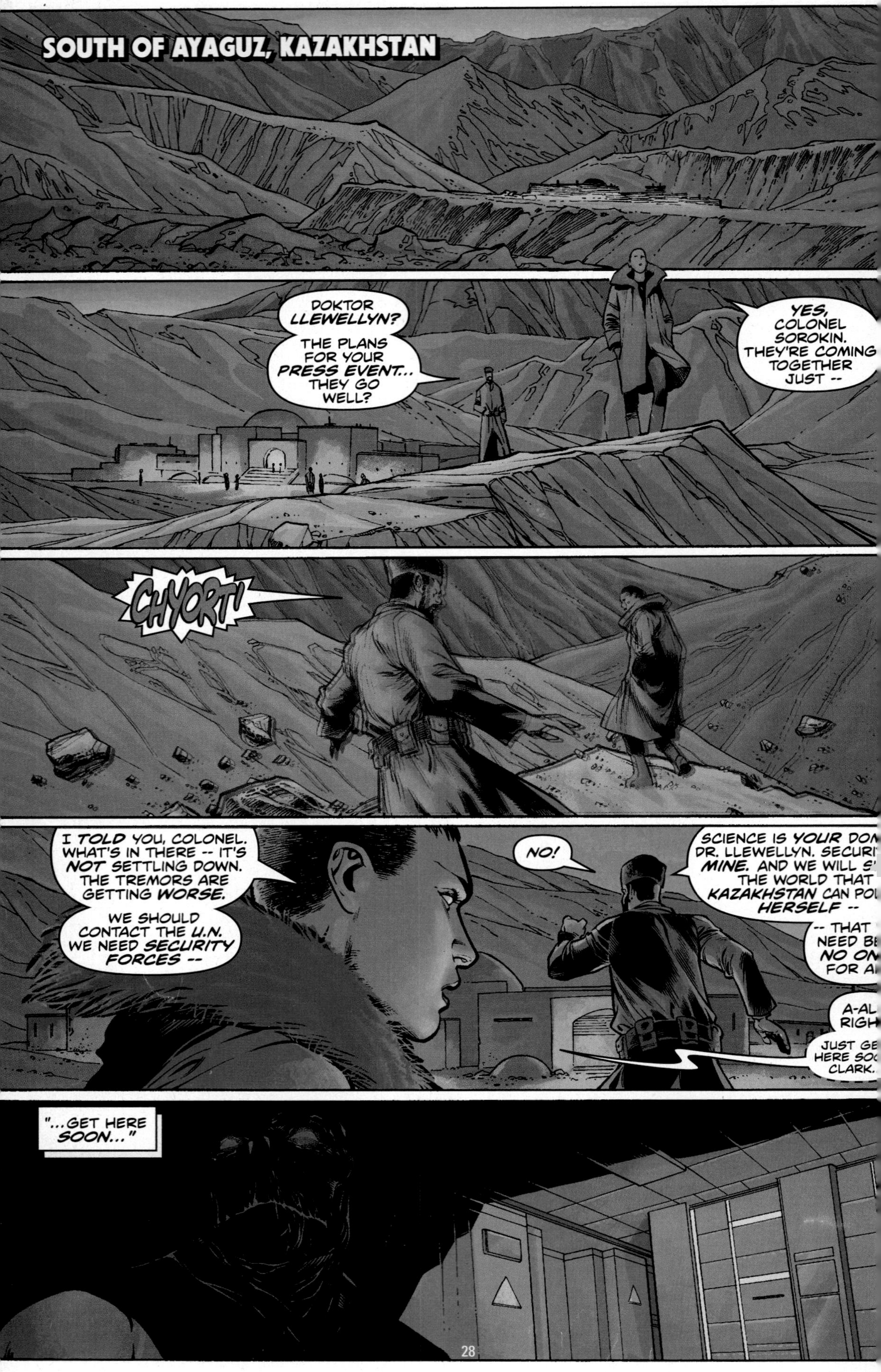

SOUTH OF AYAGUZ, KAZAKHSTAN
DOKTOR LLEWELLYN? THE PLANS FOR YOUR PRESS EVENT... THEY GO WELL?
YES, COLONEL SOROKIN. THEY'RE COMING TOGETHER JUST --
CHYORT!
I TOLD YOU, COLONEL. WHAT'S IN THERE -- IT'S NOT SETTLING DOWN. THE TREMORS ARE GETTING WORSE.
WE SHOULD CONTACT THE U.N. WE NEED SECURITY FORCES --
NO!
"...GET HERE SOON..."

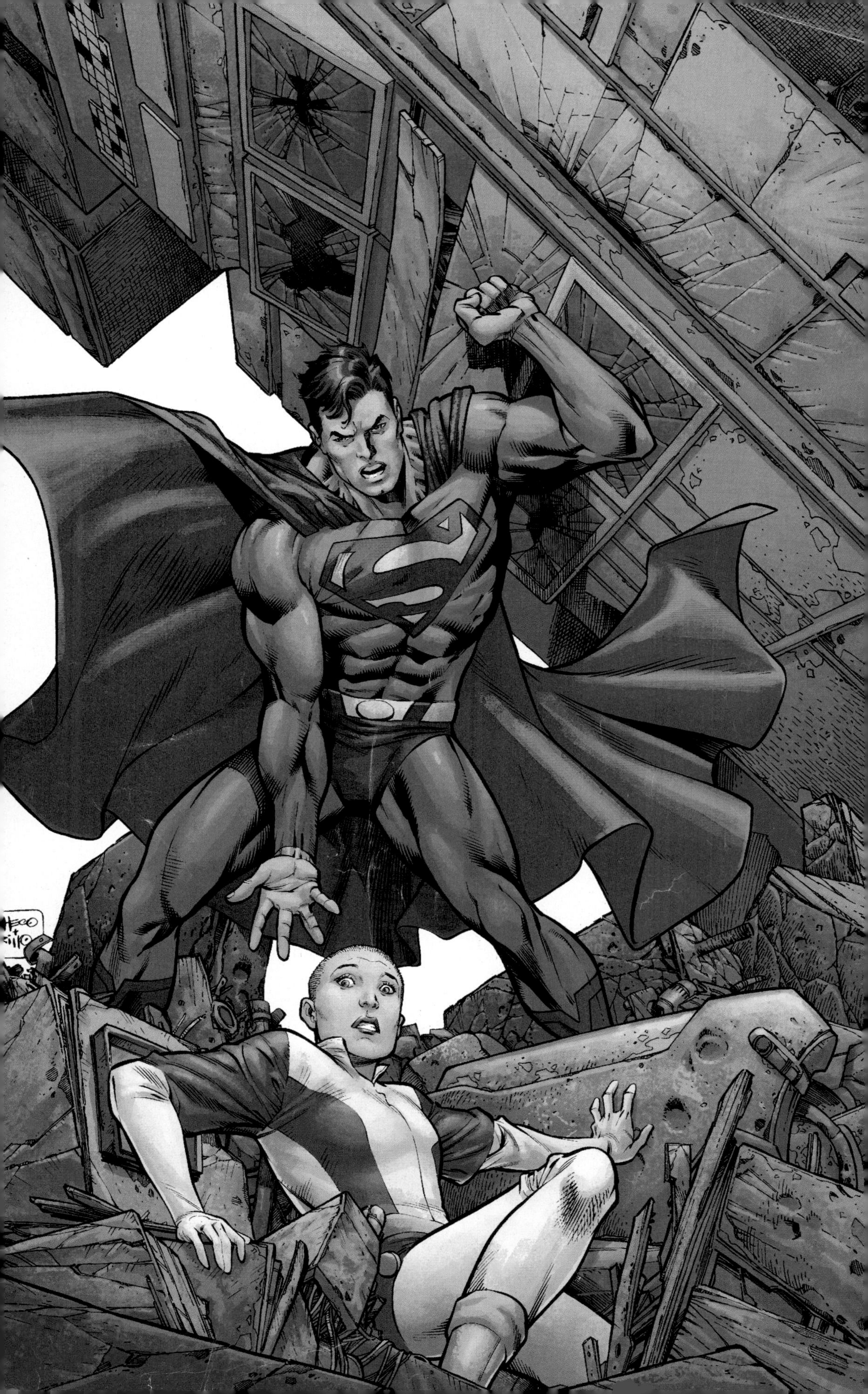

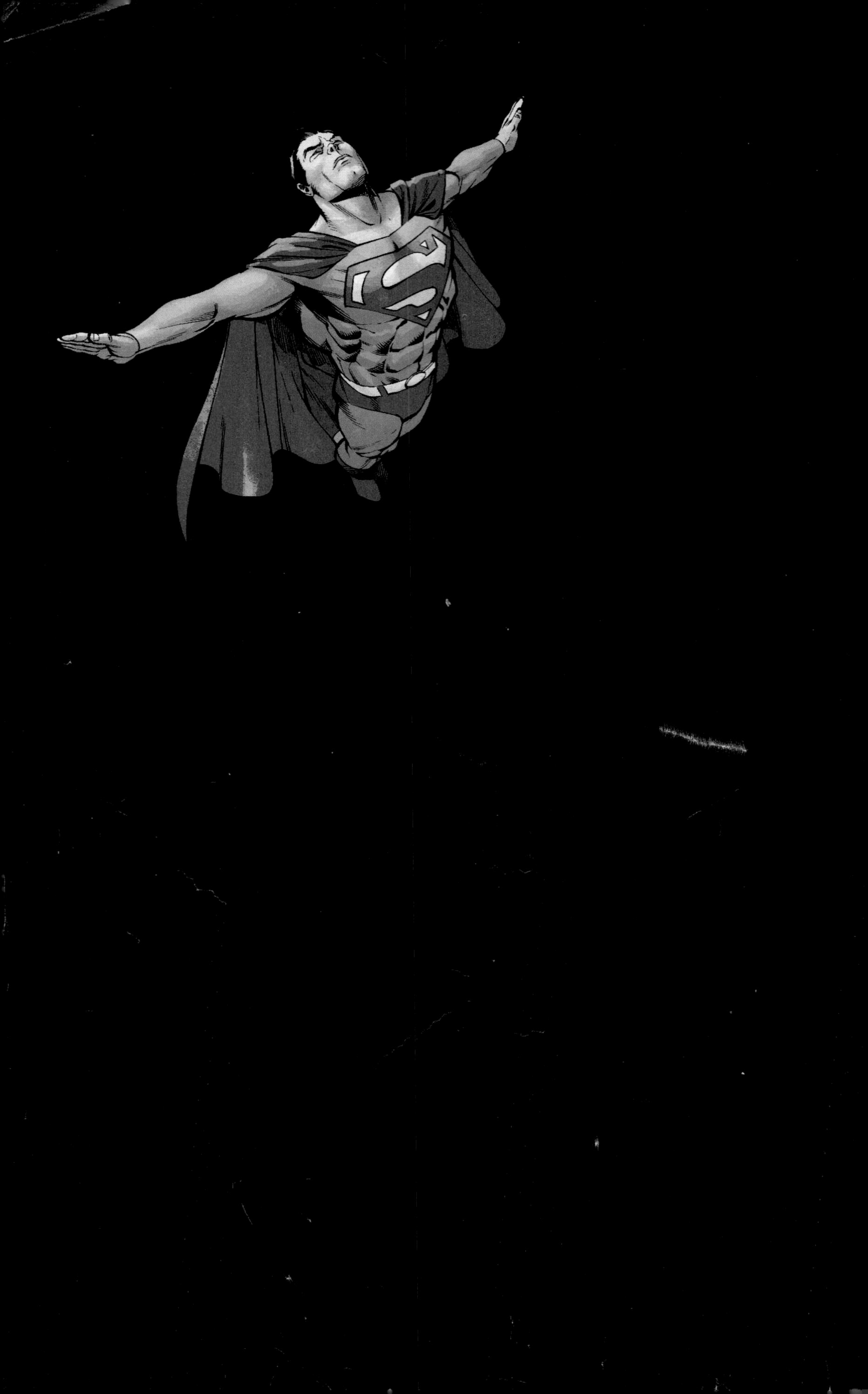

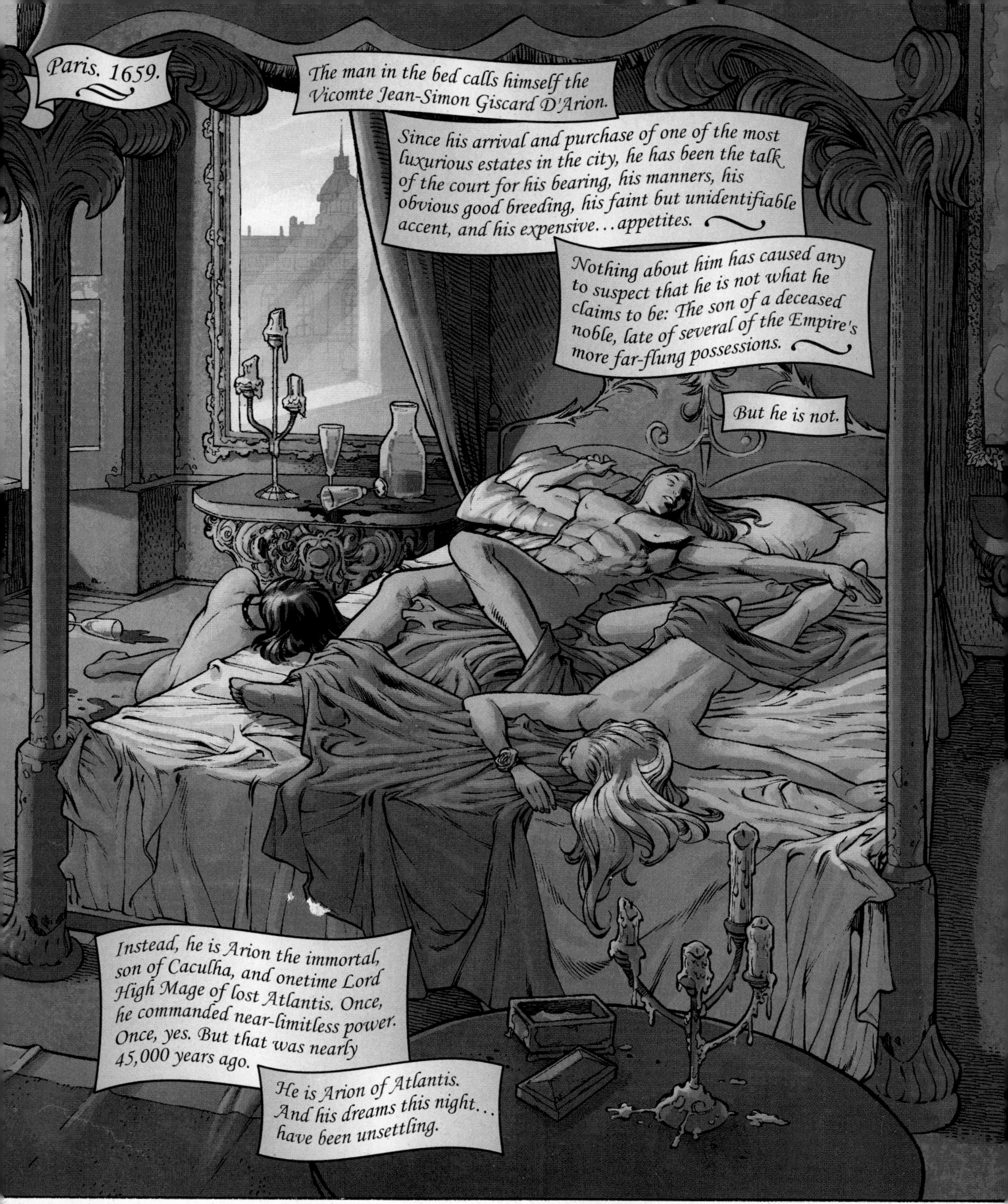
Paris. 1659.
The man in the bed calls himself the Vicomte Jean-Simon Giscard D'Arion.
Since his arrival and purchase of one of the most luxurious estates in the city, he has been the talk of the court for his bearing, his manners, his obvious good breeding, his faint but unidentifiable accent, and his expensive... appetites.
Nothing about him has caused any to suspect that he is not what he claims to be: The son of a deceased noble, late of several of the Empire's more far-flung possessions.
But he is not.
Instead, he is Arion the immortal, son of Caculha, and onetime Lord High Mage of lost Atlantis. Once, he commanded near-limitless power. Once, yes. But that was nearly 45,000 years ago.
He is Arion of Atlantis. And his dreams this night... have been unsettling.

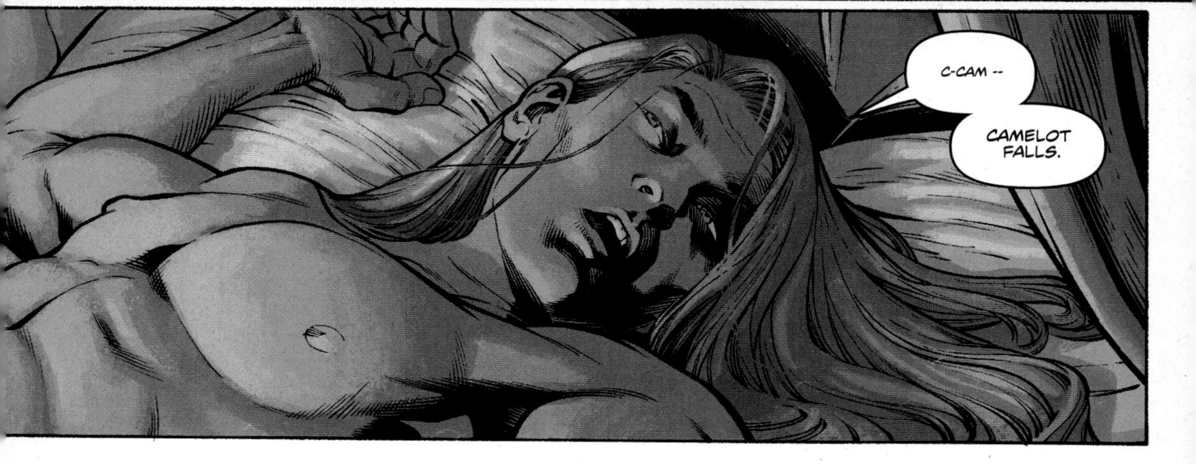
C-CAM --
CAMELOT FALLS.

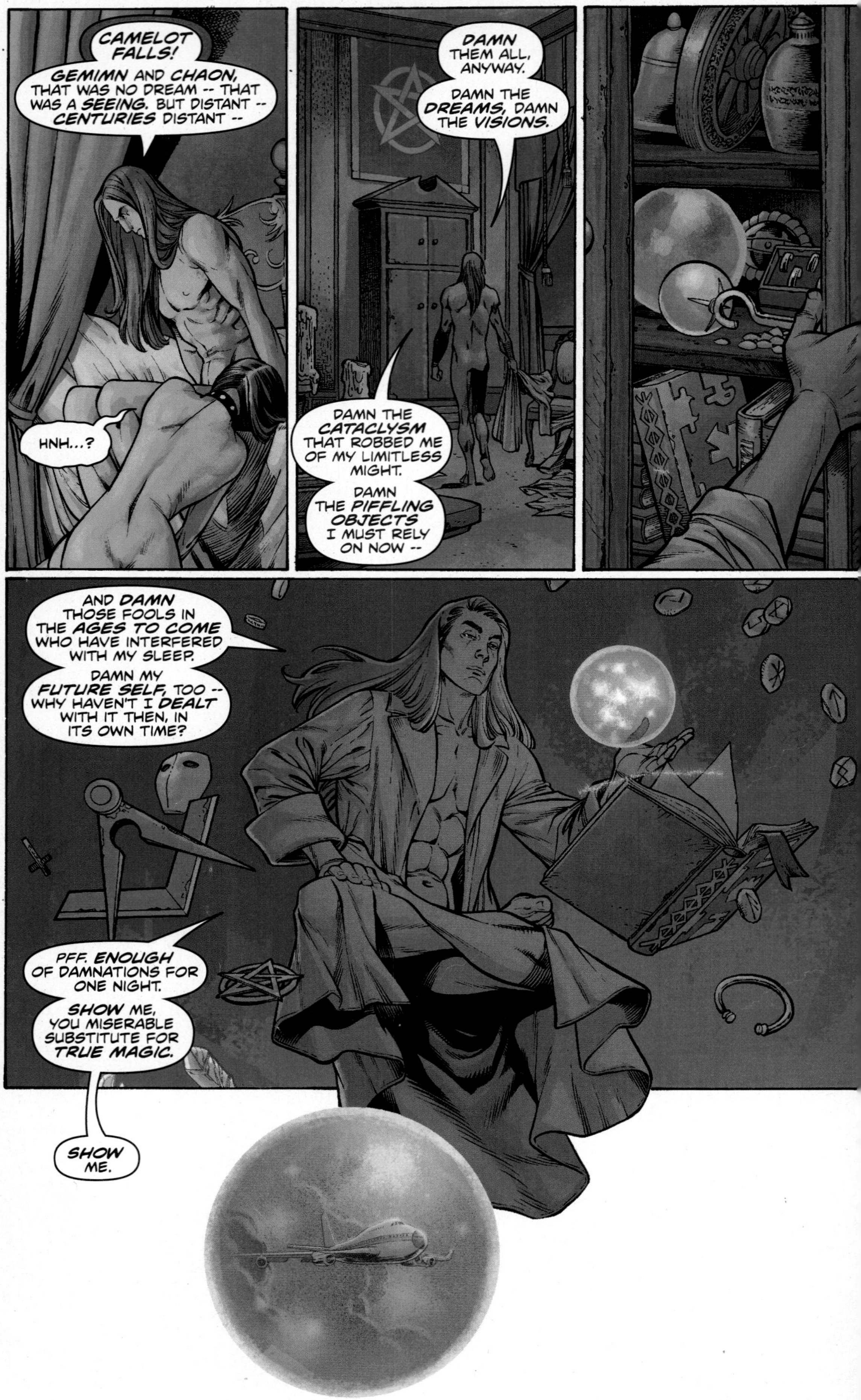
CAMELOT FALLS!
GEMIMN AND CHAON, THAT WAS NO DREAM -- THAT WAS A SEEING. BUT DISTANT -- CENTURIES DISTANT --
HNH...?
DAMN THEM ALL, ANYWAY.
DAMN THE DREAMS, DAMN THE VISIONS.
DAMN THE CATACLYSM THAT ROBBED ME OF MY LIMITLESS MIGHT.
DAMN THE PIFFLING OBJECTS I MUST RELY ON NOW --
AND DAMN THOSE FOOLS IN THE AGES TO COME WHO HAVE INTERFERED WITH MY SLEEP.
DAMN MY FUTURE SELF, TOO -- WHY HAVEN'T I DEALT WITH IT THEN, IN ITS OWN TIME?
PFF. ENOUGH OF DAMNATIONS FOR ONE NIGHT.
SHOW ME, YOU MISERABLE SUBSTITUTE FOR TRUE MAGIC.
SHOW ME.

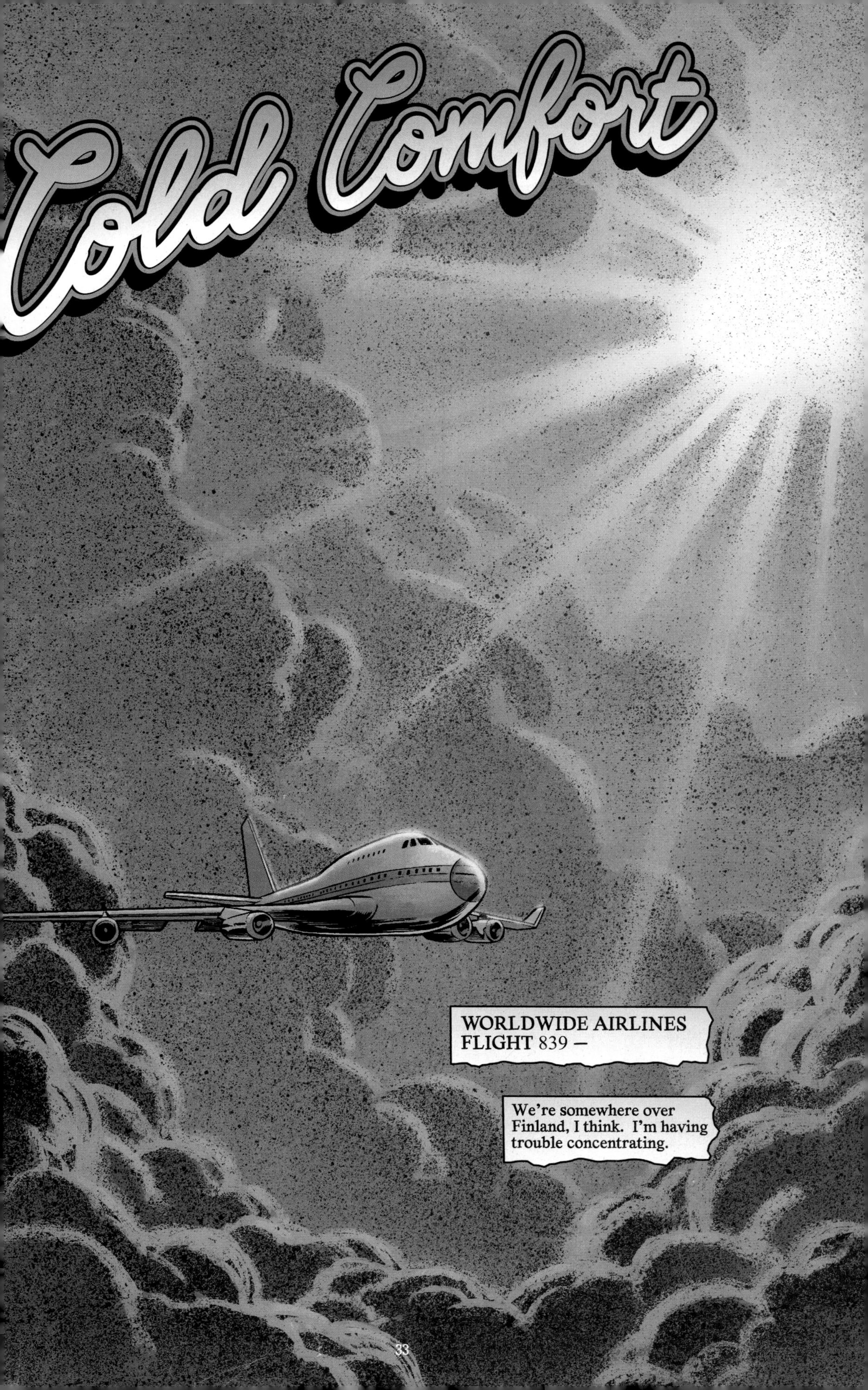
Cold Comfort
WORLDWIDE AIRLINES FLIGHT 839 –
We're somewhere over Finland, I think. I'm having trouble concentrating.

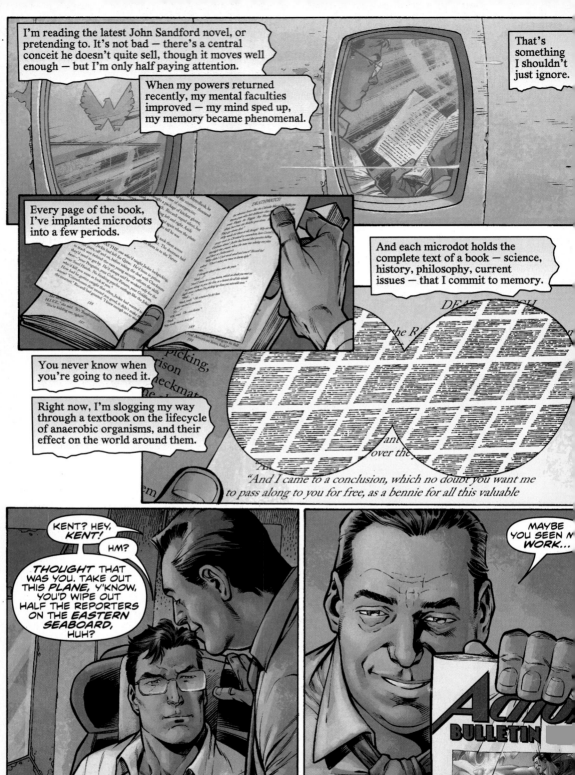

I'm reading the latest John Sandford novel, or pretending to. It's not bad — there's a central conceit he doesn't quite sell, though it moves well enough — but I'm only half paying attention.

When my powers returned recently, my mental faculties improved — my mind sped up, my memory became phenomenal.

That's something I shouldn't just ignore.

Every page of the book, I've implanted microdots into a few periods.

And each microdot holds the complete text of a book — science, history, philosophy, current issues — that I commit to memory.

You never know when you're going to need it.

Right now, I'm slogging my way through a textbook on the lifecycle of anaerobic organisms, and their effect on the world around them.

"And I came to a conclusion, which no doubt you want me to pass along to you for free, as a bennie for all this valuable

KENT? HEY, KENT!

HM?

THOUGHT THAT WAS YOU. TAKE OUT THIS *PLANE*, Y'KNOW, YOU'D WIPE OUT HALF THE REPORTERS ON THE *EASTERN SEABOARD*, HUH?

I'M JEFFRIES. *LOWELL* JEFFRIES, OF *ACTION BULLETIN NEWS*, "YOUR DAILY NEWS BULLET"?

MAYBE YOU SEEN M WORK...

I GOT THE *FRONT PAGE* ON THIS ONE. "HE'S *BACK*, BUT IS HE A *FRAUD*?"

ACTION BULLETIN

HE'S BACK, IS HE A FRAU

DEATHWATCH BY

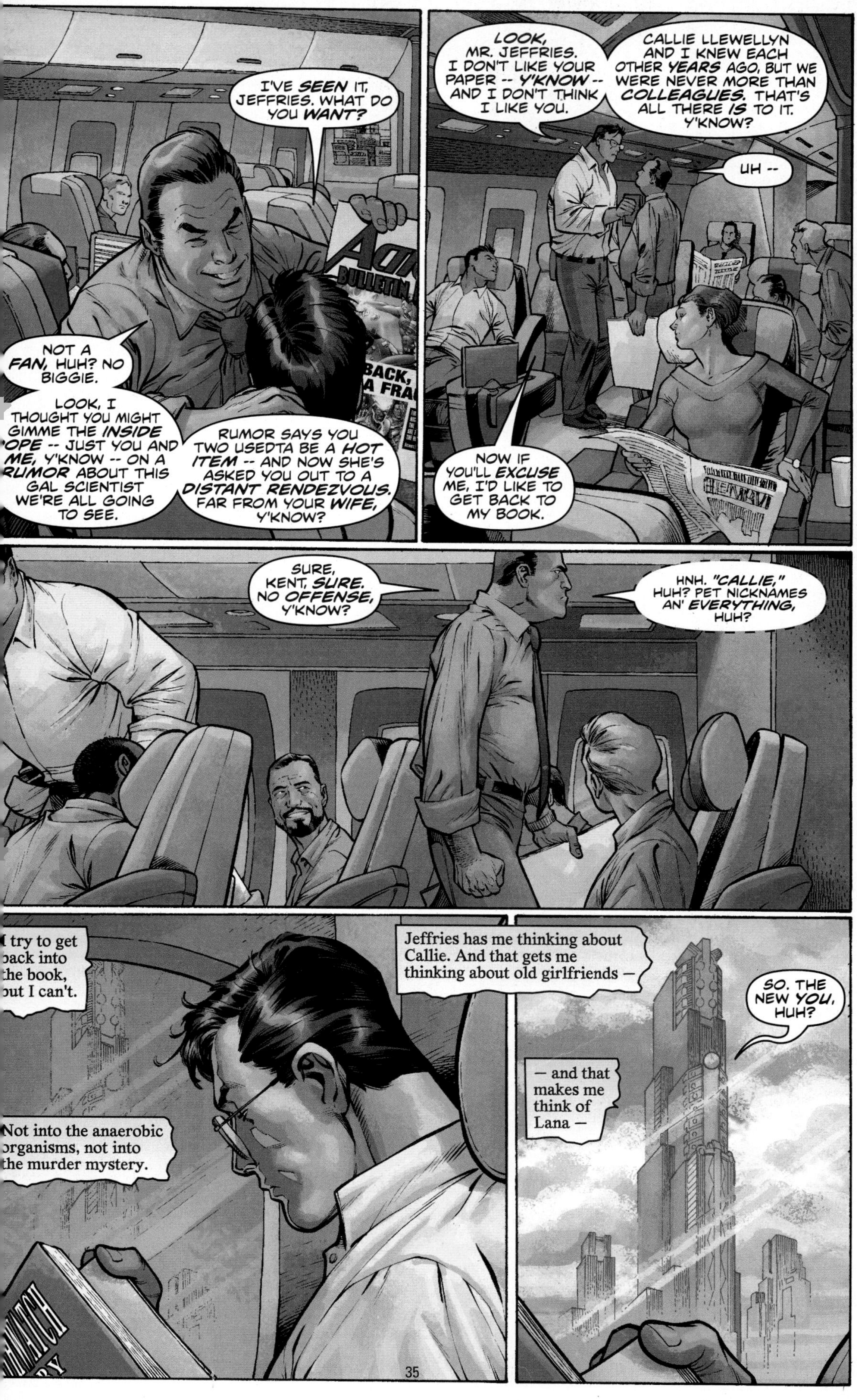
I'VE SEEN IT, JEFFRIES. WHAT DO YOU WANT?
NOT A FAN, HUH? NO BIGGIE.
LOOK, I THOUGHT YOU MIGHT GIMME THE INSIDE DOPE -- JUST YOU AND ME, Y'KNOW -- ON A RUMOR ABOUT THIS GAL SCIENTIST WE'RE ALL GOING TO SEE.
RUMOR SAYS YOU TWO USEDTA BE A HOT ITEM -- AND NOW SHE'S ASKED YOU OUT TO A DISTANT RENDEZVOUS. FAR FROM YOUR WIFE, Y'KNOW?
LOOK, MR. JEFFRIES. I DON'T LIKE YOUR PAPER -- Y'KNOW -- AND I DON'T THINK I LIKE YOU.
CALLIE LLEWELLYN AND I KNEW EACH OTHER YEARS AGO, BUT WE WERE NEVER MORE THAN COLLEAGUES. THAT'S ALL THERE IS TO IT. Y'KNOW?
UH --
NOW IF YOU'LL EXCUSE ME, I'D LIKE TO GET BACK TO MY BOOK.
SURE, KENT, SURE. NO OFFENSE, Y'KNOW?
HNH. "CALLIE," HUH? PET NICKNAMES AN' EVERYTHING, HUH?
I try to get back into the book, but I can't.
Not into the anaerobic organisms, not into the murder mystery.
Jeffries has me thinking about Callie. And that gets me thinking about old girlfriends —
— and that makes me think of Lana —
SO. THE NEW YOU, HUH?

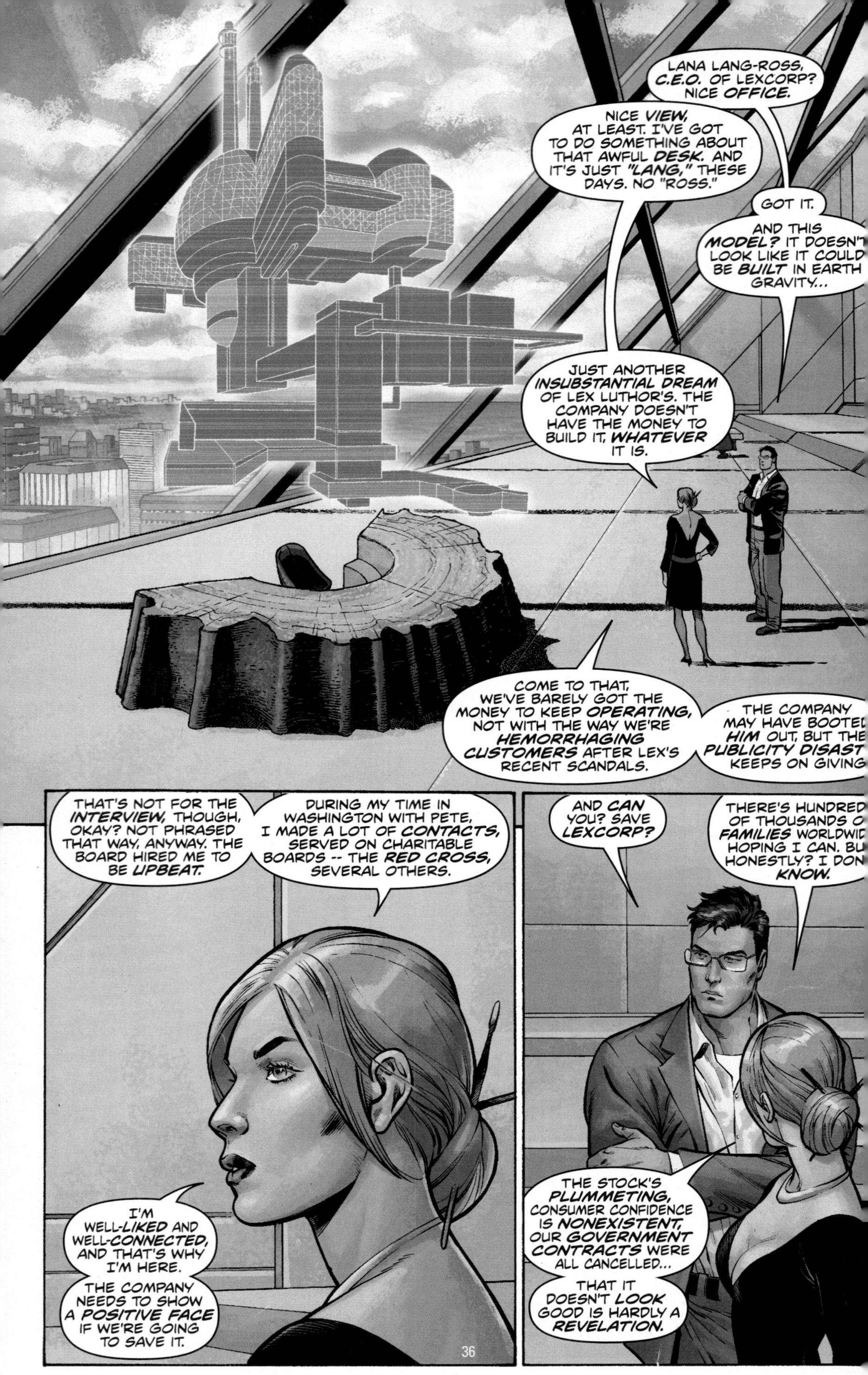
LANA LANG-ROSS, C.E.O. OF LEXCORP? NICE OFFICE.
NICE VIEW, AT LEAST. I'VE GOT TO DO SOMETHING ABOUT THAT AWFUL DESK. AND IT'S JUST "LANG," THESE DAYS. NO "ROSS."
GOT IT.
AND THIS MODEL? IT DOESN'T LOOK LIKE IT COULD BE BUILT IN EARTH GRAVITY...
JUST ANOTHER INSUBSTANTIAL DREAM OF LEX LUTHOR'S. THE COMPANY DOESN'T HAVE THE MONEY TO BUILD IT, WHATEVER IT IS.
COME TO THAT, WE'VE BARELY GOT THE MONEY TO KEEP OPERATING, NOT WITH THE WAY WE'RE HEMORRHAGING CUSTOMERS AFTER LEX'S RECENT SCANDALS.
THE COMPANY MAY HAVE BOOTED HIM OUT, BUT THE PUBLICITY DISAST KEEPS ON GIVING
THAT'S NOT FOR THE INTERVIEW, THOUGH, OKAY? NOT PHRASED THAT WAY, ANYWAY. THE BOARD HIRED ME TO BE UPBEAT.
DURING MY TIME IN WASHINGTON WITH PETE, I MADE A LOT OF CONTACTS, SERVED ON CHARITABLE BOARDS -- THE RED CROSS, SEVERAL OTHERS.
I'M WELL-LIKED AND WELL-CONNECTED, AND THAT'S WHY I'M HERE.
THE COMPANY NEEDS TO SHOW A POSITIVE FACE IF WE'RE GOING TO SAVE IT.
AND CAN YOU? SAVE LEXCORP?
THERE'S HUNDRED OF THOUSANDS O FAMILIES WORLDWID HOPING I CAN. BU HONESTLY? I DON KNOW.
THE STOCK'S PLUMMETING, CONSUMER CONFIDENCE IS NONEXISTENT, OUR GOVERNMENT CONTRACTS WERE ALL CANCELLED...
THAT IT DOESN'T LOOK GOOD IS HARDLY A REVELATION.

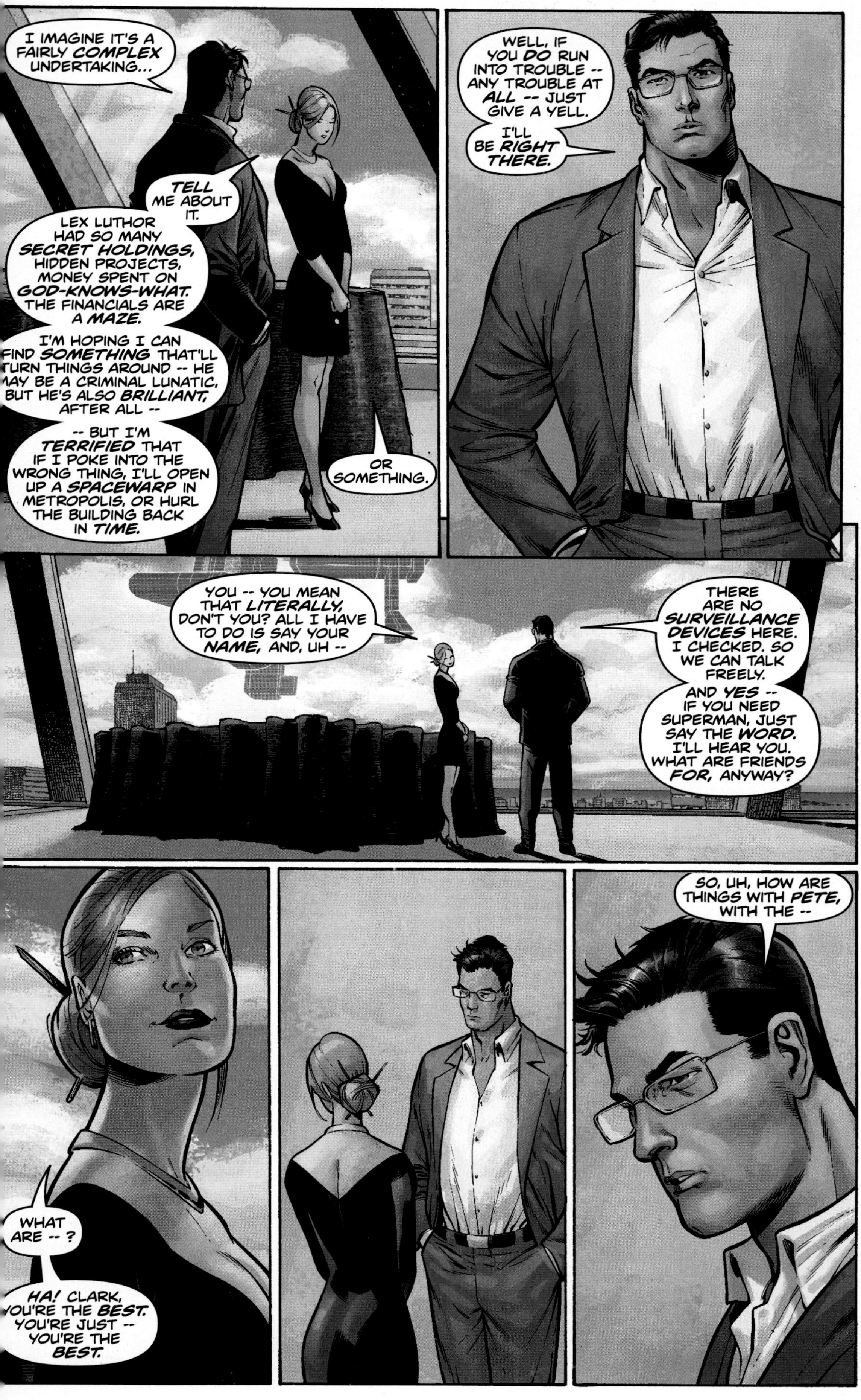
I IMAGINE IT'S A FAIRLY COMPLEX UNDERTAKING...
TELL ME ABOUT IT.
LEX LUTHOR HAD SO MANY SECRET HOLDINGS, HIDDEN PROJECTS, MONEY SPENT ON GOD-KNOWS-WHAT. THE FINANCIALS ARE A MAZE.
I'M HOPING I CAN FIND SOMETHING THAT'LL TURN THINGS AROUND -- HE MAY BE A CRIMINAL LUNATIC, BUT HE'S ALSO BRILLIANT, AFTER ALL --
-- BUT I'M TERRIFIED THAT IF I POKE INTO THE WRONG THING, I'LL OPEN UP A SPACEWARP IN METROPOLIS, OR HURL THE BUILDING BACK IN TIME.
OR SOMETHING.
WELL, IF YOU DO RUN INTO TROUBLE -- ANY TROUBLE AT ALL -- JUST GIVE A YELL.
I'LL BE RIGHT THERE.
YOU -- YOU MEAN THAT LITERALLY, DON'T YOU? ALL I HAVE TO DO IS SAY YOUR NAME, AND, UH --
THERE ARE NO SURVEILLANCE DEVICES HERE. I CHECKED. SO WE CAN TALK FREELY.
AND YES -- IF YOU NEED SUPERMAN, JUST SAY THE WORD. I'LL HEAR YOU. WHAT ARE FRIENDS FOR, ANYWAY?
WHAT ARE -- ?
HA! CLARK, YOU'RE THE BEST. YOU'RE JUST -- YOU'RE THE BEST.
SO, UH, HOW ARE THINGS WITH PETE, WITH THE --

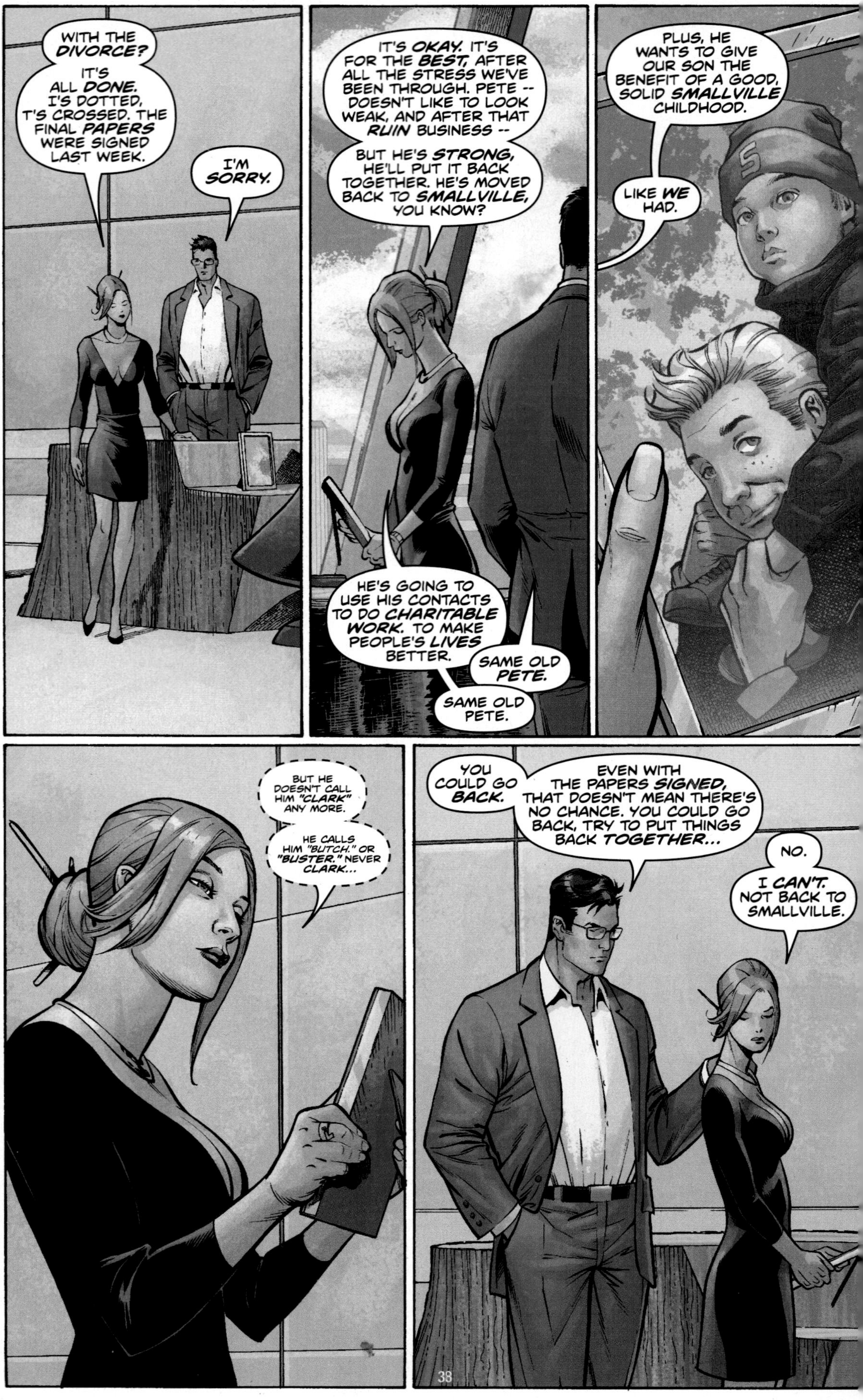

WITH THE DIVORCE?
IT'S ALL DONE. I'S DOTTED, T'S CROSSED. THE FINAL PAPERS WERE SIGNED LAST WEEK.
I'M SORRY.
IT'S OKAY. IT'S FOR THE BEST, AFTER ALL THE STRESS WE'VE BEEN THROUGH. PETE -- DOESN'T LIKE TO LOOK WEAK, AND AFTER THAT RUIN BUSINESS --
BUT HE'S STRONG, HE'LL PUT IT BACK TOGETHER. HE'S MOVED BACK TO SMALLVILLE, YOU KNOW?
HE'S GOING TO USE HIS CONTACTS TO DO CHARITABLE WORK. TO MAKE PEOPLE'S LIVES BETTER.
SAME OLD PETE.
SAME OLD PETE.
PLUS, HE WANTS TO GIVE OUR SON THE BENEFIT OF A GOOD, SOLID SMALLVILLE CHILDHOOD.
LIKE WE HAD.
BUT HE DOESN'T CALL HIM "CLARK" ANY MORE.
HE CALLS HIM "BUTCH," OR "BUSTER." NEVER CLARK...
YOU COULD GO BACK.
EVEN WITH THE PAPERS SIGNED, THAT DOESN'T MEAN THERE'S NO CHANCE. YOU COULD GO BACK, TRY TO PUT THINGS BACK TOGETHER...
NO.
I CAN'T. NOT BACK TO SMALLVILLE.

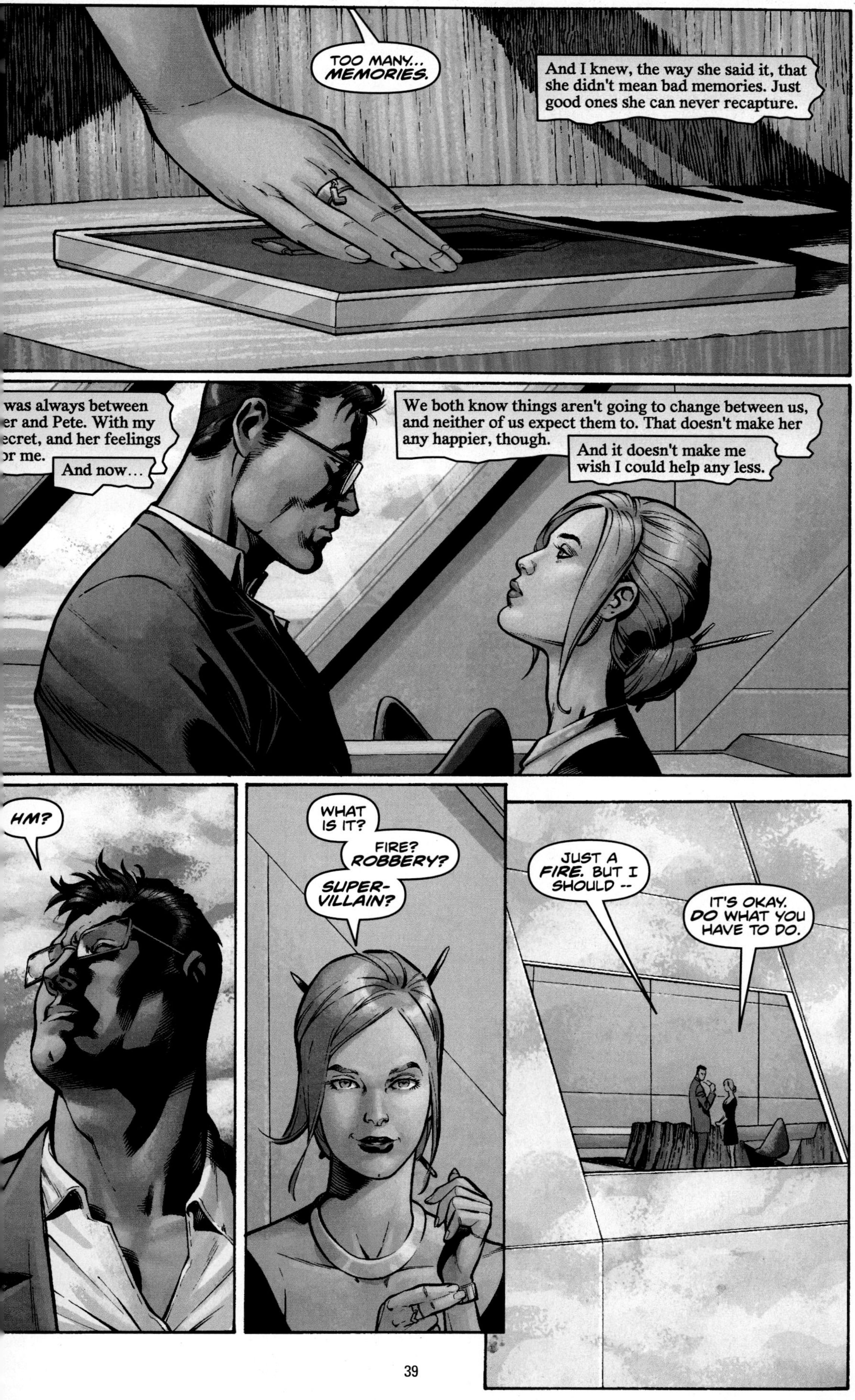
TOO MANY... MEMORIES.
And I knew, the way she said it, that she didn't mean bad memories. Just good ones she can never recapture.
was always between er and Pete. With my ecret, and her feelings or me.
And now...
We both know things aren't going to change between us, and neither of us expect them to. That doesn't make her any happier, though.
And it doesn't make me wish I could help any less.
HM?
WHAT IS IT?
FIRE? ROBBERY?
SUPER-VILLAIN?
JUST A FIRE. BUT I SHOULD --
IT'S OKAY. DO WHAT YOU HAVE TO DO.

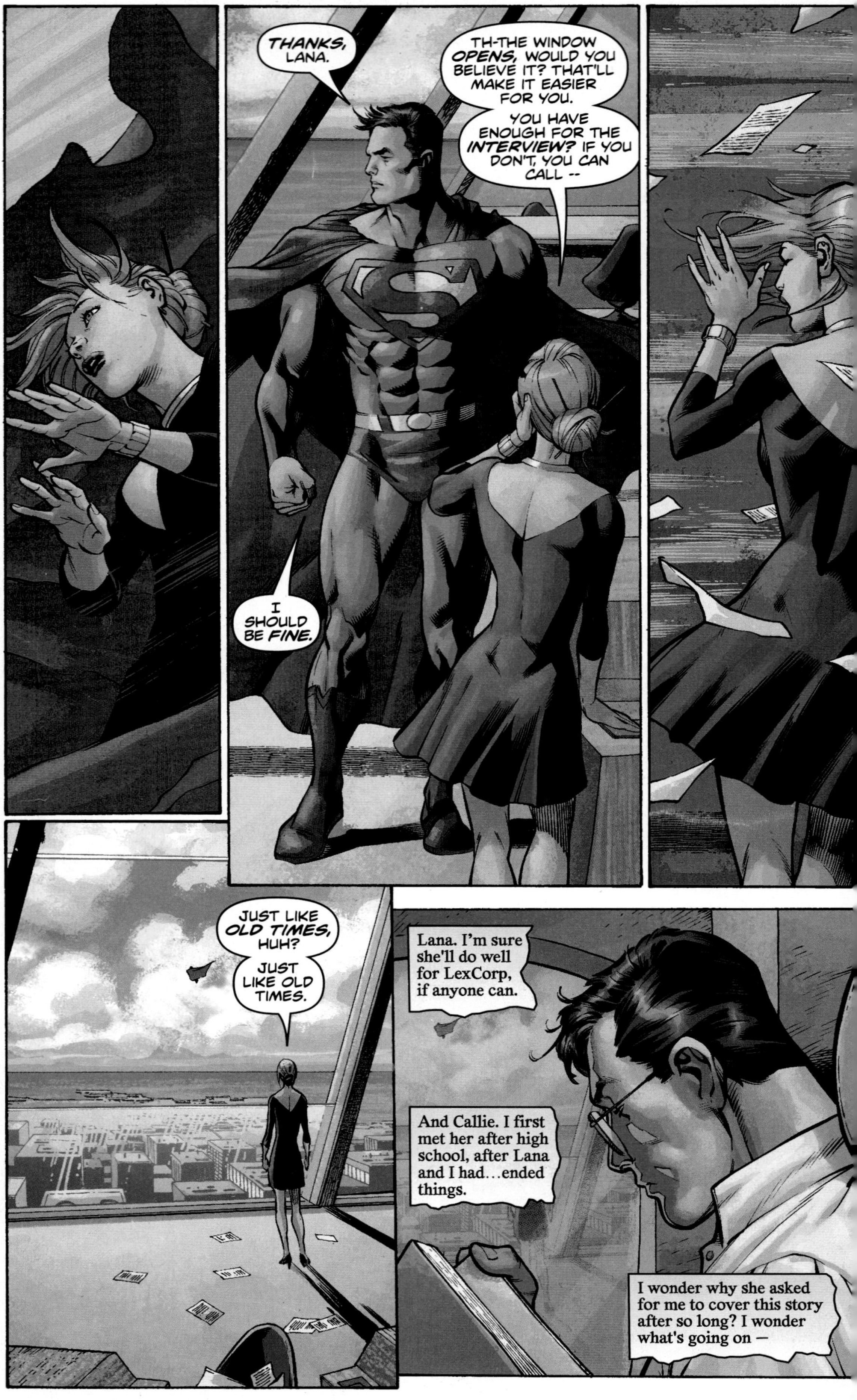
THANKS, LANA.
TH-THE WINDOW OPENS, WOULD YOU BELIEVE IT? THAT'LL MAKE IT EASIER FOR YOU.
YOU HAVE ENOUGH FOR THE INTERVIEW? IF YOU DON'T, YOU CAN CALL --
I SHOULD BE FINE.
JUST LIKE OLD TIMES, HUH?
JUST LIKE OLD TIMES.
Lana. I'm sure she'll do well for LexCorp, if anyone can.
And Callie. I first met her after high school, after Lana and I had…ended things.
I wonder why she asked for me to cover this story after so long? I wonder what's going on —

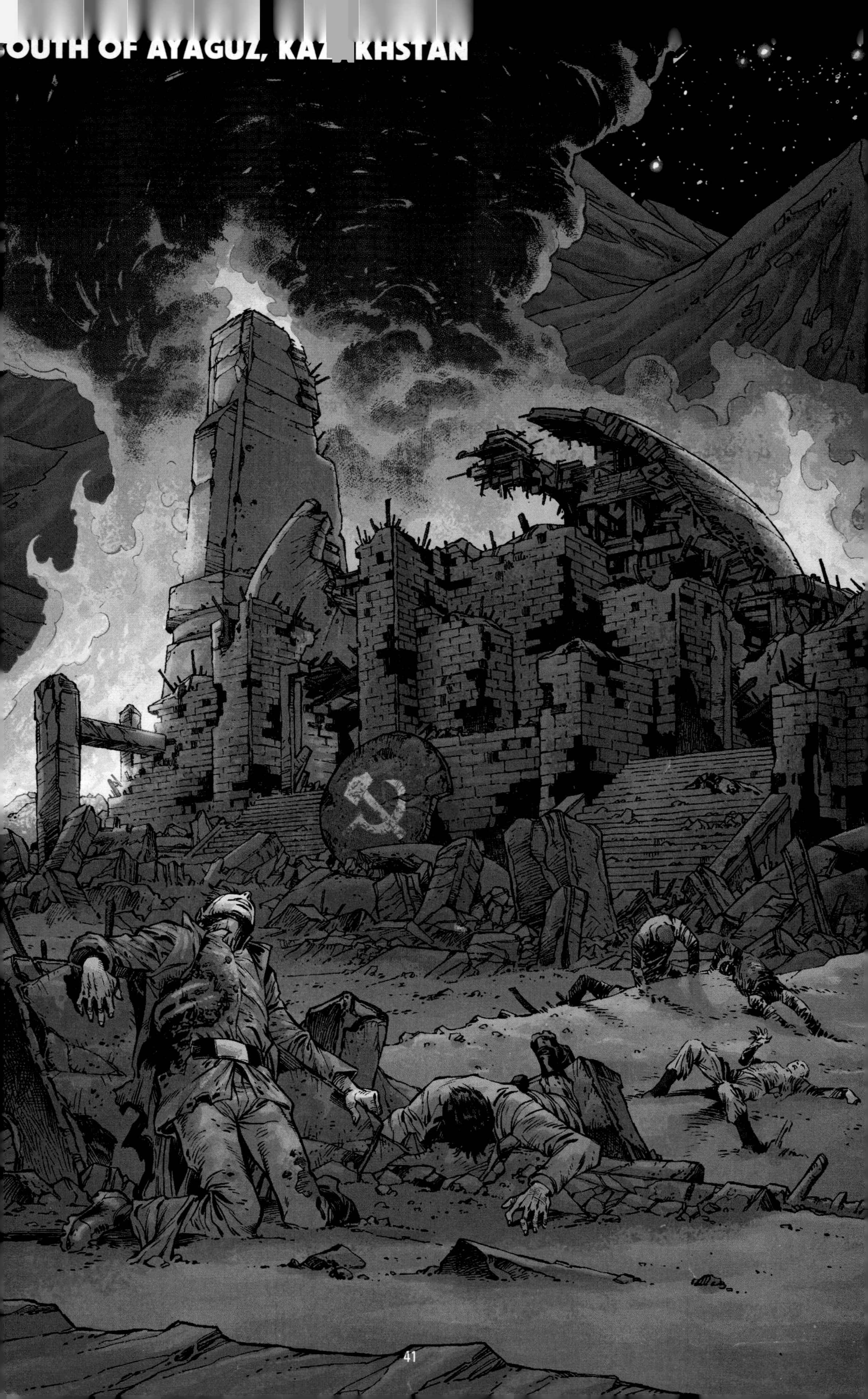
OUTH OF AYAGUZ, KAZ KHSTAN

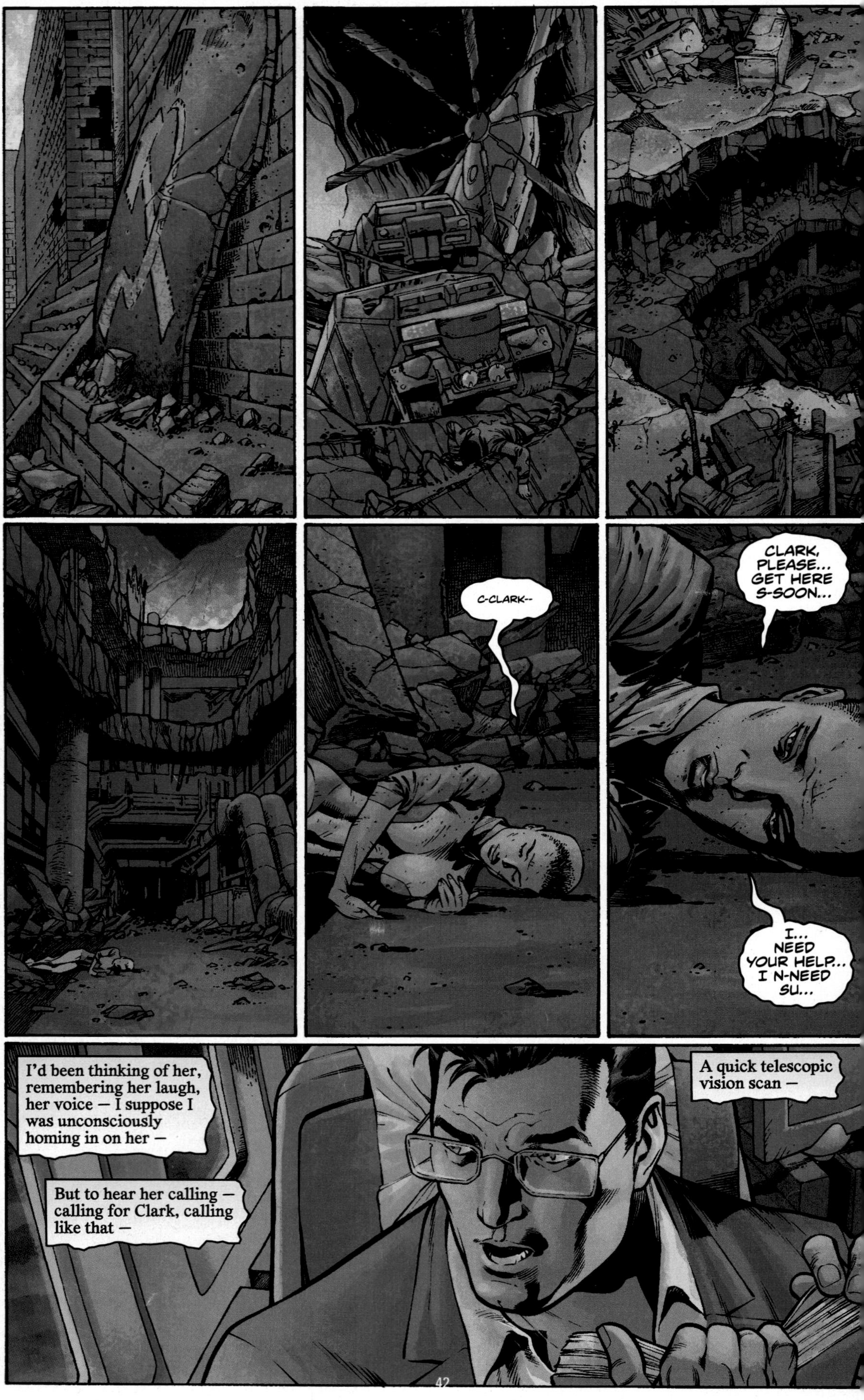
C-CLARK--
CLARK, PLEASE... GET HERE S-SOON...
I... NEED YOUR HELP... I N-NEED SU...
I'd been thinking of her, remembering her laugh, her voice — I suppose I was unconsciously homing in on her —
But to hear her calling — calling for Clark, calling like that —
A quick telescopic vision scan —

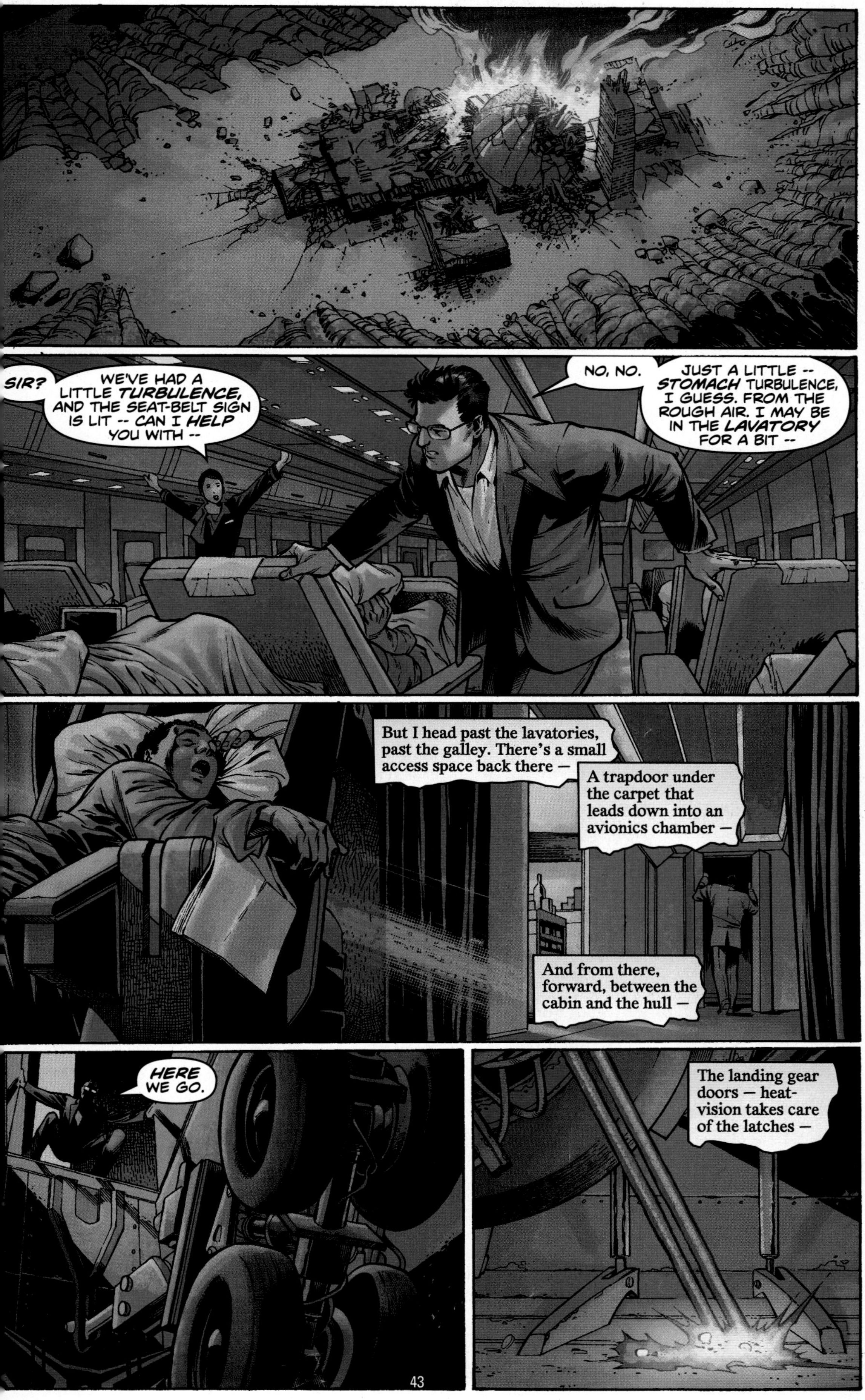
SIR?
WE'VE HAD A LITTLE TURBULENCE, AND THE SEAT-BELT SIGN IS LIT -- CAN I HELP YOU WITH --
NO, NO.
JUST A LITTLE -- STOMACH TURBULENCE, I GUESS. FROM THE ROUGH AIR. I MAY BE IN THE LAVATORY FOR A BIT --
But I head past the lavatories, past the galley. There's a small access space back there —
A trapdoor under the carpet that leads down into an avionics chamber —
And from there, forward, between the cabin and the hull —
HERE WE GO.
The landing gear doors — heat-vision takes care of the latches —

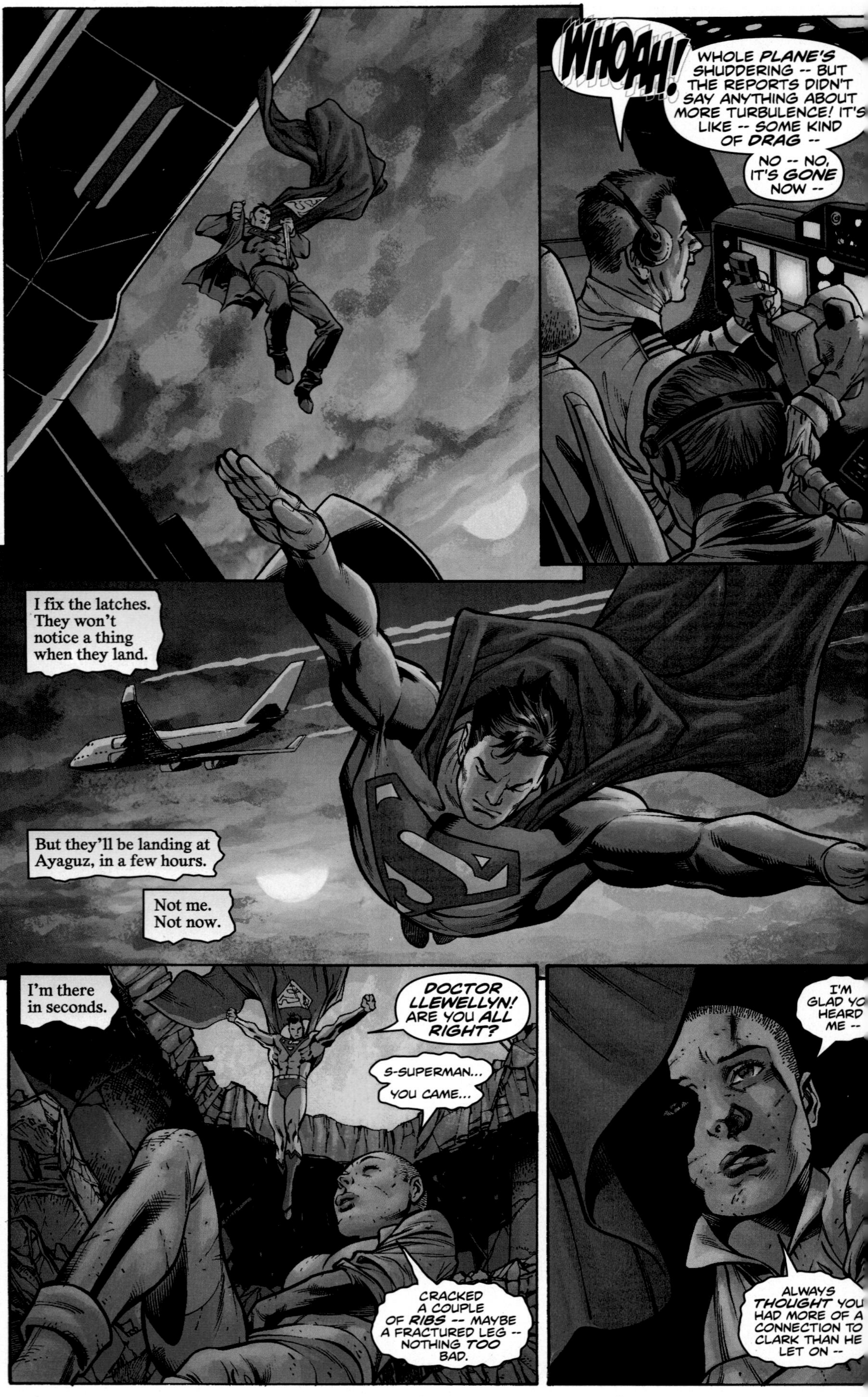
WHOAH!
WHOLE PLANE'S SHUDDERING -- BUT THE REPORTS DIDN'T SAY ANYTHING ABOUT MORE TURBULENCE! IT'S LIKE -- SOME KIND OF DRAG --
NO -- NO, IT'S GONE NOW --
I fix the latches. They won't notice a thing when they land.
But they'll be landing at Ayaguz, in a few hours.
Not me. Not now.
I'm there in seconds.
DOCTOR LLEWELLYN! ARE YOU ALL RIGHT?
S-SUPERMAN...
YOU CAME...
CRACKED A COUPLE OF RIBS -- MAYBE A FRACTURED LEG -- NOTHING TOO BAD.
I'M GLAD YO HEARD ME --
ALWAYS THOUGHT YOU HAD MORE OF A CONNECTION TO CLARK THAN HE LET ON --

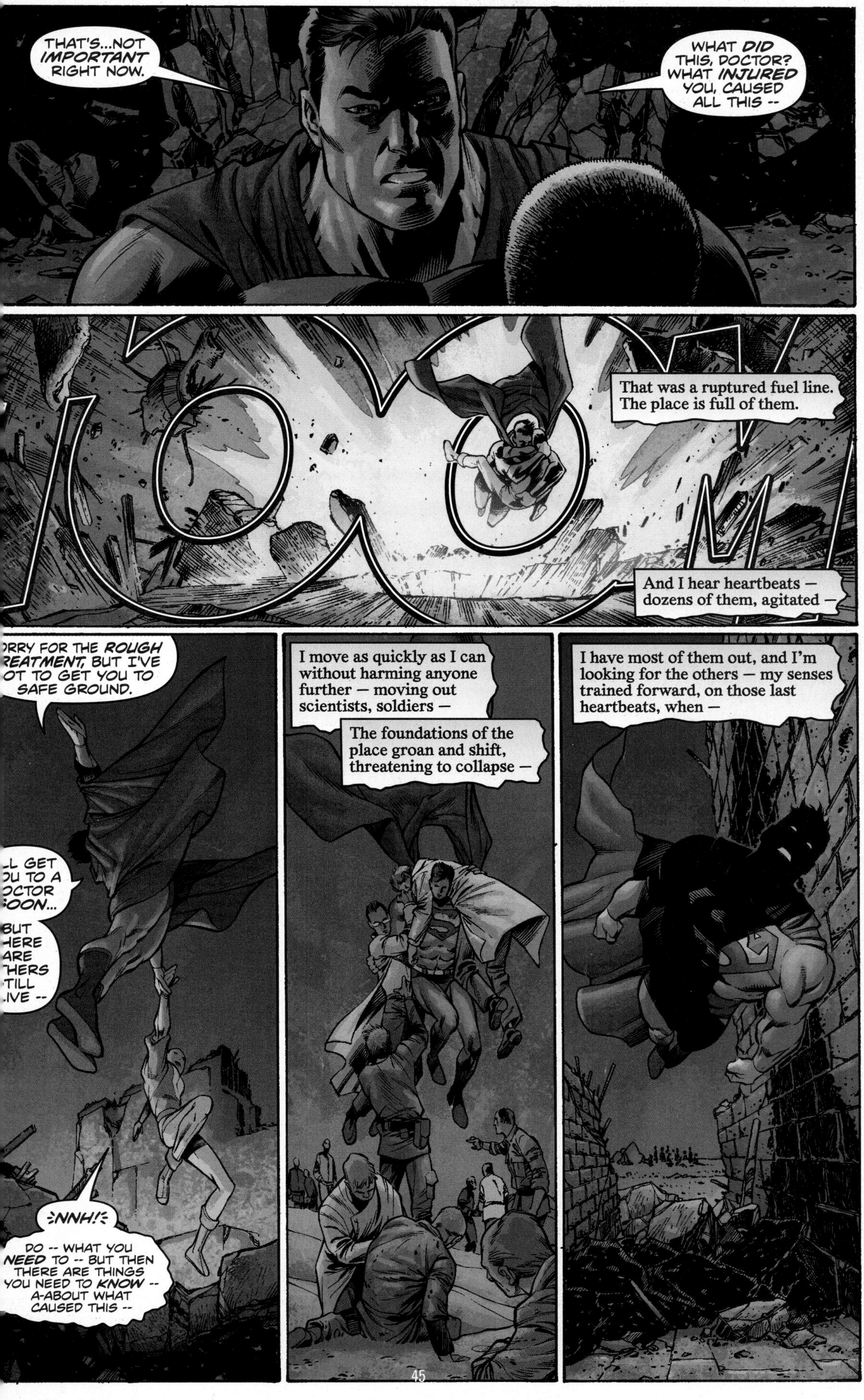
THAT'S...NOT IMPORTANT RIGHT NOW.
WHAT DID THIS, DOCTOR? WHAT INJURED YOU, CAUSED ALL THIS --
That was a ruptured fuel line. The place is full of them.
And I hear heartbeats — dozens of them, agitated —
RRY FOR THE ROUGH REATMENT, BUT I'VE OT TO GET YOU TO SAFE GROUND.
L GET OU TO A OCTOR OON...
BUT HERE ARE THERS TILL IVE --
NNH!
DO -- WHAT YOU NEED TO -- BUT THEN THERE ARE THINGS YOU NEED TO KNOW -- A-ABOUT WHAT CAUSED THIS --
I move as quickly as I can without harming anyone further — moving out scientists, soldiers —
The foundations of the place groan and shift, threatening to collapse —
I have most of them out, and I'm looking for the others — my senses trained forward, on those last heartbeats, when —

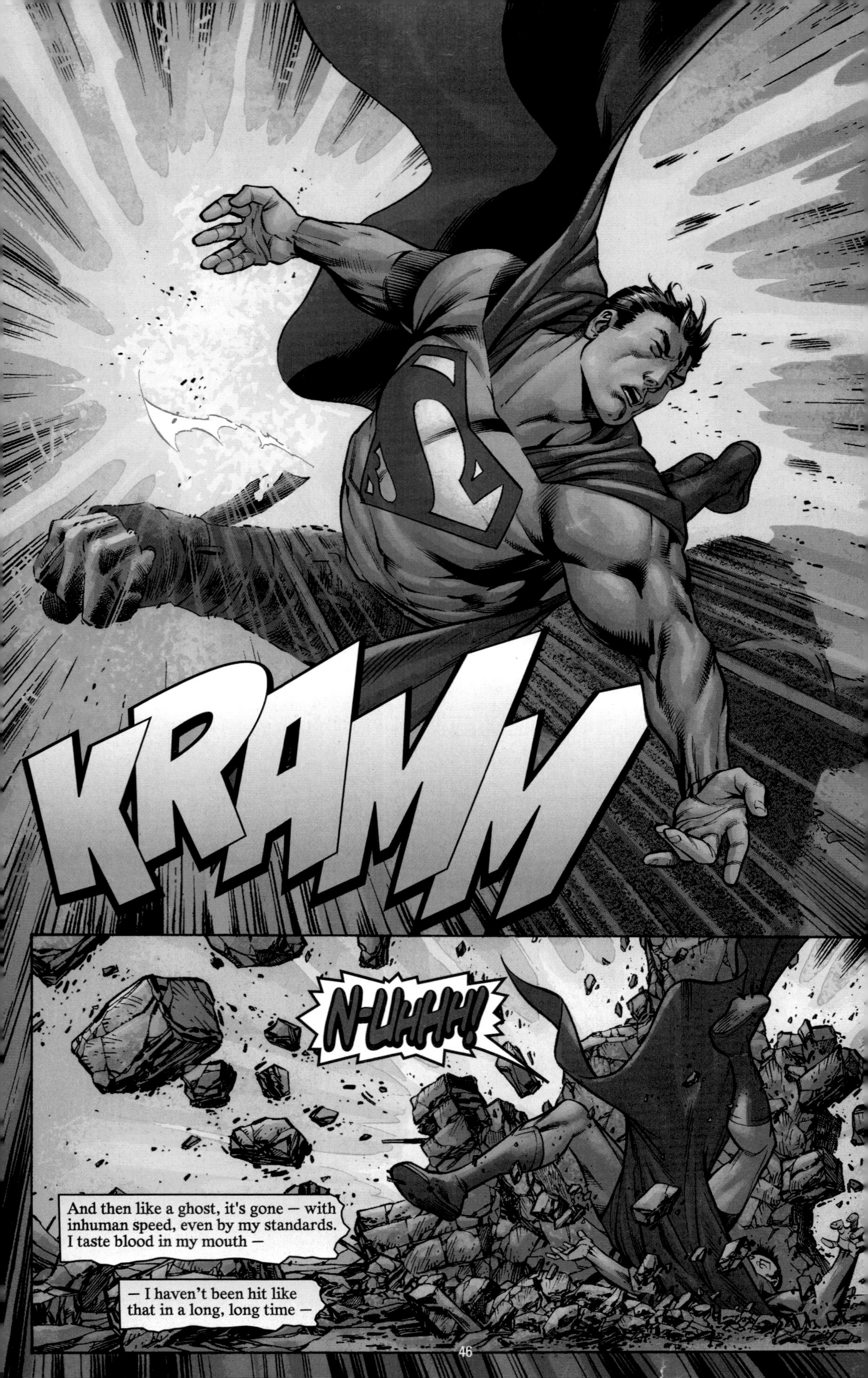
KRAMM
N-UHHH!
And then like a ghost, it's gone — with inhuman speed, even by my standards. I taste blood in my mouth —
— I haven't been hit like that in a long, long time —

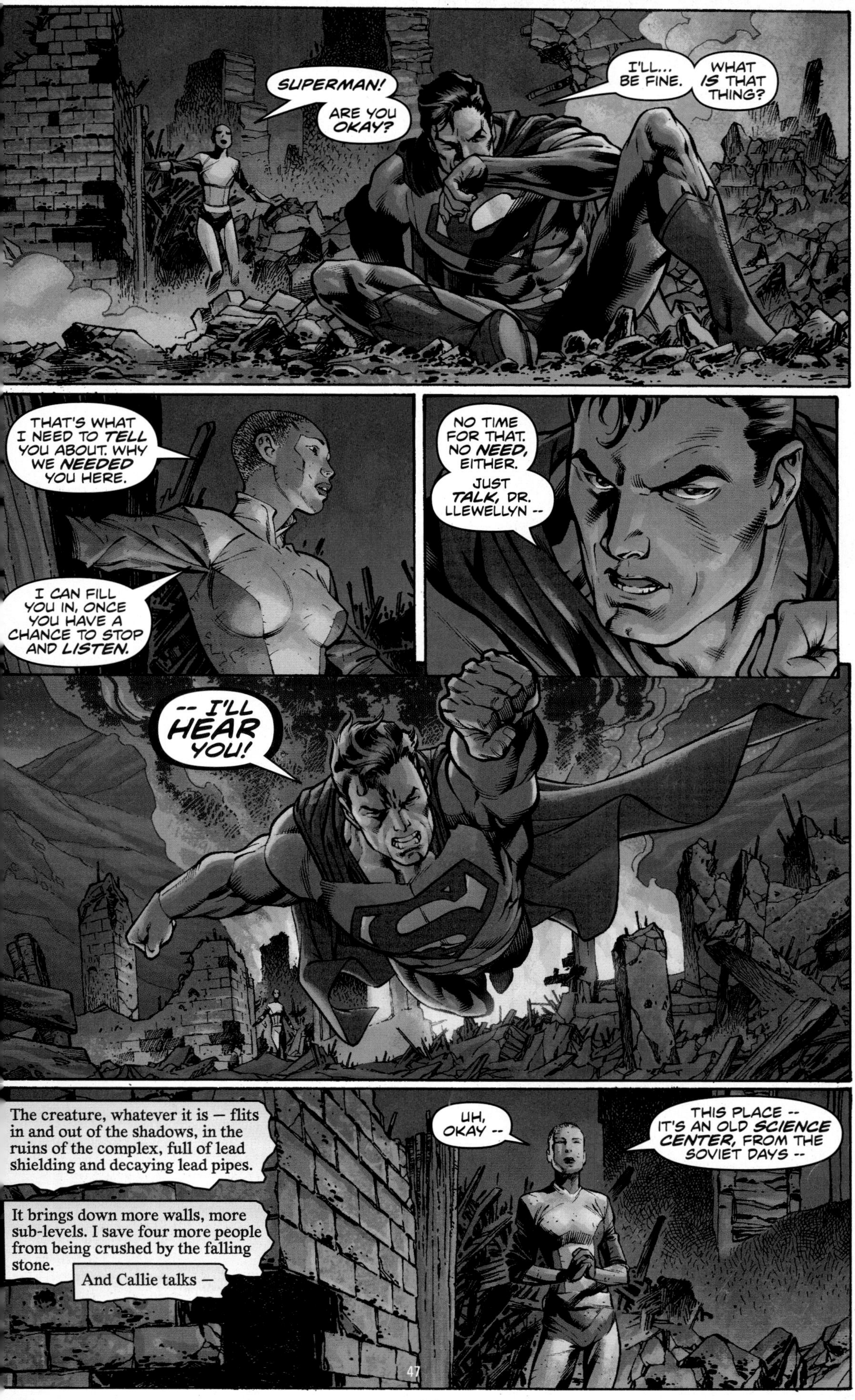
SUPERMAN! ARE YOU OKAY?
I'LL... BE FINE.
WHAT IS THAT THING?
THAT'S WHAT I NEED TO TELL YOU ABOUT. WHY WE NEEDED YOU HERE.
I CAN FILL YOU IN, ONCE YOU HAVE A CHANCE TO STOP AND LISTEN.
NO TIME FOR THAT. NO NEED, EITHER.
JUST TALK, DR. LLEWELLYN --
-- I'LL HEAR YOU!
The creature, whatever it is — flits in and out of the shadows, in the ruins of the complex, full of lead shielding and decaying lead pipes.
It brings down more walls, more sub-levels. I save four more people from being crushed by the falling stone.
And Callie talks —
UH, OKAY --
THIS PLACE -- IT'S AN OLD SCIENCE CENTER, FROM THE SOVIET DAYS --

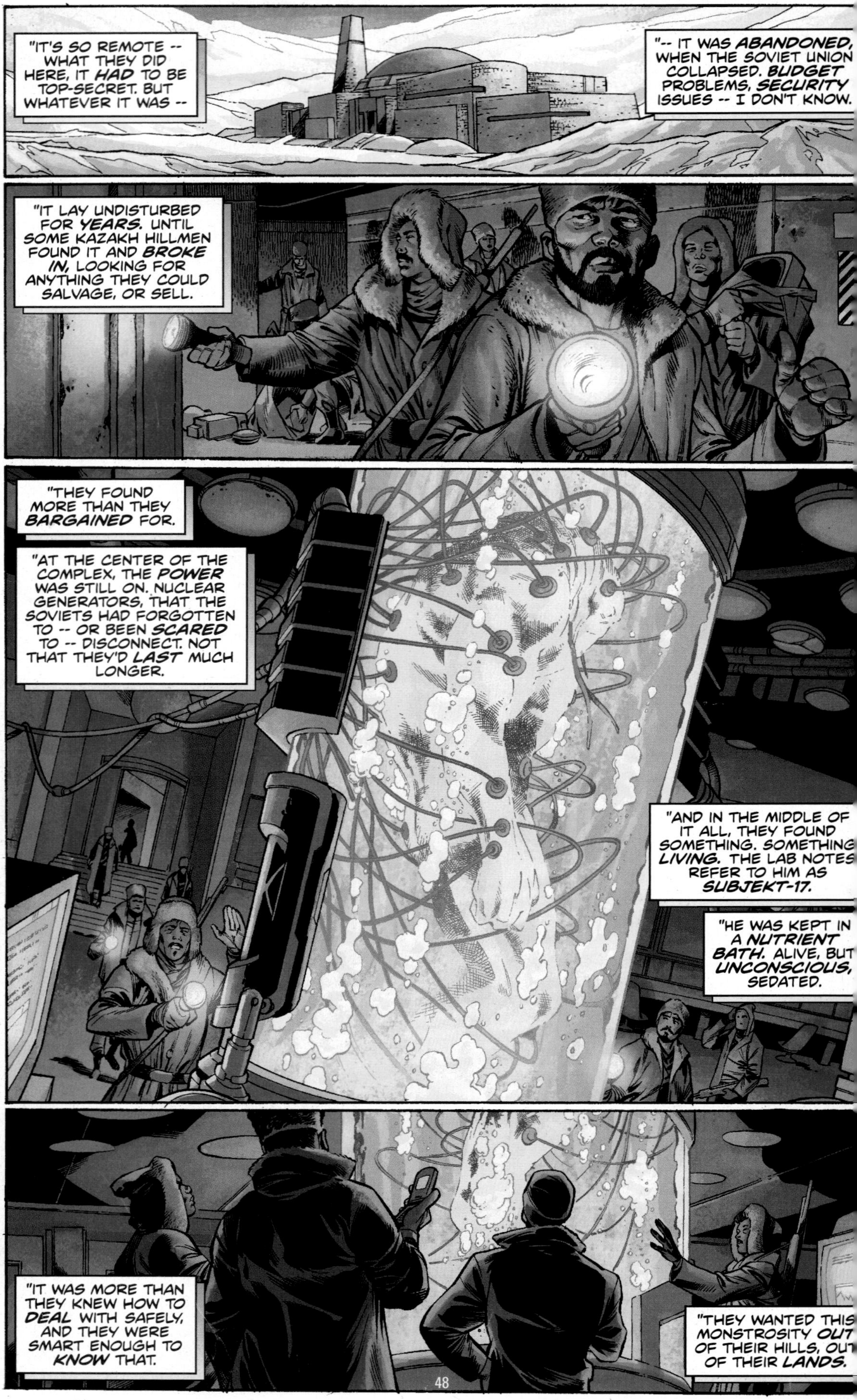
"IT'S SO REMOTE -- WHAT THEY DID HERE, IT HAD TO BE TOP-SECRET. BUT WHATEVER IT WAS --
"-- IT WAS ABANDONED, WHEN THE SOVIET UNION COLLAPSED. BUDGET PROBLEMS, SECURITY ISSUES -- I DON'T KNOW.
"IT LAY UNDISTURBED FOR YEARS. UNTIL SOME KAZAKH HILLMEN FOUND IT AND BROKE IN, LOOKING FOR ANYTHING THEY COULD SALVAGE, OR SELL.
"THEY FOUND MORE THAN THEY BARGAINED FOR.
"AT THE CENTER OF THE COMPLEX, THE POWER WAS STILL ON. NUCLEAR GENERATORS, THAT THE SOVIETS HAD FORGOTTEN TO -- OR BEEN SCARED TO -- DISCONNECT. NOT THAT THEY'D LAST MUCH LONGER.
"AND IN THE MIDDLE OF IT ALL, THEY FOUND SOMETHING. SOMETHING LIVING. THE LAB NOTES REFER TO HIM AS SUBJEKT-17.
"HE WAS KEPT IN A NUTRIENT BATH. ALIVE, BUT UNCONSCIOUS, SEDATED.
"IT WAS MORE THAN THEY KNEW HOW TO DEAL WITH SAFELY, AND THEY WERE SMART ENOUGH TO KNOW THAT.
"THEY WANTED THIS MONSTROSITY OUT OF THEIR HILLS, OUT OF THEIR LANDS.

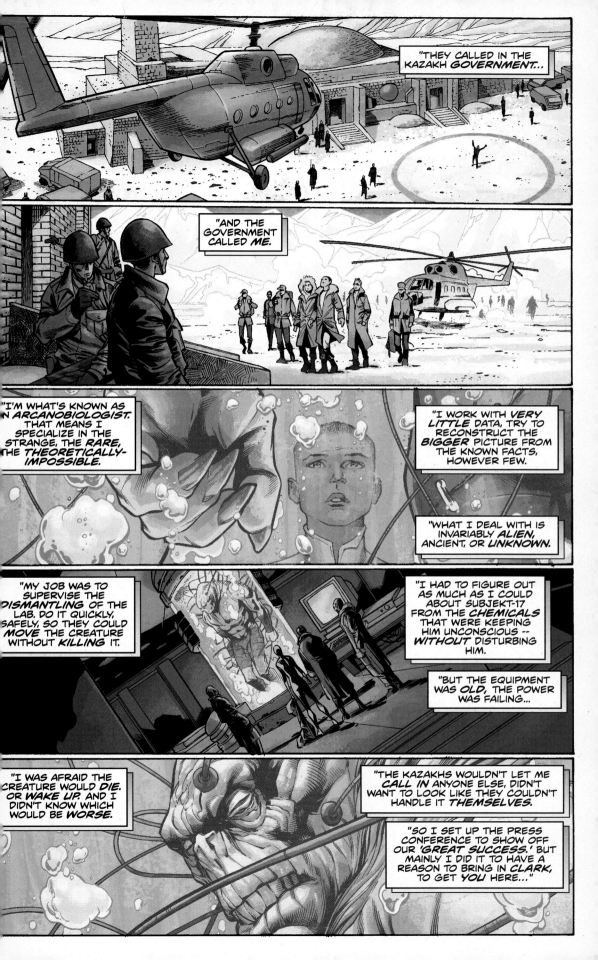

"THEY CALLED IN THE KAZAKH *GOVERNMENT*...

"AND THE GOVERNMENT CALLED *ME.*

"I'M WHAT'S KNOWN AS AN *ARCANOBIOLOGIST.* THAT MEANS I SPECIALIZE IN THE STRANGE, THE *RARE*, THE *THEORETICALLY-IMPOSSIBLE.*

"I WORK WITH *VERY LITTLE* DATA, TRY TO RECONSTRUCT THE *BIGGER* PICTURE FROM THE KNOWN FACTS, HOWEVER FEW.

"WHAT I DEAL WITH IS INVARIABLY *ALIEN*, ANCIENT, OR *UNKNOWN.*

"MY JOB WAS TO SUPERVISE THE *DISMANTLING* OF THE LAB. DO IT QUICKLY, SAFELY, SO THEY COULD *MOVE* THE CREATURE WITHOUT *KILLING* IT.

"I HAD TO FIGURE OUT AS MUCH AS I COULD ABOUT SUBJEKT-17 FROM THE *CHEMICALS* THAT WERE KEEPING HIM UNCONSCIOUS -- *WITHOUT* DISTURBING HIM.

"BUT THE EQUIPMENT WAS *OLD*, THE POWER WAS FAILING...

"I WAS AFRAID THE CREATURE WOULD *DIE.* OR *WAKE UP.* AND I DIDN'T KNOW WHICH WOULD BE *WORSE.*

"THE KAZAKHS WOULDN'T LET ME *CALL IN* ANYONE ELSE, DIDN'T WANT TO LOOK LIKE THEY COULDN'T HANDLE IT *THEMSELVES.*

"SO I SET UP THE PRESS CONFERENCE TO SHOW OFF OUR *'GREAT SUCCESS.'* BUT MAINLY I DID IT TO HAVE A REASON TO BRING IN *CLARK*, TO GET *YOU* HERE..."

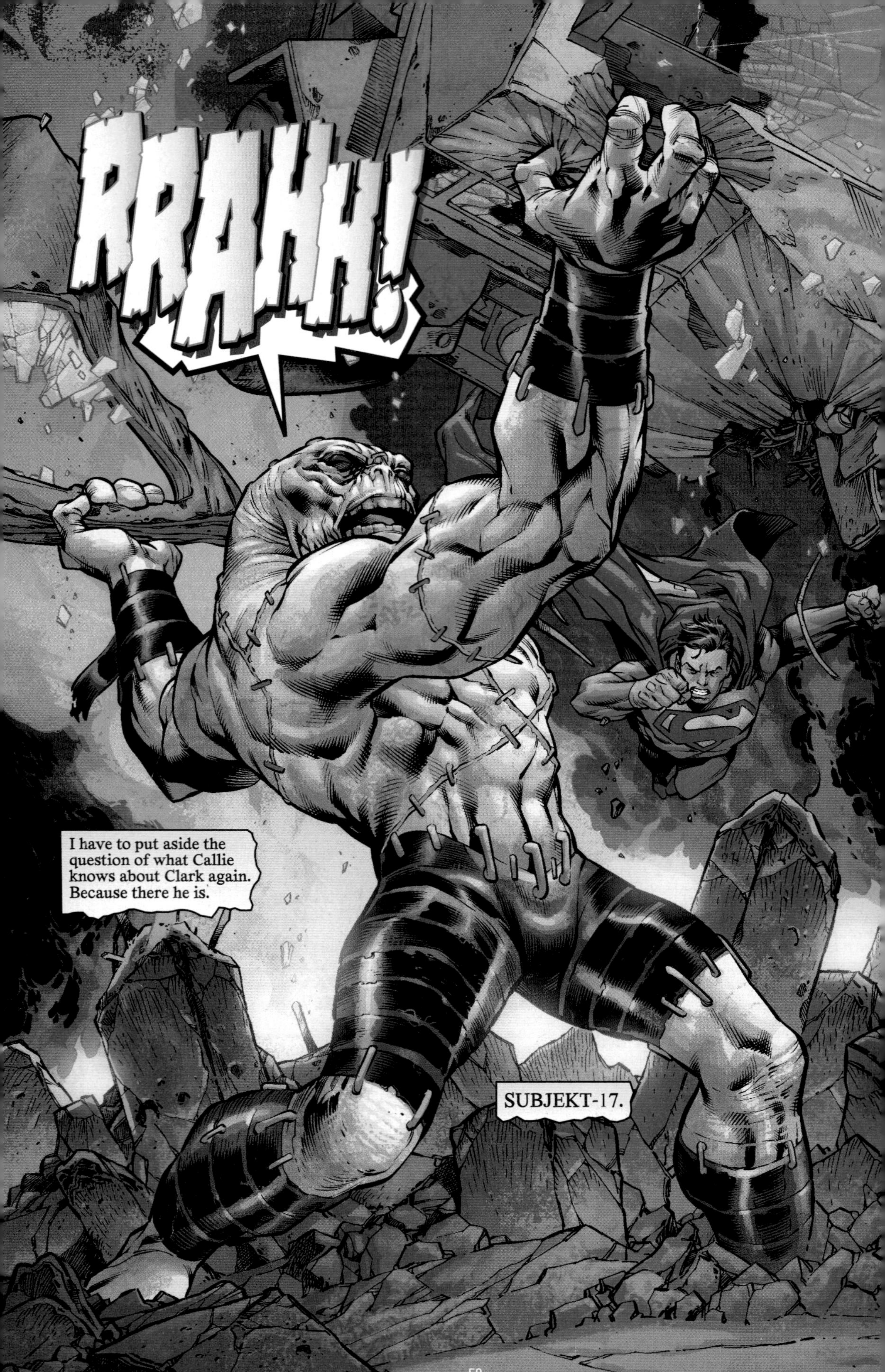
RRAHH!
I have to put aside the question of what Callie knows about Clark again. Because there he is.
SUBJEKT-17.

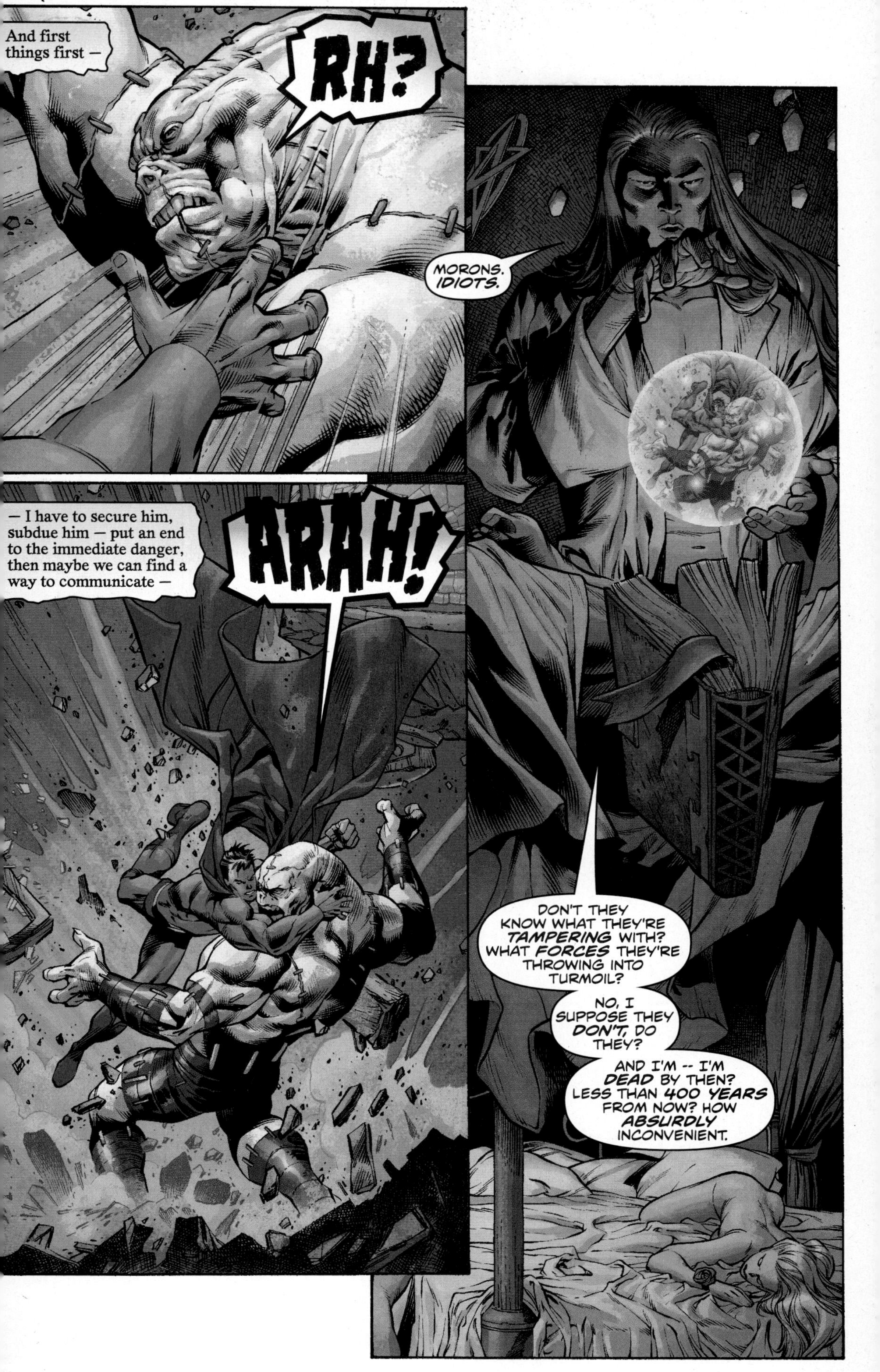

And first things first —
RH?
MORONS. IDIOTS.
— I have to secure him, subdue him — put an end to the immediate danger, then maybe we can find a way to communicate —
ARAH!
DON'T THEY KNOW WHAT THEY'RE TAMPERING WITH? WHAT FORCES THEY'RE THROWING INTO TURMOIL?
NO, I SUPPOSE THEY DON'T, DO THEY?
AND I'M -- I'M DEAD BY THEN? LESS THAN 400 YEARS FROM NOW? HOW ABSURDLY INCONVENIENT.

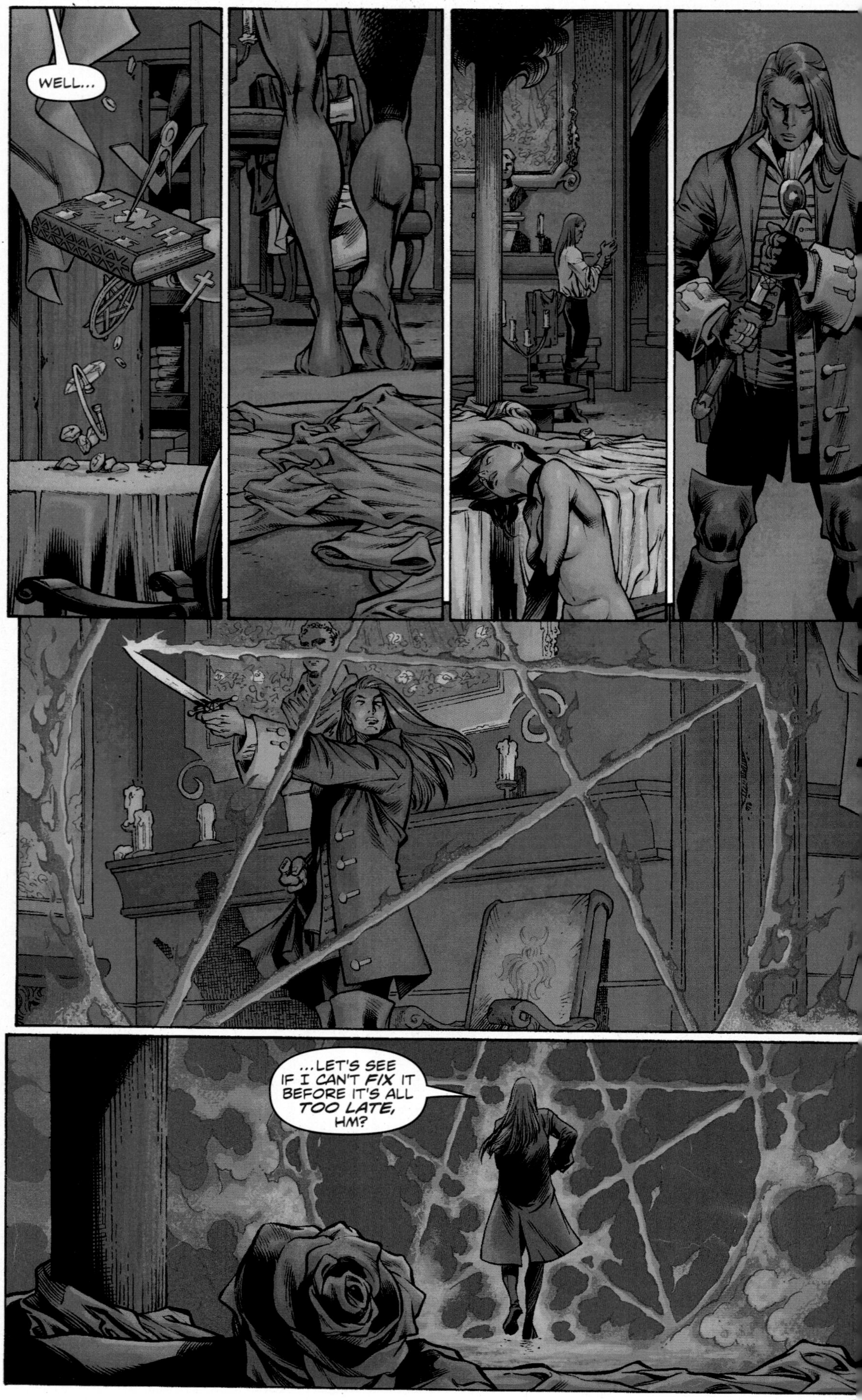
WELL...
...LET'S SEE IF I CAN'T FIX IT BEFORE IT'S ALL TOO LATE, HM?

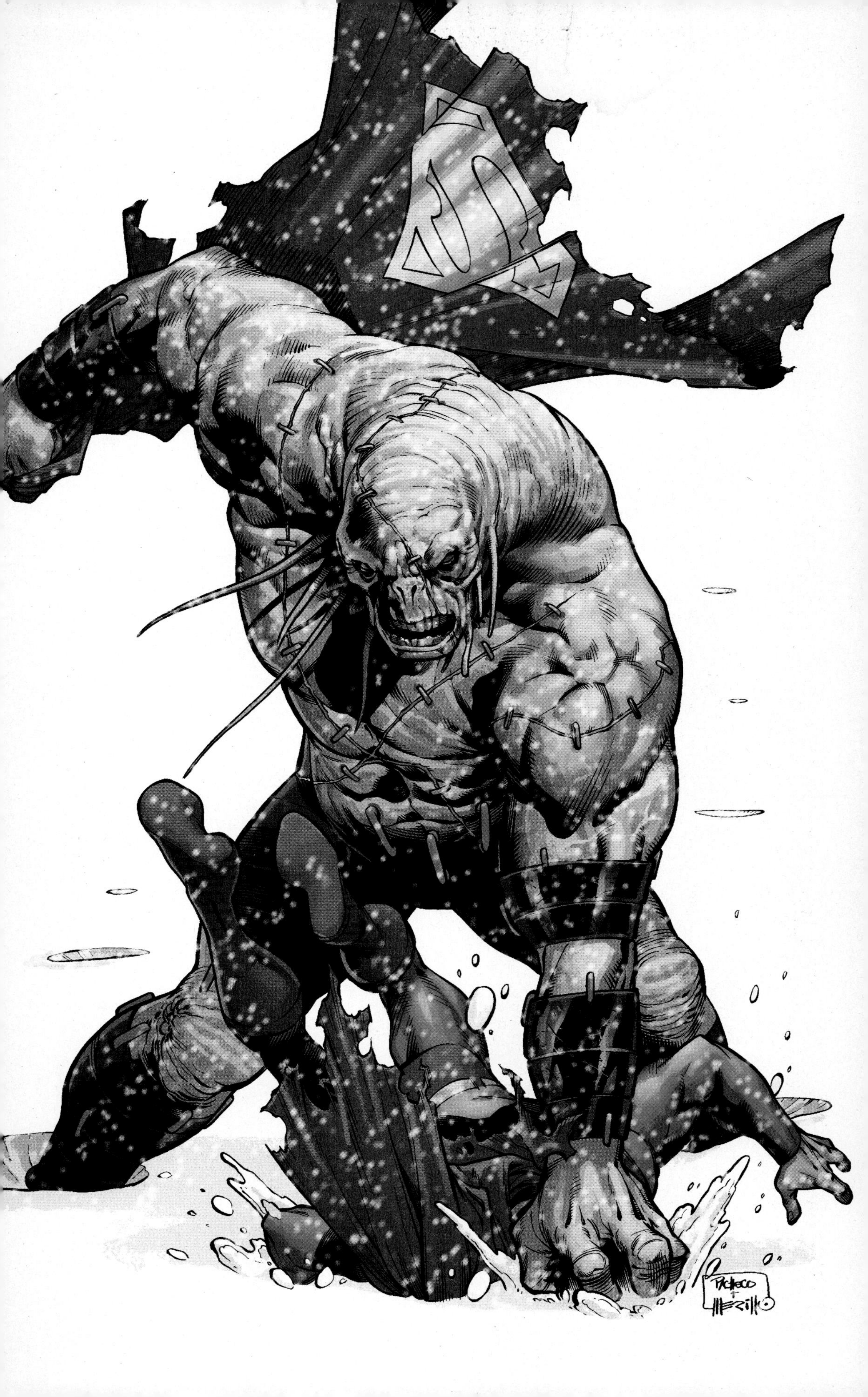

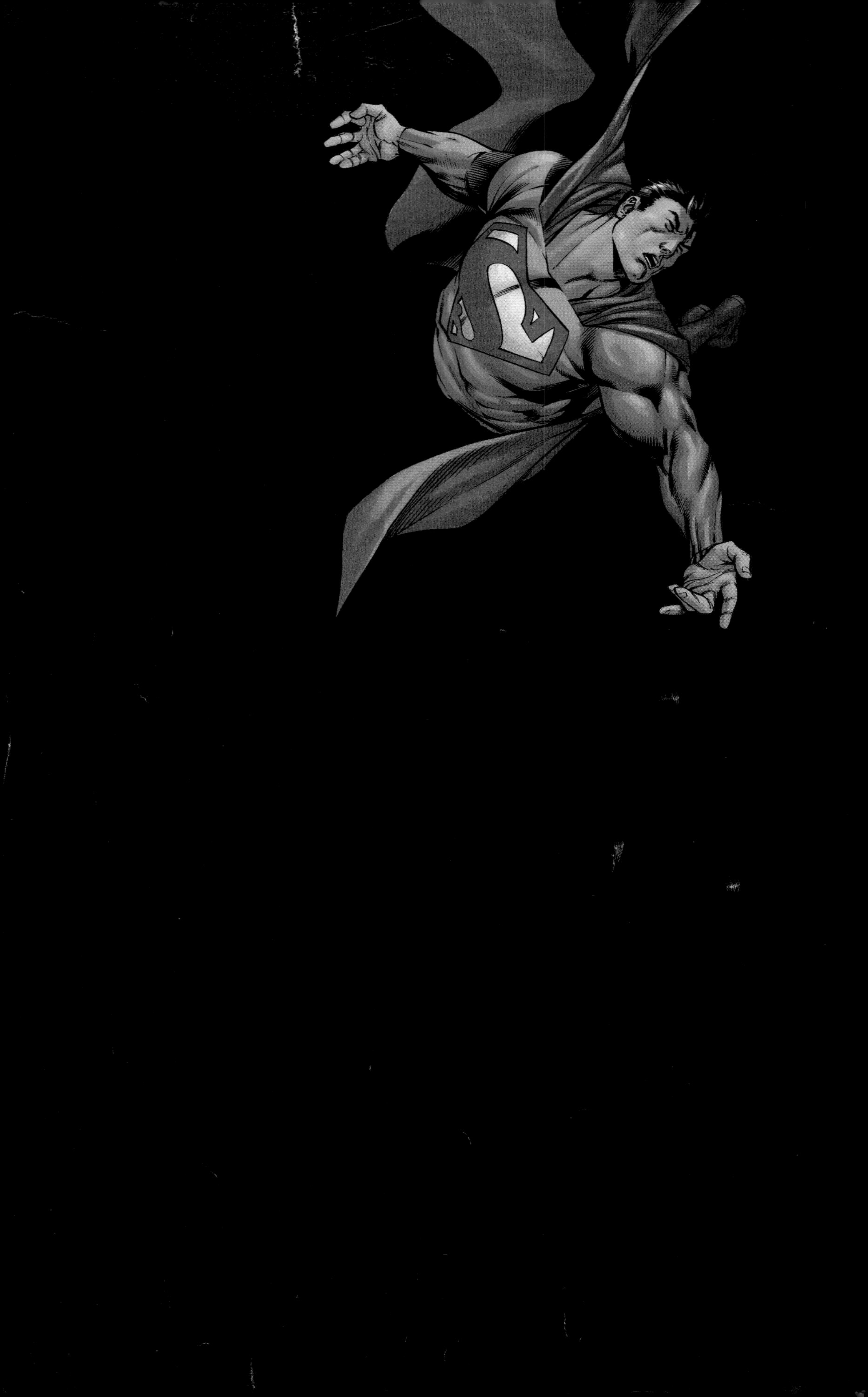

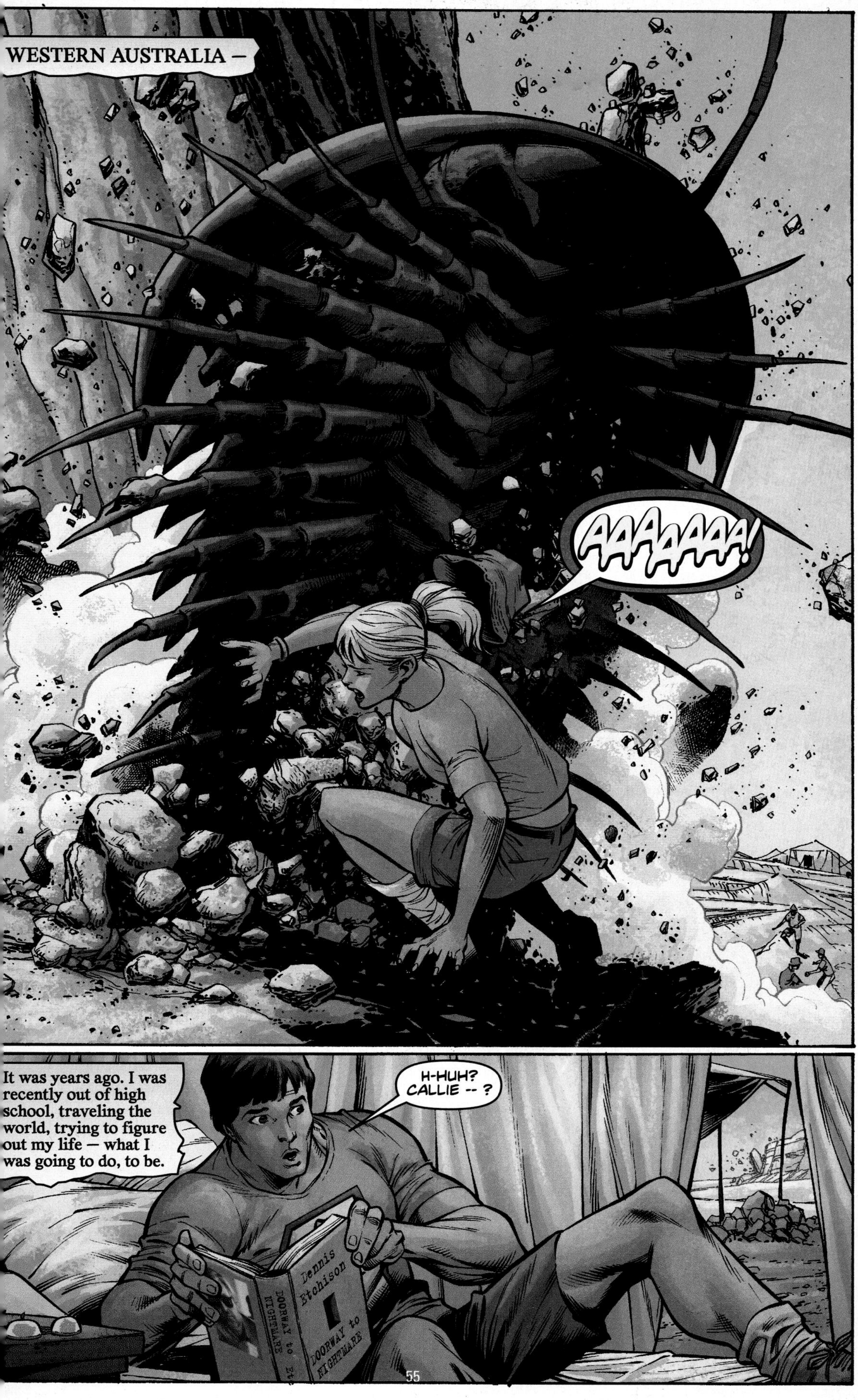
WESTERN AUSTRALIA —
AAAAAA!
It was years ago. I was recently out of high school, traveling the world, trying to figure out my life — what I was going to do, to be.
H-HUH? CALLIE -- ?
Dennis Etchison
DOORWAY to NIGHTMARE

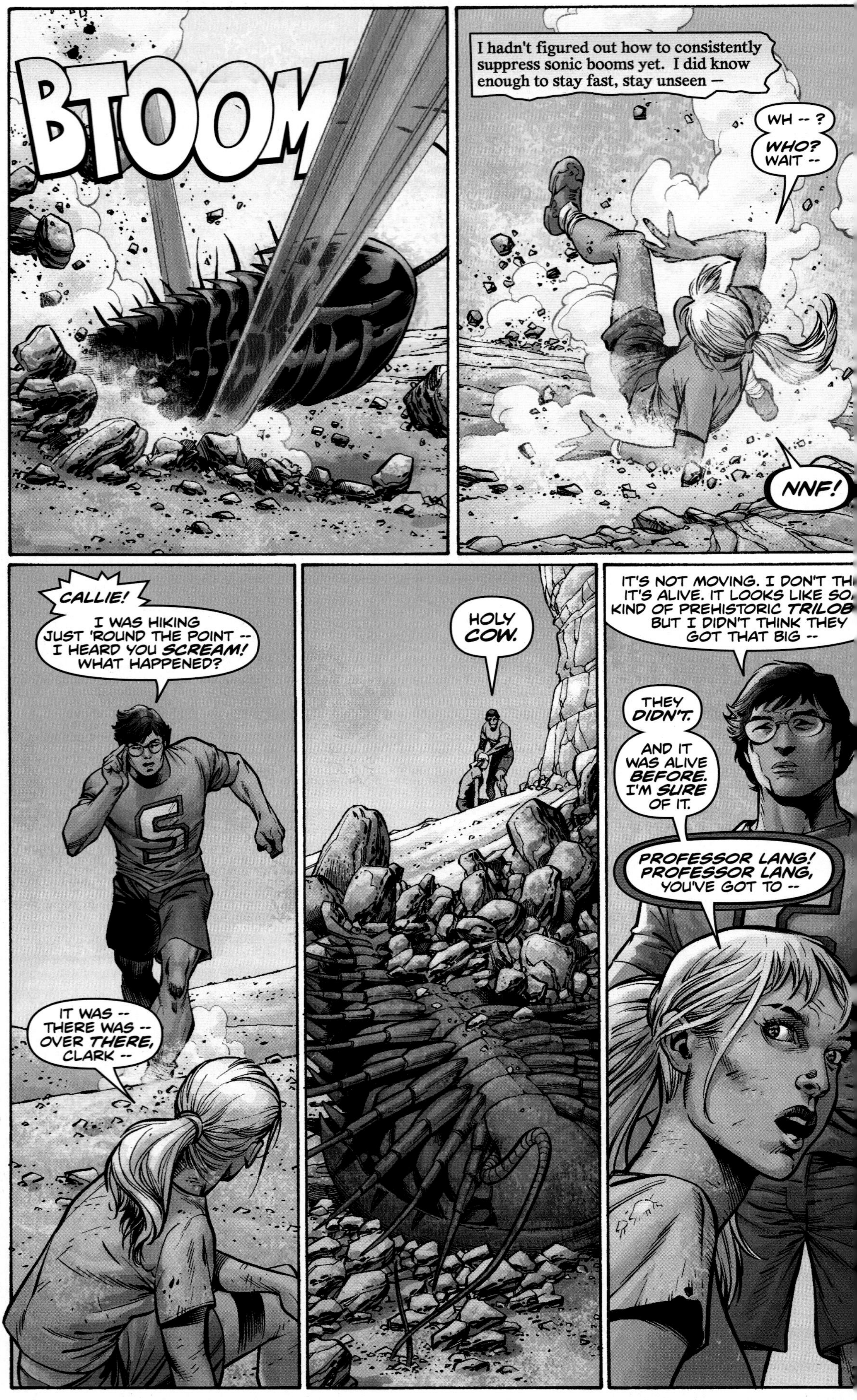
BTOOM
I hadn't figured out how to consistently suppress sonic booms yet. I did know enough to stay fast, stay unseen —
WH -- ? WHO? WAIT --
NNF!
CALLIE!
I WAS HIKING JUST 'ROUND THE POINT -- I HEARD YOU SCREAM! WHAT HAPPENED?
IT WAS -- THERE WAS -- OVER THERE, CLARK --
HOLY COW.
IT'S NOT MOVING. I DON'T TH
IT'S ALIVE. IT LOOKS LIKE SO
KIND OF PREHISTORIC TRILOB
BUT I DIDN'T THINK THEY GOT THAT BIG --
THEY DIDN'T.
AND IT WAS ALIVE BEFORE. I'M SURE OF IT.
PROFESSOR LANG! PROFESSOR LANG, YOU'VE GOT TO --

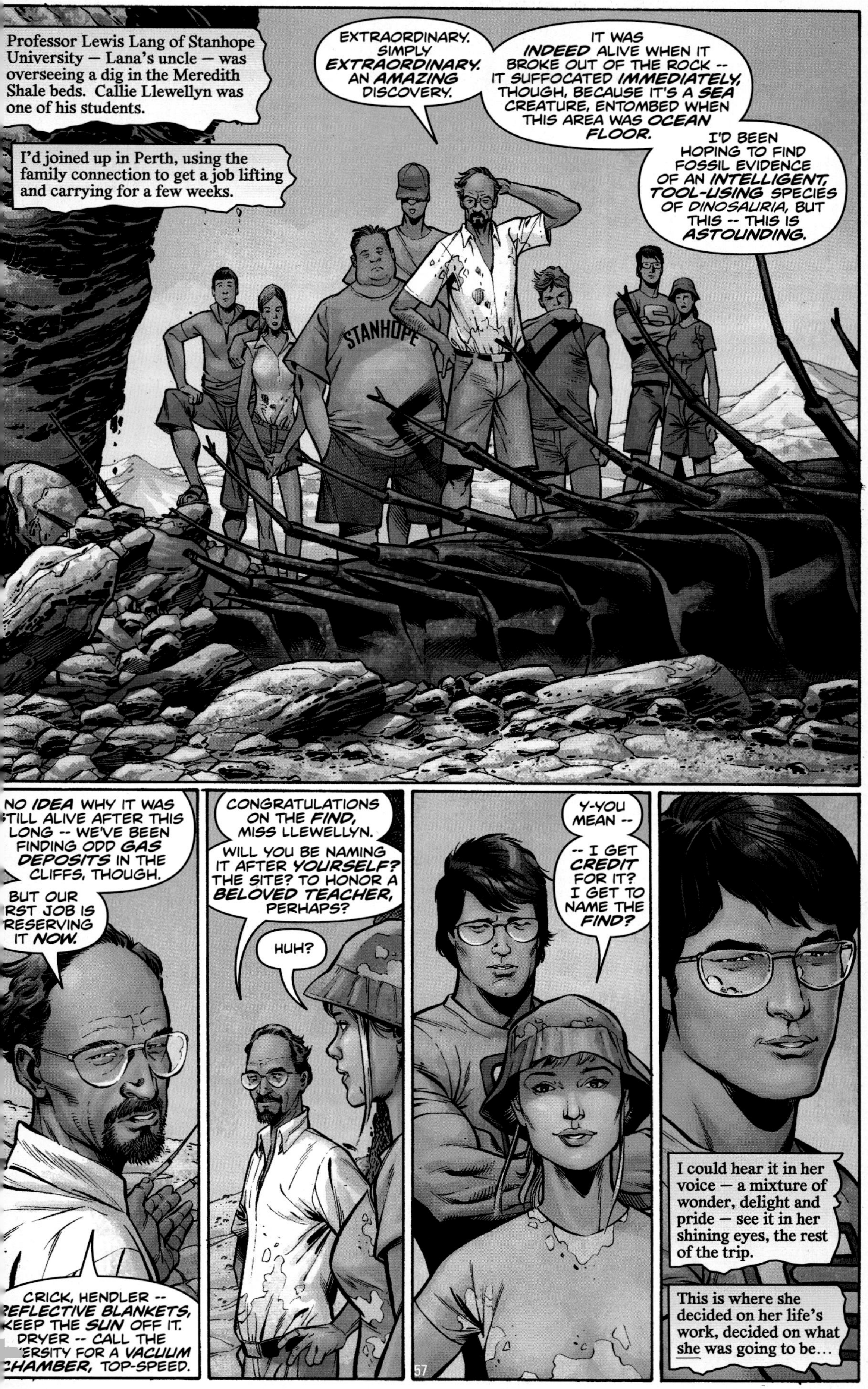
Professor Lewis Lang of Stanhope University — Lana's uncle — was overseeing a dig in the Meredith Shale beds. Callie Llewellyn was one of his students.
I'd joined up in Perth, using the family connection to get a job lifting and carrying for a few weeks.
EXTRAORDINARY. SIMPLY EXTRAORDINARY. AN AMAZING DISCOVERY.
IT WAS INDEED ALIVE WHEN IT BROKE OUT OF THE ROCK -- IT SUFFOCATED IMMEDIATELY, THOUGH, BECAUSE IT'S A SEA CREATURE, ENTOMBED WHEN THIS AREA WAS OCEAN FLOOR.
I'D BEEN HOPING TO FIND FOSSIL EVIDENCE OF AN INTELLIGENT, TOOL-USING SPECIES OF DINOSAURIA, BUT THIS -- THIS IS ASTOUNDING.
STANHOPE
NO IDEA WHY IT WAS STILL ALIVE AFTER THIS LONG -- WE'VE BEEN FINDING ODD GAS DEPOSITS IN THE CLIFFS, THOUGH.
BUT OUR RST JOB IS RESERVING IT NOW.
CRICK, HENDLER -- REFLECTIVE BLANKETS, KEEP THE SUN OFF IT. DRYER -- CALL THE ERSITY FOR A VACUUM CHAMBER, TOP-SPEED.
CONGRATULATIONS ON THE FIND, MISS LLEWELLYN.
WILL YOU BE NAMING IT AFTER YOURSELF? THE SITE? TO HONOR A BELOVED TEACHER, PERHAPS?
HUH?
Y-YOU MEAN --
-- I GET CREDIT FOR IT? I GET TO NAME THE FIND?
I could hear it in her voice — a mixture of wonder, delight and pride — see it in her shining eyes, the rest of the trip.
This is where she decided on her life's work, decided on what she was going to be…

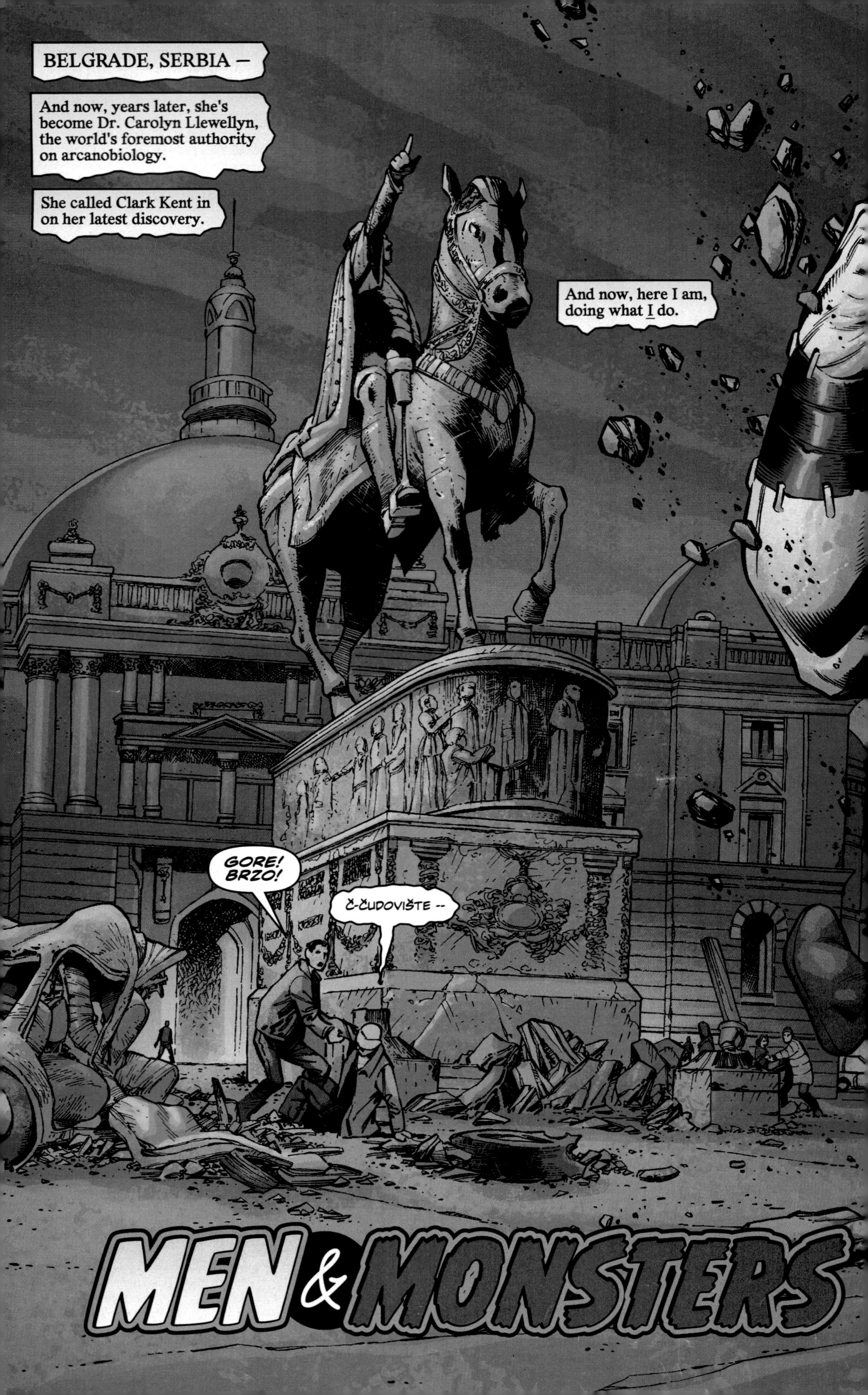
BELGRADE, SERBIA —
And now, years later, she's become Dr. Carolyn Llewellyn, the world's foremost authority on arcanobiology.
She called Clark Kent in on her latest discovery.
And now, here I am, doing what I do.
GORE! BRZO!
Č-ČUDOVIŠTE --
MEN & MONSTERS

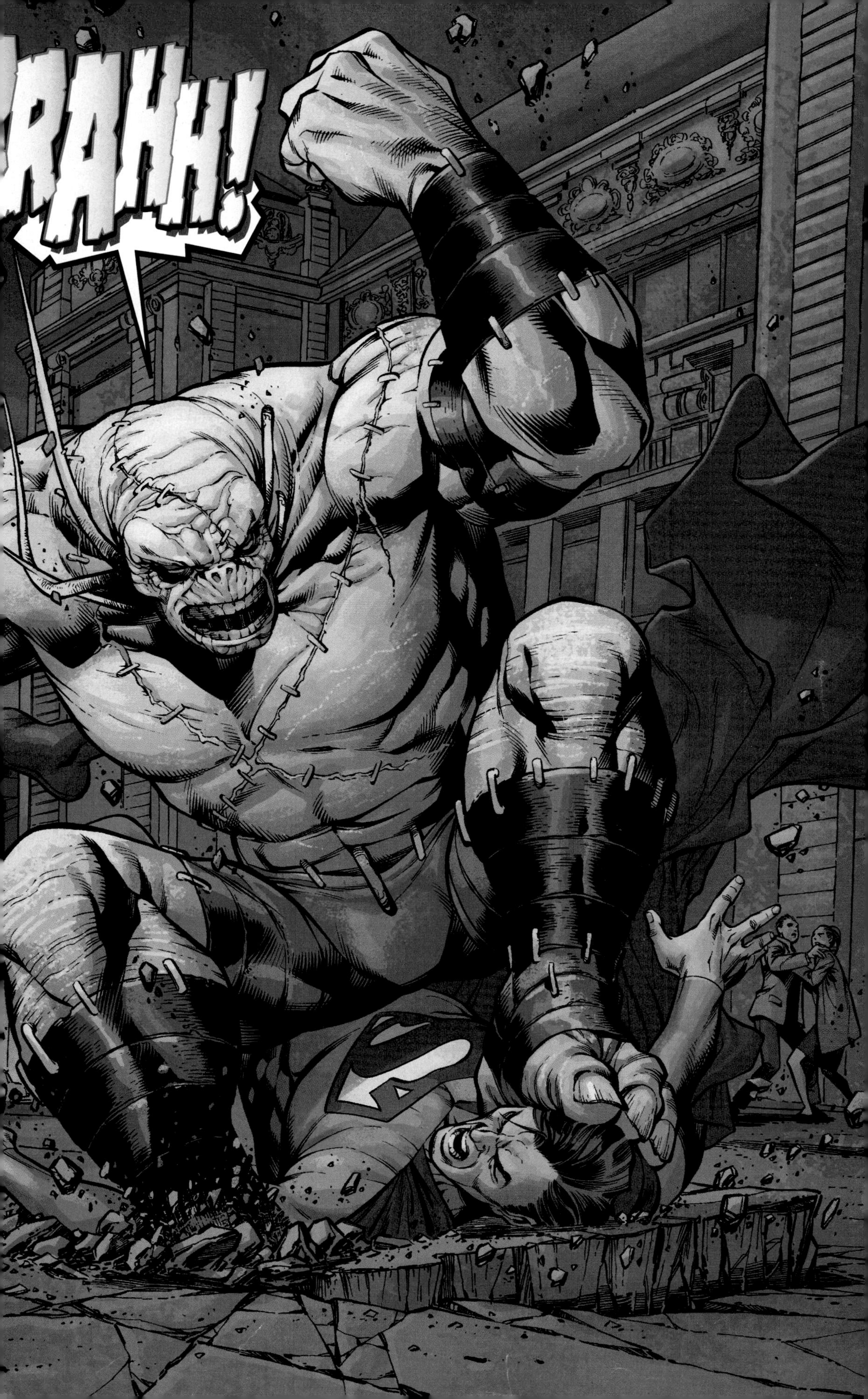
RAHH!

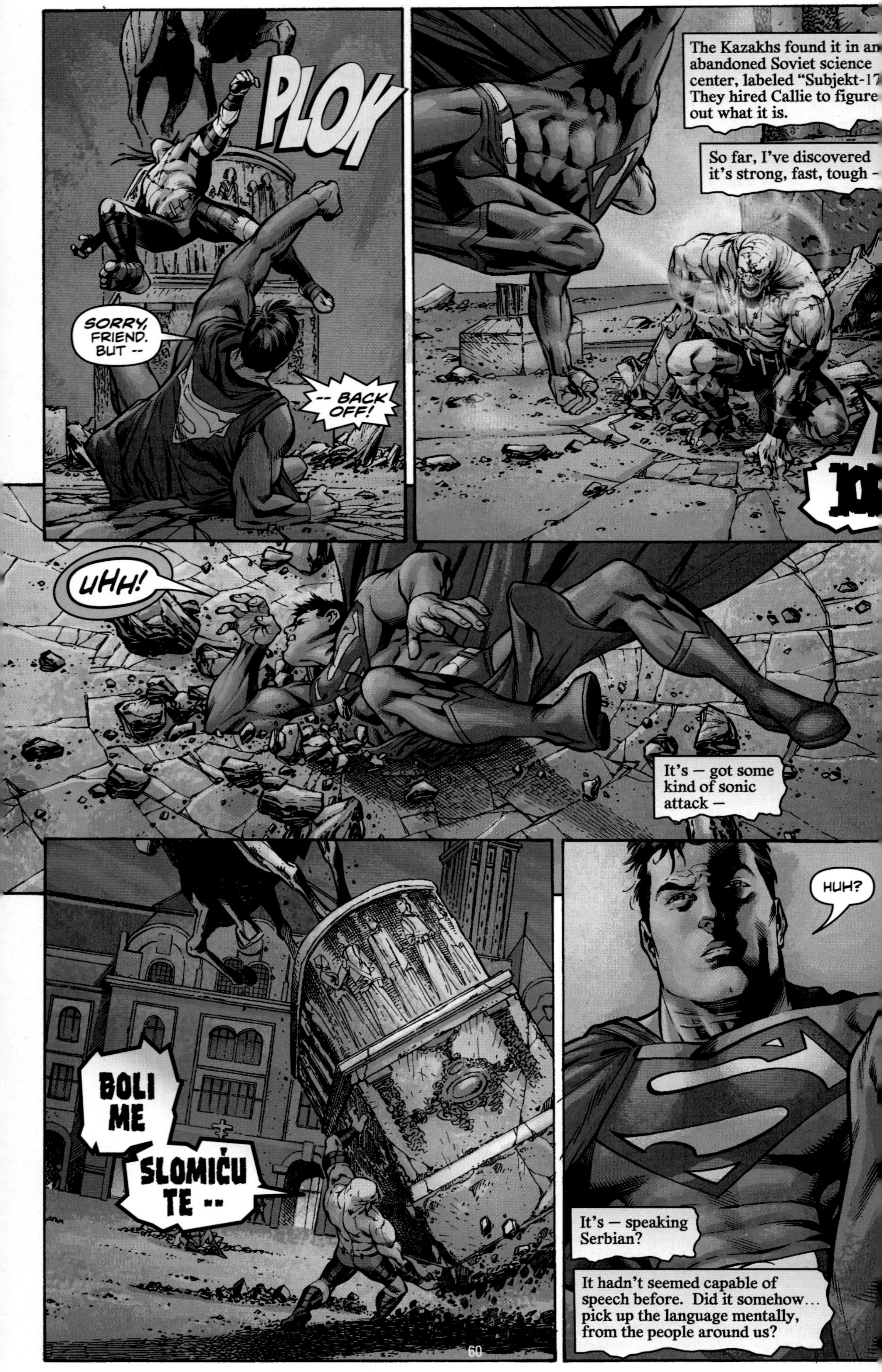
PLOK
SORRY, FRIEND. BUT --
-- BACK OFF!
The Kazakhs found it in an abandoned Soviet science center, labeled "Subjekt-17 They hired Callie to figure out what it is.
So far, I've discovered it's strong, fast, tough –
UHH!
It's – got some kind of sonic attack –
BOLI ME
SLOMIČU TE --
HUH?
It's – speaking Serbian?
It hadn't seemed capable of speech before. Did it somehow… pick up the language mentally, from the people around us?

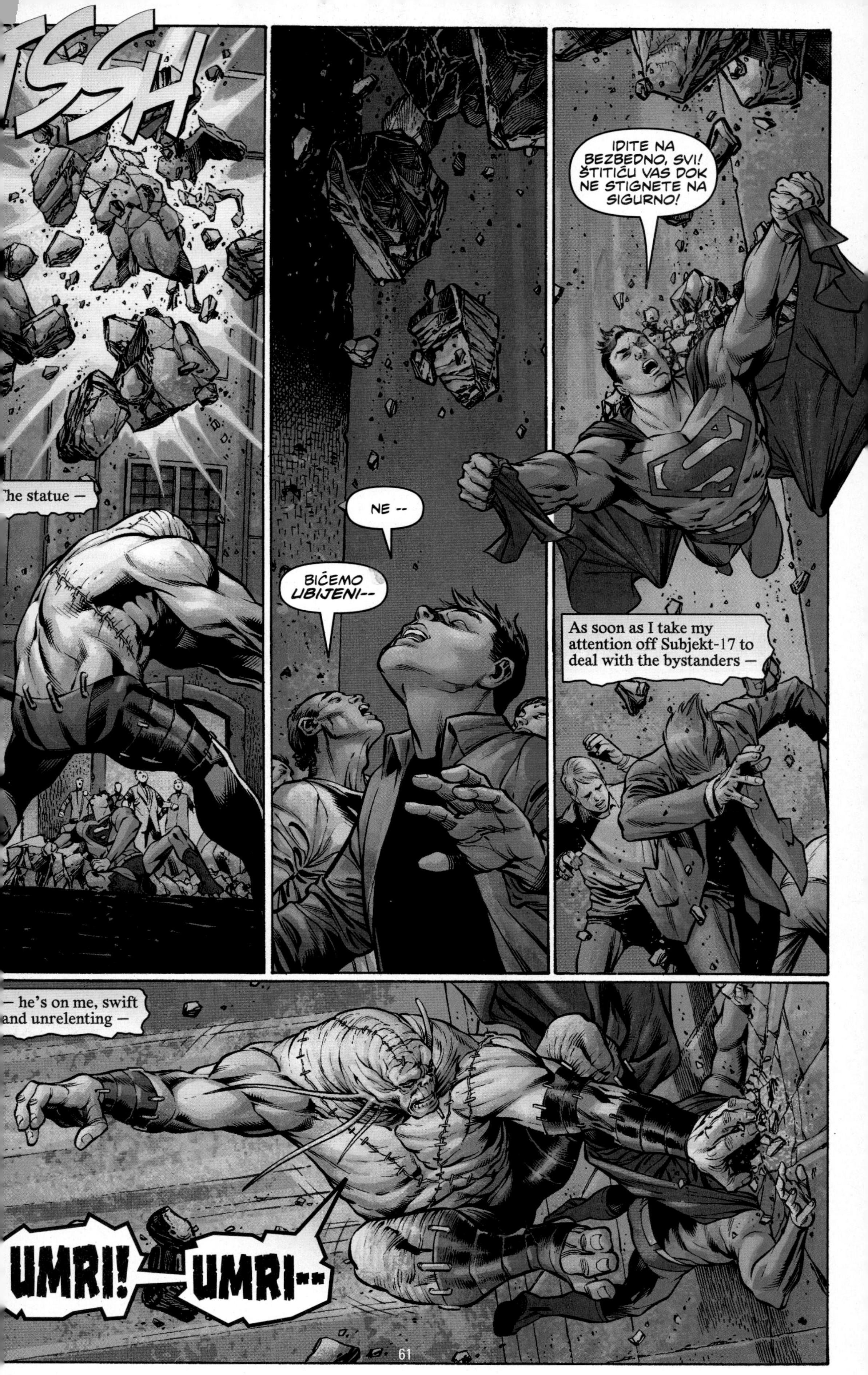
TSSH
The statue —
NE --
BIĆEMO UBIJENI--
IDITE NA BEZBEDNO, SVI! ŠTITIĆU VAS DOK NE STIGNETE NA SIGURNO!
As soon as I take my attention off Subjekt-17 to deal with the bystanders —
— he's on me, swift and unrelenting —
UMRI! UMRI--

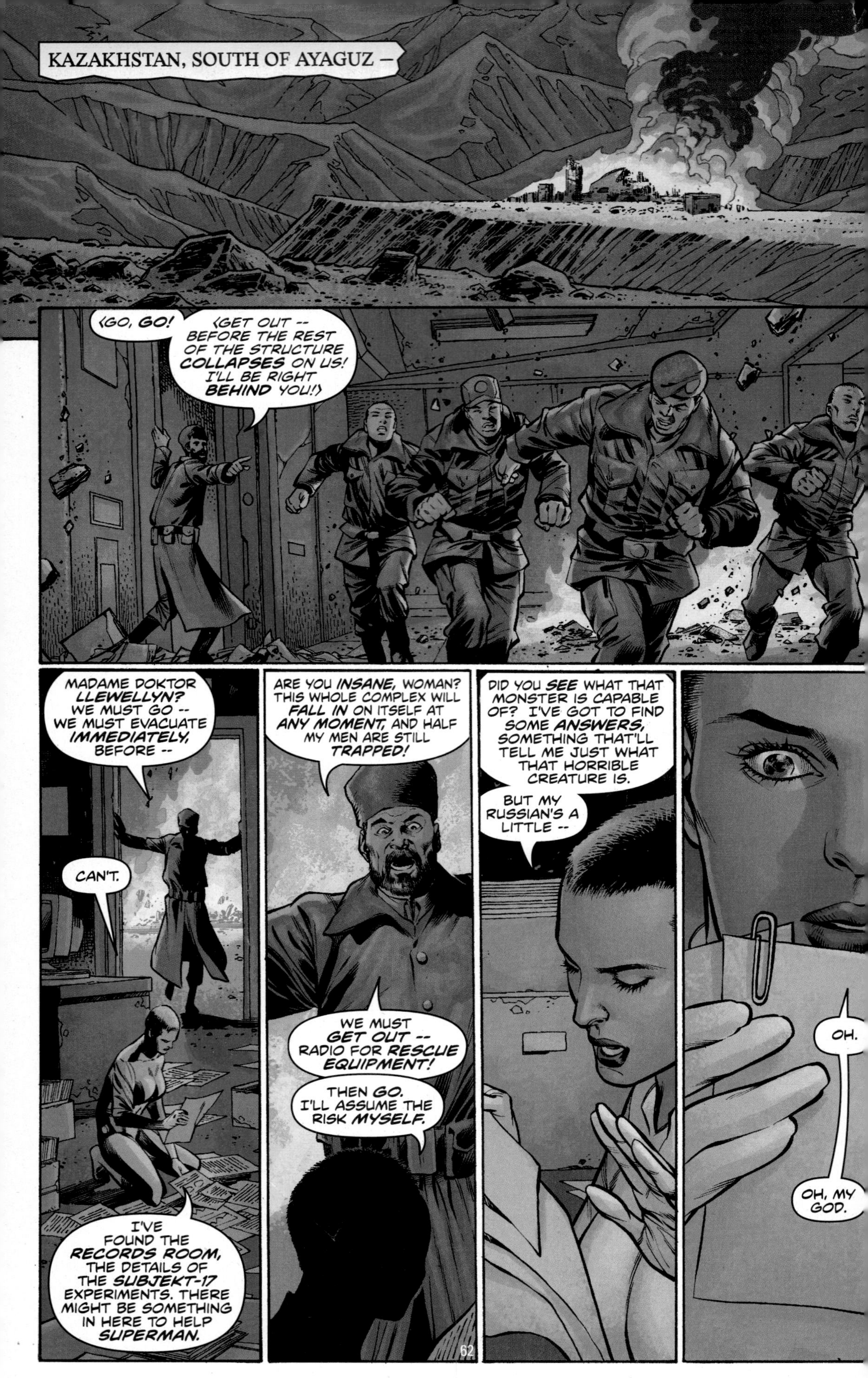

KAZAKHSTAN, SOUTH OF AYAGUZ —
‹GO, GO!
‹GET OUT -- BEFORE THE REST OF THE STRUCTURE COLLAPSES ON US! I'LL BE RIGHT BEHIND YOU!›
MADAME DOKTOR LLEWELLYN? WE MUST GO -- WE MUST EVACUATE IMMEDIATELY, BEFORE --
CAN'T.
I'VE FOUND THE RECORDS ROOM, THE DETAILS OF THE SUBJEKT-17 EXPERIMENTS. THERE MIGHT BE SOMETHING IN HERE TO HELP SUPERMAN.
ARE YOU INSANE, WOMAN? THIS WHOLE COMPLEX WILL FALL IN ON ITSELF AT ANY MOMENT, AND HALF MY MEN ARE STILL TRAPPED!
WE MUST GET OUT -- RADIO FOR RESCUE EQUIPMENT!
THEN GO. I'LL ASSUME THE RISK MYSELF.
DID YOU SEE WHAT THAT MONSTER IS CAPABLE OF? I'VE GOT TO FIND SOME ANSWERS, SOMETHING THAT'LL TELL ME JUST WHAT THAT HORRIBLE CREATURE IS.
BUT MY RUSSIAN'S A LITTLE --
OH.
OH, MY GOD.

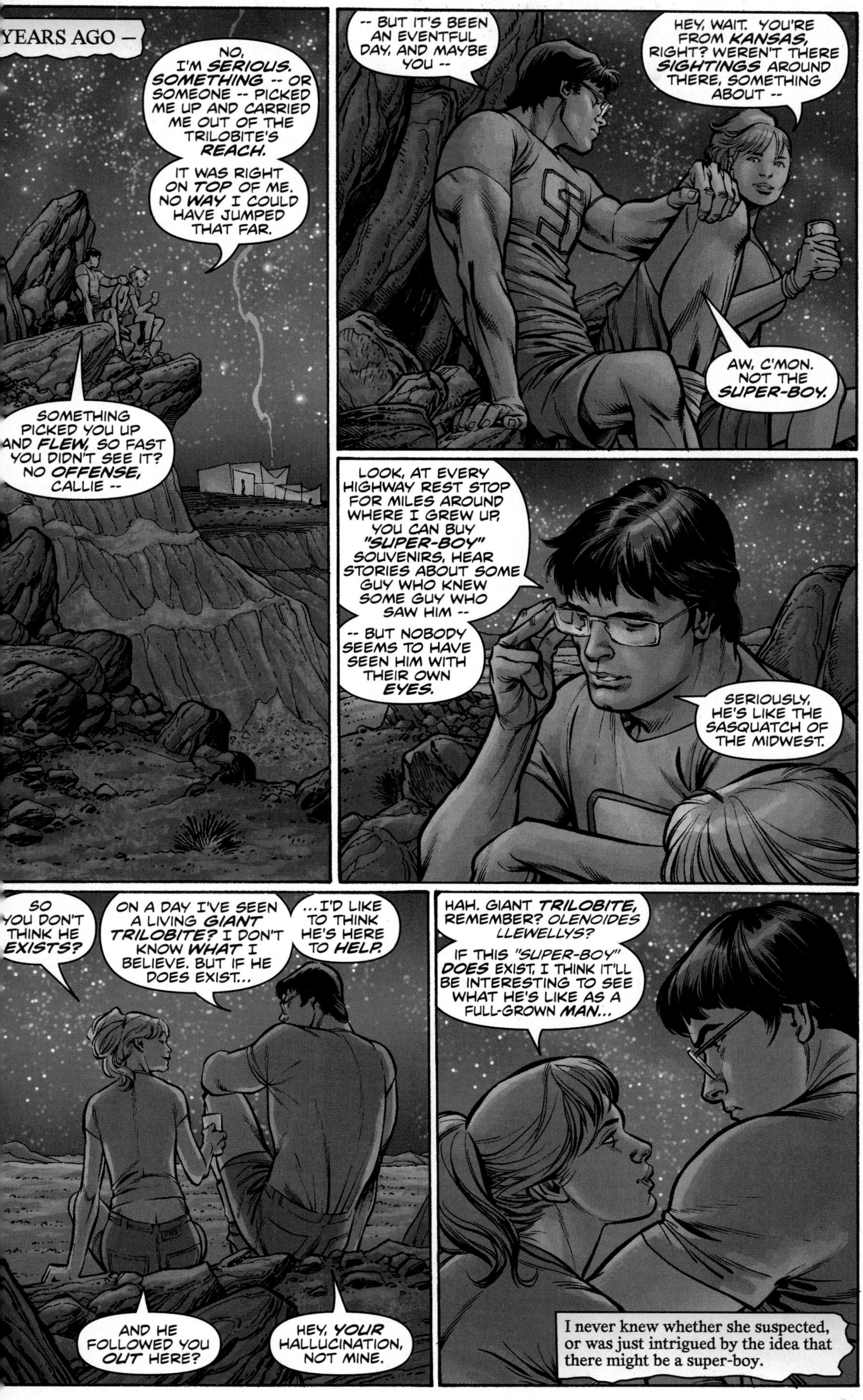

YEARS AGO —
NO, I'M SERIOUS. SOMETHING -- OR SOMEONE -- PICKED ME UP AND CARRIED ME OUT OF THE TRILOBITE'S REACH.
IT WAS RIGHT ON TOP OF ME. NO WAY I COULD HAVE JUMPED THAT FAR.
SOMETHING PICKED YOU UP AND FLEW, SO FAST YOU DIDN'T SEE IT? NO OFFENSE, CALLIE --
-- BUT IT'S BEEN AN EVENTFUL DAY, AND MAYBE YOU --
HEY, WAIT. YOU'RE FROM KANSAS, RIGHT? WEREN'T THERE SIGHTINGS AROUND THERE, SOMETHING ABOUT --
AW, C'MON. NOT THE SUPER-BOY.
LOOK, AT EVERY HIGHWAY REST STOP FOR MILES AROUND WHERE I GREW UP, YOU CAN BUY "SUPER-BOY" SOUVENIRS, HEAR STORIES ABOUT SOME GUY WHO KNEW SOME GUY WHO SAW HIM --
-- BUT NOBODY SEEMS TO HAVE SEEN HIM WITH THEIR OWN EYES.
SERIOUSLY, HE'S LIKE THE SASQUATCH OF THE MIDWEST.
SO YOU DON'T THINK HE EXISTS?
ON A DAY I'VE SEEN A LIVING GIANT TRILOBITE? I DON'T KNOW WHAT I BELIEVE. BUT IF HE DOES EXIST...
...I'D LIKE TO THINK HE'S HERE TO HELP.
AND HE FOLLOWED YOU OUT HERE?
HEY, YOUR HALLUCINATION, NOT MINE.
HAH. GIANT TRILOBITE, REMEMBER? OLENOIDES LLEWELLYS?
IF THIS "SUPER-BOY" DOES EXIST, I THINK IT'LL BE INTERESTING TO SEE WHAT HE'S LIKE AS A FULL-GROWN MAN...
I never knew whether she suspected, or was just intrigued by the idea that there might be a super-boy.

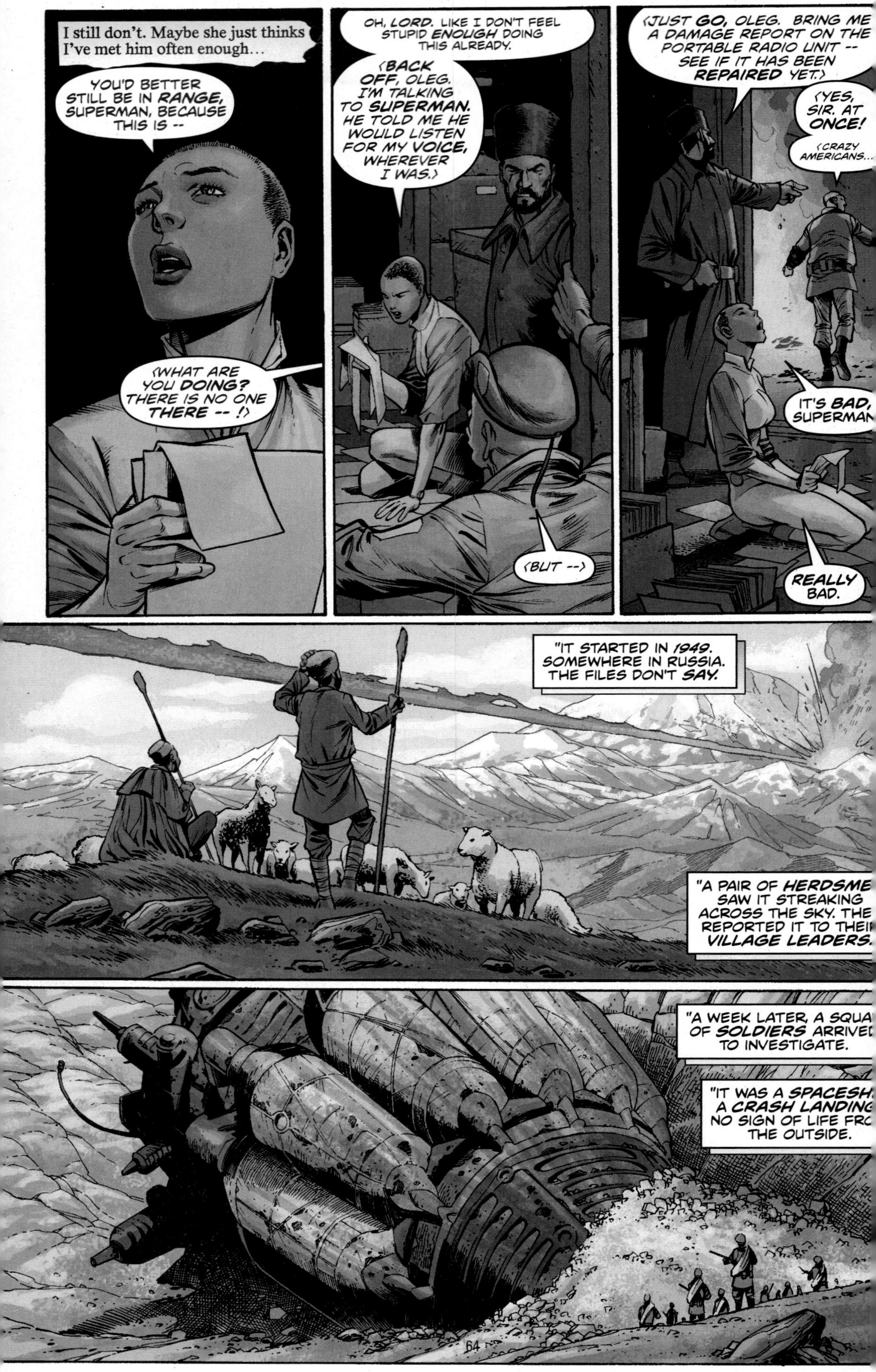

I still don't. Maybe she just thinks I've met him often enough…
YOU'D BETTER STILL BE IN RANGE, SUPERMAN, BECAUSE THIS IS --
‹WHAT ARE YOU DOING? THERE IS NO ONE THERE -- !›
OH, LORD. LIKE I DON'T FEEL STUPID ENOUGH DOING THIS ALREADY.
‹BACK OFF, OLEG. I'M TALKING TO SUPERMAN. HE TOLD ME HE WOULD LISTEN FOR MY VOICE, WHEREVER I WAS.›
‹BUT --›
‹JUST GO, OLEG. BRING ME A DAMAGE REPORT ON THE PORTABLE RADIO UNIT -- SEE IF IT HAS BEEN REPAIRED YET.›
‹YES, SIR. AT ONCE!
‹CRAZY AMERICANS...
IT'S BAD, SUPERMAN
REALLY BAD.
"IT STARTED IN 1949. SOMEWHERE IN RUSSIA. THE FILES DON'T SAY.
"A PAIR OF HERDSME SAW IT STREAKING ACROSS THE SKY. THE REPORTED IT TO THEI VILLAGE LEADERS.
"A WEEK LATER, A SQUA OF SOLDIERS ARRIVE TO INVESTIGATE.
"IT WAS A SPACESH. A CRASH LANDING NO SIGN OF LIFE FR THE OUTSIDE.

"THE CRASH HAD RIPPED HOLES IN THE *HULL*, THOUGH --

"-- AND THE SOLDIERS ENTERED. *WARY*, CAUTIOUS.

[TH]EY FOUND [TH]E *CONTROL* CENTER.

[TH]E SHIP HAD [I]NTERNAL [DA]MAGE FROM [TH]E CRASH AS WELL.

"THE PILOT HAD *DIED* AT THE CONTROLS, TRYING TO BRING THE SHIP IN *SAFELY.*

[I]N AN *INNER* [C]HAMBER, [TH]EY FOUND [W]HAT HE'D [TRI]ED TRYING [TO] *PROTECT.*"

UPACI BOZHE.

"SHE WAS STILL [A]LIVE, BUT JUST [B]ARELY. AND SHE [W]AS *PREGNANT.*

⊕...

"THEY TOOK HER FROM THE WRECK, TRANSPORTED HER *HERE* --

65

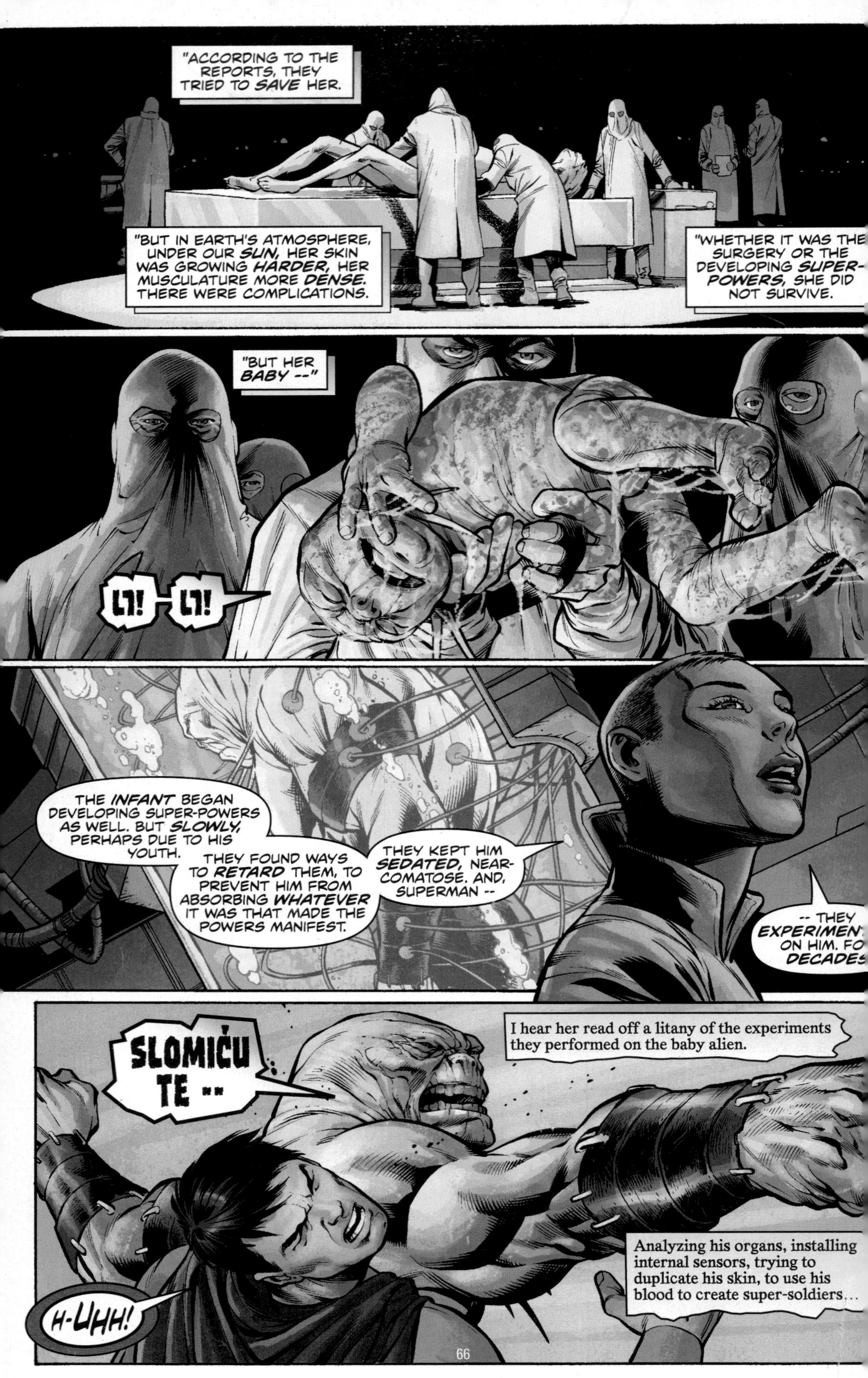

"ACCORDING TO THE REPORTS, THEY TRIED TO SAVE HER.
"BUT IN EARTH'S ATMOSPHERE, UNDER OUR SUN, HER SKIN WAS GROWING HARDER, HER MUSCULATURE MORE DENSE. THERE WERE COMPLICATIONS.
"WHETHER IT WAS THE SURGERY OR THE DEVELOPING SUPER-POWERS, SHE DID NOT SURVIVE.
"BUT HER BABY --"
L7! L7!
THE INFANT BEGAN DEVELOPING SUPER-POWERS AS WELL. BUT SLOWLY, PERHAPS DUE TO HIS YOUTH.
THEY FOUND WAYS TO RETARD THEM, TO PREVENT HIM FROM ABSORBING WHATEVER IT WAS THAT MADE THE POWERS MANIFEST.
THEY KEPT HIM SEDATED, NEAR-COMATOSE. AND, SUPERMAN --
-- THEY EXPERIMEN ON HIM. FO DECADES
I hear her read off a litany of the experiments they performed on the baby alien.
SLOMIČU TE --
Analyzing his organs, installing internal sensors, trying to duplicate his skin, to use his blood to create super-soldiers…
H-UHH!

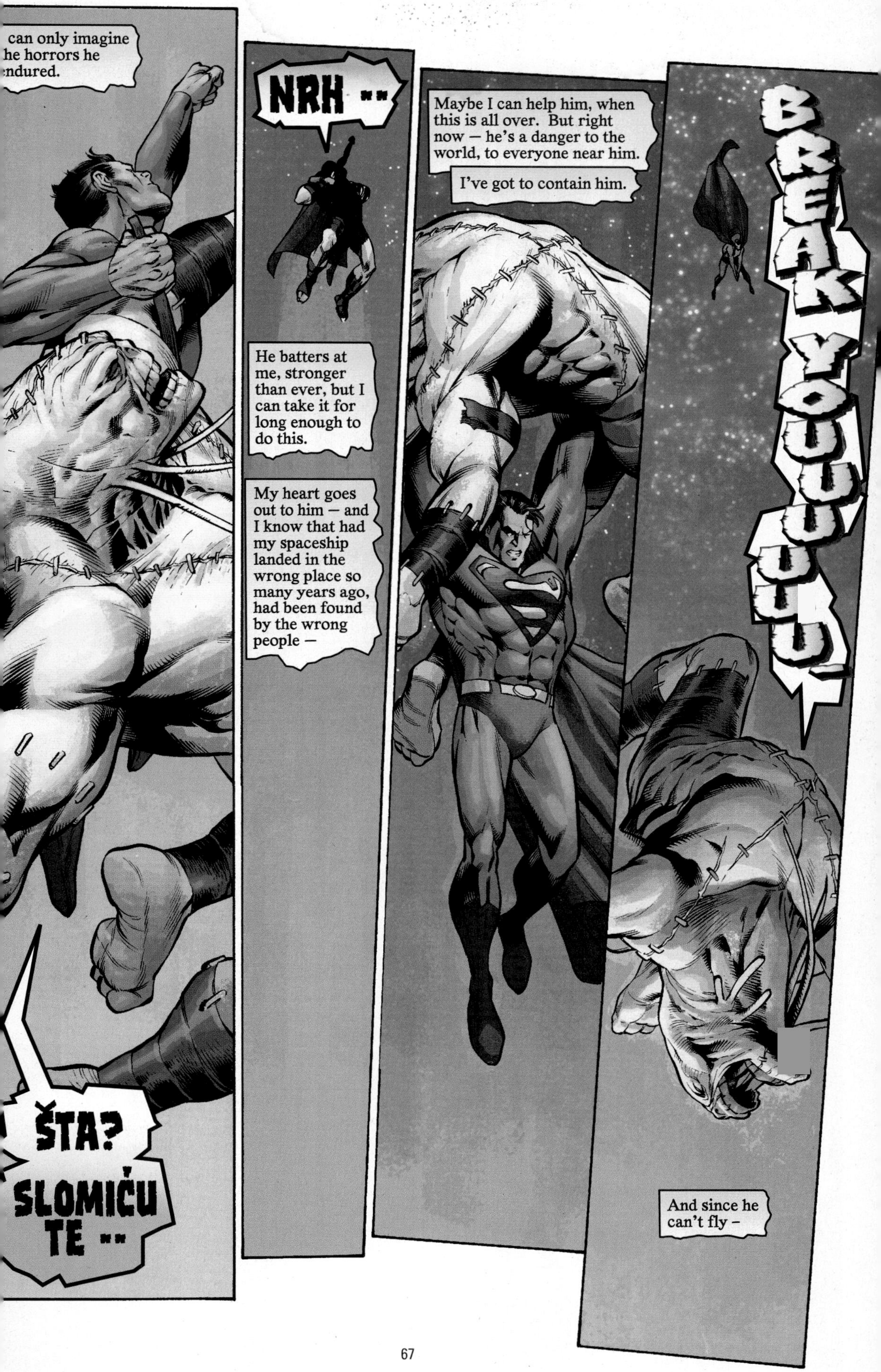
can only imagine he horrors he ndured.
ŠTA? SLOMIČU TE ..
NRH ..
He batters at me, stronger than ever, but I can take it for long enough to do this.
My heart goes out to him — and I know that had my spaceship landed in the wrong place so many years ago, had been found by the wrong people —
Maybe I can help him, when this is all over. But right now — he's a danger to the world, to everyone near him.
I've got to contain him.
BREAK YOUUUUU–
And since he can't fly –

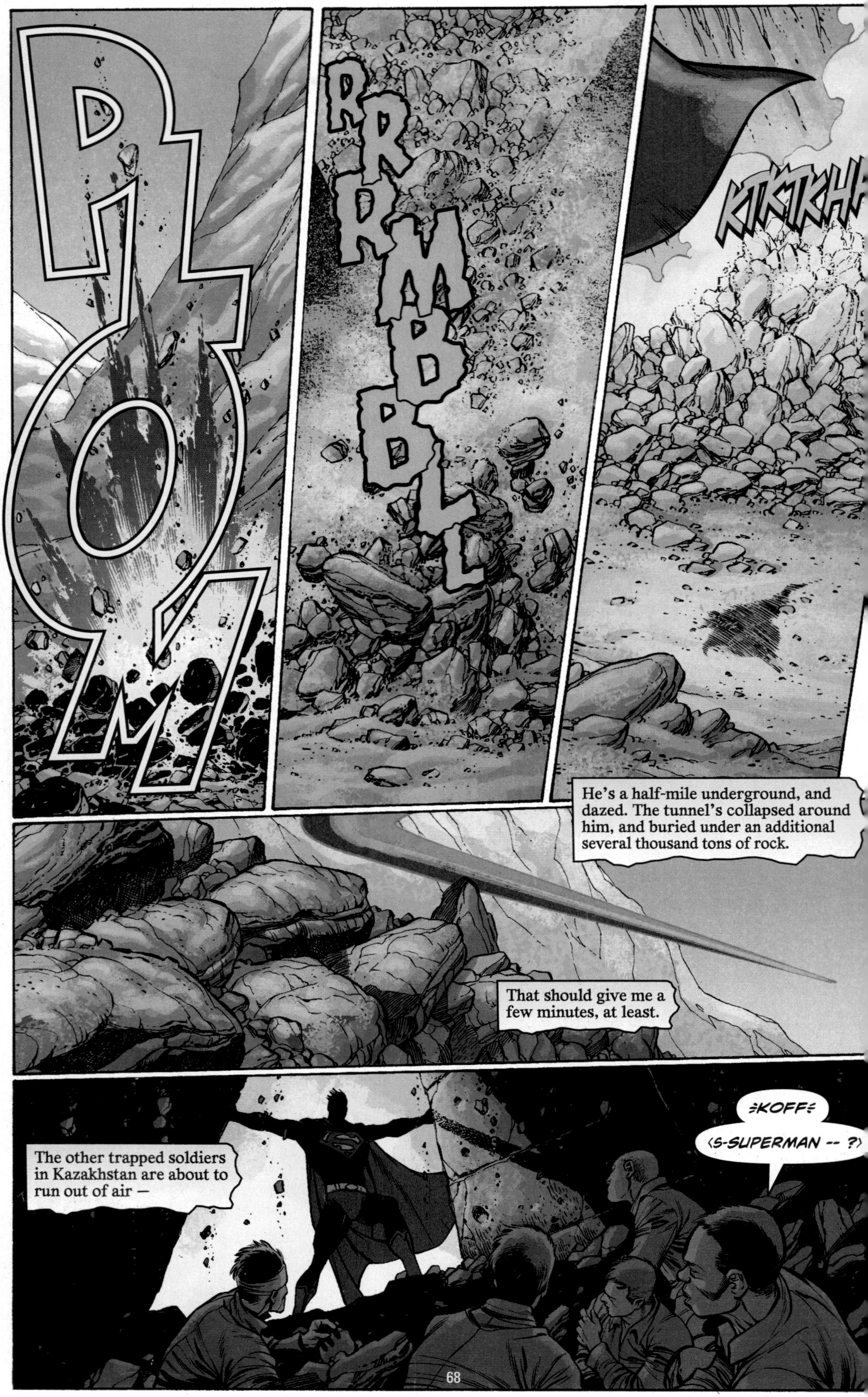
DOOM
RRRMMBBLL
KTKTKH
He's a half-mile underground, and dazed. The tunnel's collapsed around him, and buried under an additional several thousand tons of rock.
That should give me a few minutes, at least.
The other trapped soldiers in Kazakhstan are about to run out of air –
KOFF
‹S-SUPERMAN -- ?›

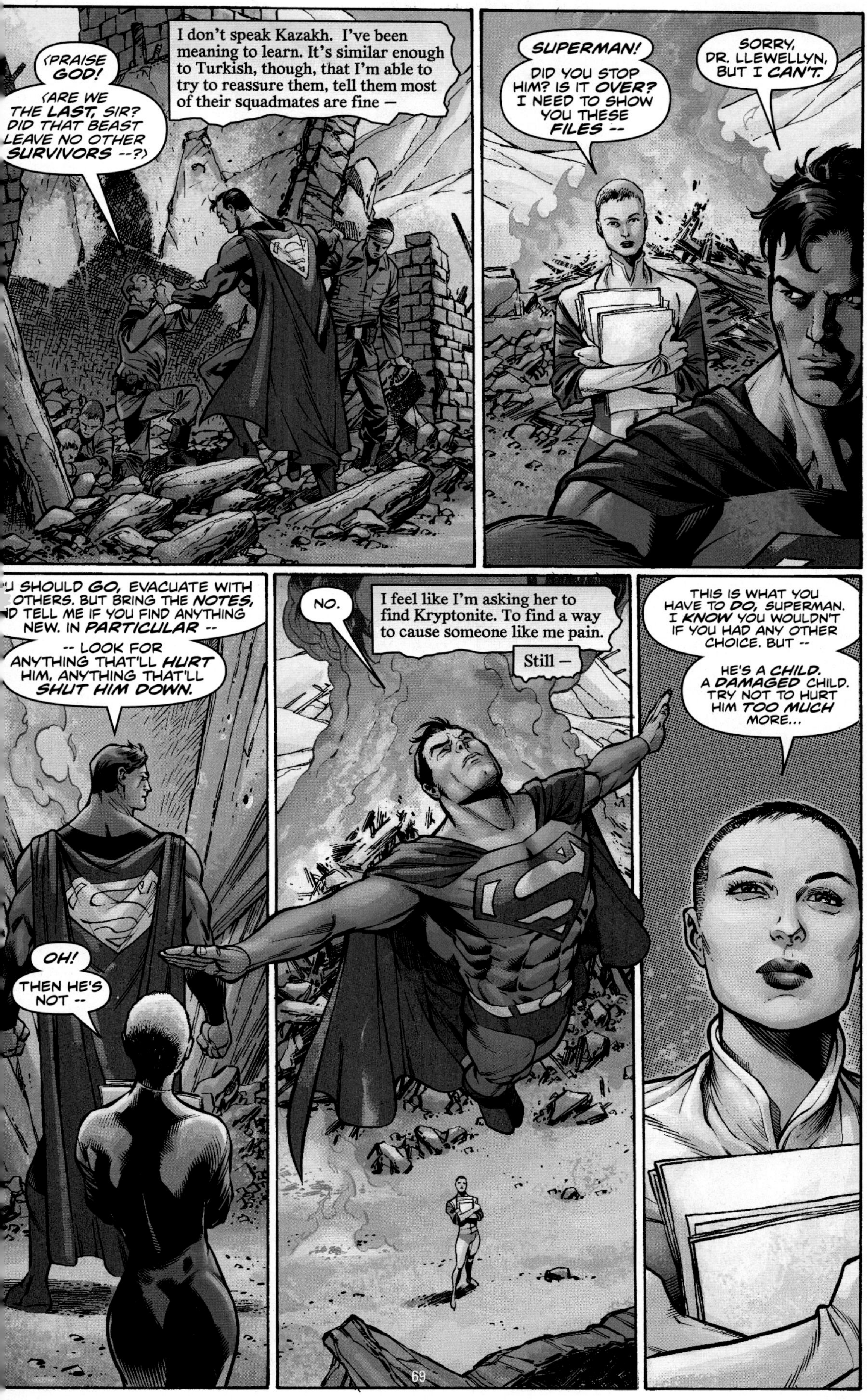

I don't speak Kazakh. I've been meaning to learn. It's similar enough to Turkish, though, that I'm able to try to reassure them, tell them most of their squadmates are fine —
‹PRAISE GOD!
‹ARE WE THE LAST, SIR? DID THAT BEAST LEAVE NO OTHER SURVIVORS --?›
SUPERMAN!
DID YOU STOP HIM? IS IT OVER? I NEED TO SHOW YOU THESE FILES --
SORRY, DR. LLEWELLYN, BUT I CAN'T.
U SHOULD GO, EVACUATE WITH OTHERS. BUT BRING THE NOTES, D TELL ME IF YOU FIND ANYTHING NEW. IN PARTICULAR --
-- LOOK FOR ANYTHING THAT'LL HURT HIM, ANYTHING THAT'LL SHUT HIM DOWN.
OH!
THEN HE'S NOT --
NO.
I feel like I'm asking her to find Kryptonite. To find a way to cause someone like me pain.
Still —
THIS IS WHAT YOU HAVE TO DO, SUPERMAN. I KNOW YOU WOULDN'T IF YOU HAD ANY OTHER CHOICE. BUT --
HE'S A CHILD. A DAMAGED CHILD. TRY NOT TO HURT HIM TOO MUCH MORE...

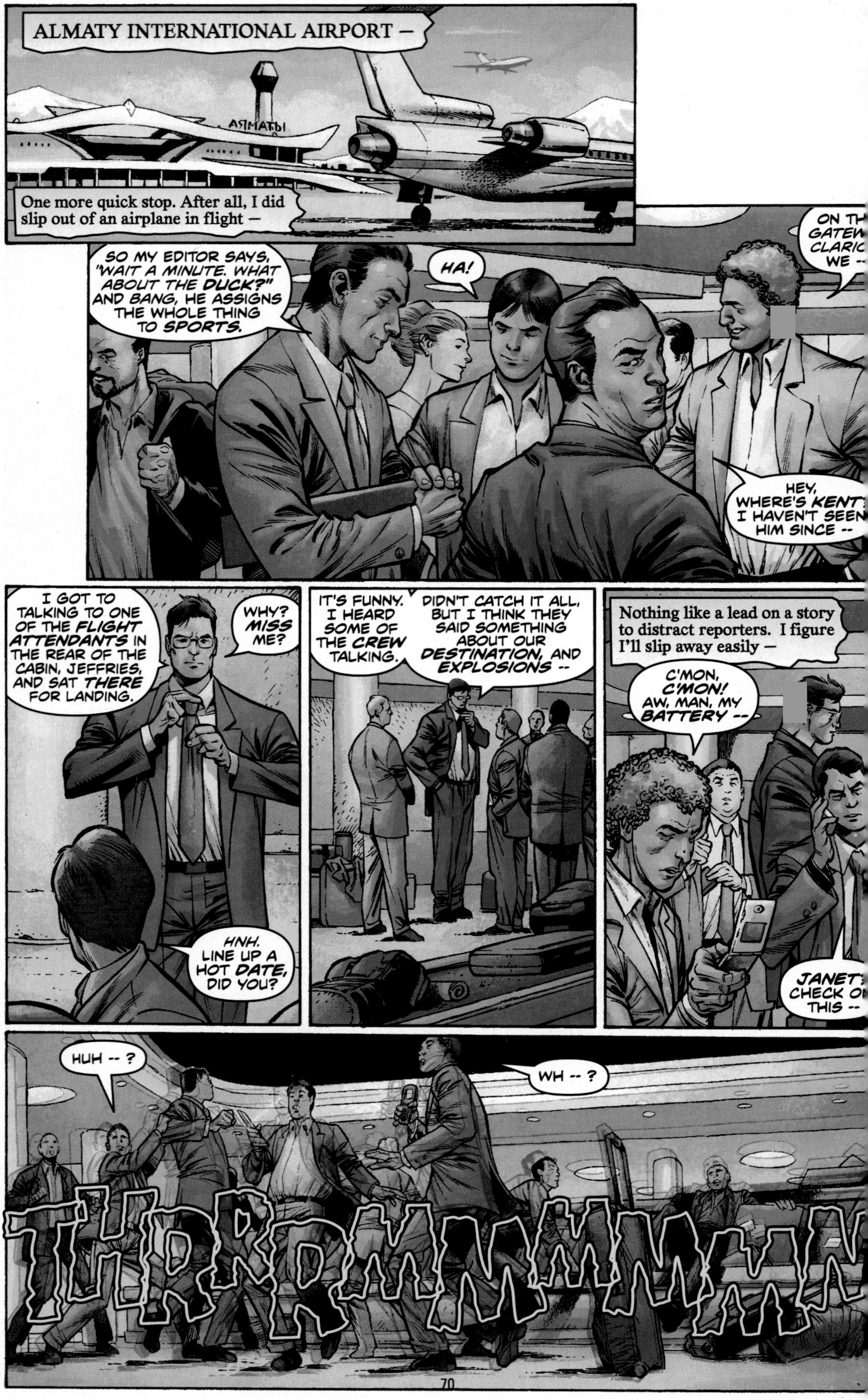
ALMATY INTERNATIONAL AIRPORT —
АЛМАТЫ
One more quick stop. After all, I did slip out of an airplane in flight —
SO MY EDITOR SAYS, "WAIT A MINUTE. WHAT ABOUT THE DUCK?" AND BANG, HE ASSIGNS THE WHOLE THING TO SPORTS.
HA!
ON TH GATEW CLARIC WE --
HEY, WHERE'S KENT I HAVEN'T SEEN HIM SINCE --
I GOT TO TALKING TO ONE OF THE FLIGHT ATTENDANTS IN THE REAR OF THE CABIN, JEFFRIES, AND SAT THERE FOR LANDING.
WHY? MISS ME?
HNH. LINE UP A HOT DATE, DID YOU?
IT'S FUNNY. I HEARD SOME OF THE CREW TALKING.
DIDN'T CATCH IT ALL, BUT I THINK THEY SAID SOMETHING ABOUT OUR DESTINATION, AND EXPLOSIONS --
Nothing like a lead on a story to distract reporters. I figure I'll slip away easily —
C'MON, C'MON! AW, MAN, MY BATTERY --
JANET CHECK O THIS --
HUH -- ?
WH -- ?
THRRMMMMM

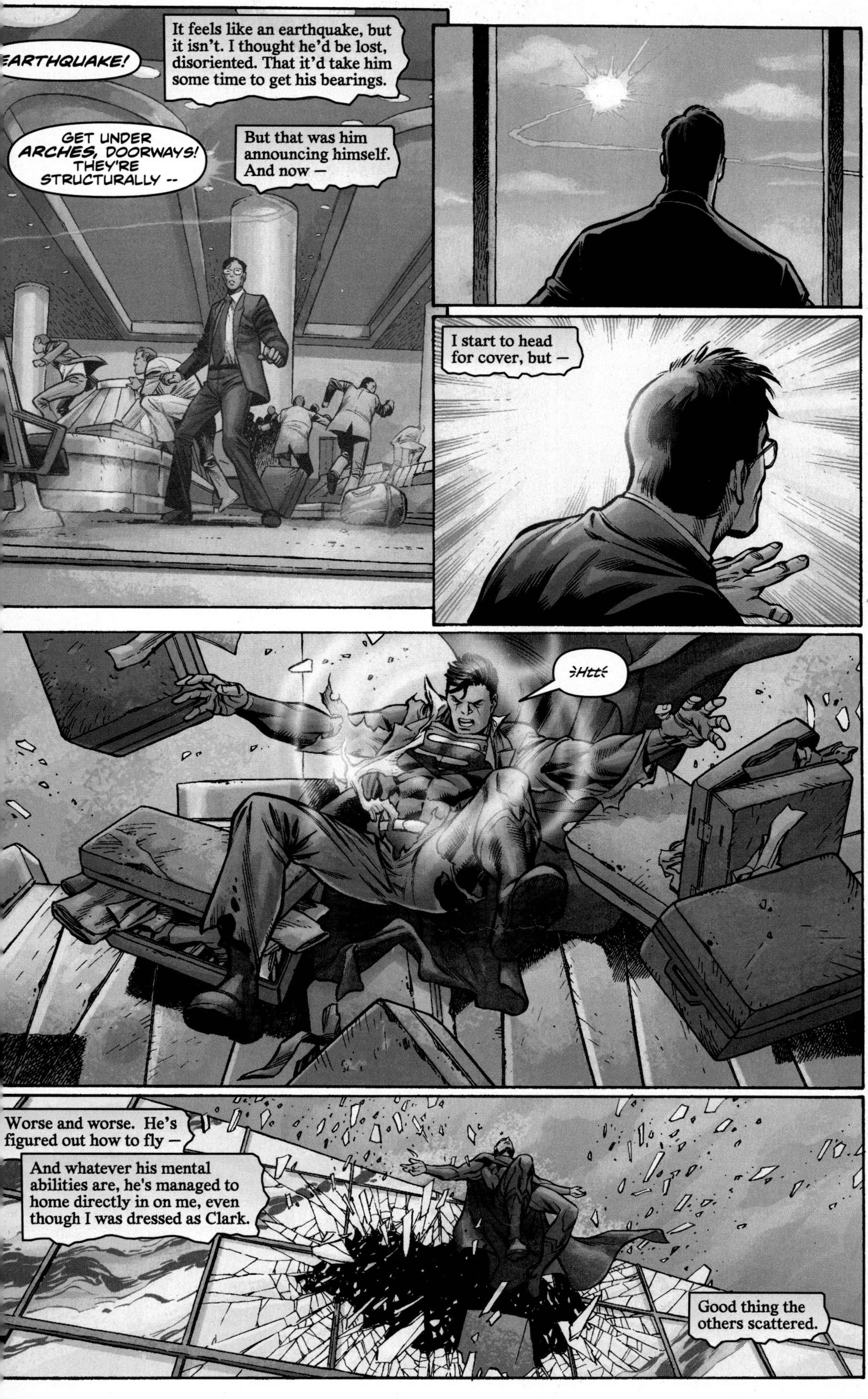
EARTHQUAKE!
It feels like an earthquake, but it isn't. I thought he'd be lost, disoriented. That it'd take him some time to get his bearings.
GET UNDER ARCHES, DOORWAYS! THEY'RE STRUCTURALLY --
But that was him announcing himself. And now —
I start to head for cover, but —
Htt
Worse and worse. He's figured out how to fly —
And whatever his mental abilities are, he's managed to home directly in on me, even though I was dressed as Clark.
Good thing the others scattered.

YOU -- YOU -- I FEEL YOU -- SEE -- SEE **THROUGH** YOU --

He's got me in a telekinetic hold. And he's speaking English — I thought he'd started to, before.

I can feel his power, playing over me —

YOU -- NOT LIKE THEM. NOT MONSTER, NOT "**HUMAN**."

YOU -- **OTHER.** ALIEN. LIKE **SUBJEKT** LIKE **ME**.

Callie was wrong. He's not a child.

He's an adult. An adult that was never socialized, never taught anything. He learned from what he was subjected to — cruelty and pain.

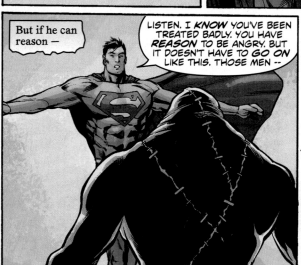

But if he can reason —

LISTEN. I **KNOW** YOU'VE BEEN TREATED BADLY. YOU HAVE **REASON** TO BE ANGRY. BUT IT DOESN'T HAVE TO **GO ON** LIKE THIS. THOSE MEN --

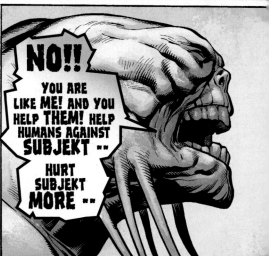

NO!! YOU ARE LIKE **ME**! AND YOU HELP **THEM**! HELP HUMANS AGAINST **SUBJEKT** --

HURT SUBJEKT **MORE** --

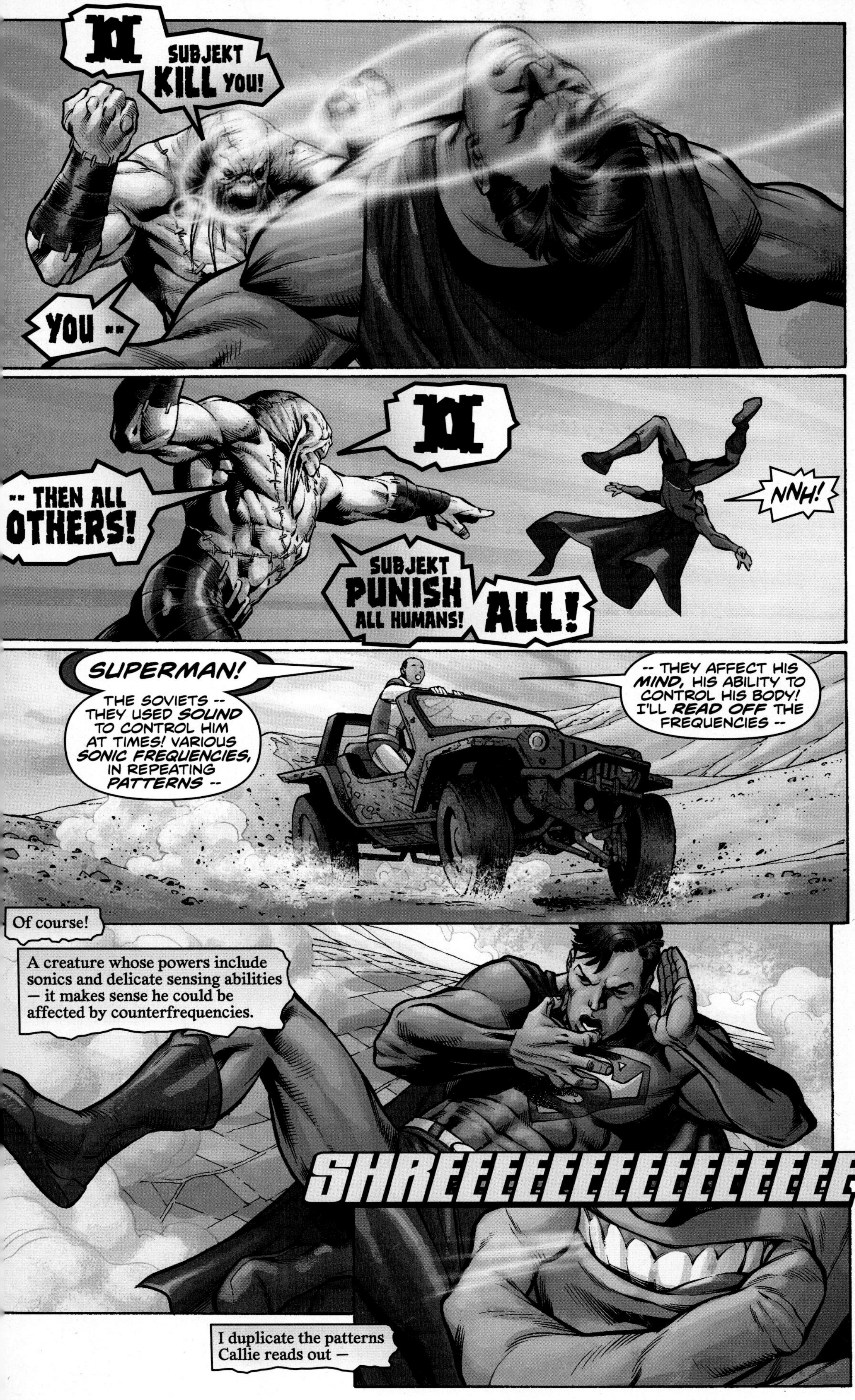
Ж
SUBJEKT KILL YOU!
YOU --
-- THEN ALL OTHERS!
Ж
SUBJEKT PUNISH ALL HUMANS!
ALL!
NNH!
SUPERMAN!
THE SOVIETS -- THEY USED SOUND TO CONTROL HIM AT TIMES! VARIOUS SONIC FREQUENCIES, IN REPEATING PATTERNS --
-- THEY AFFECT HIS MIND, HIS ABILITY TO CONTROL HIS BODY! I'LL READ OFF THE FREQUENCIES --
Of course!
A creature whose powers include sonics and delicate sensing abilities — it makes sense he could be affected by counterfrequencies.
SHREEEEEEEEEEEEEEEE
I duplicate the patterns Callie reads out —

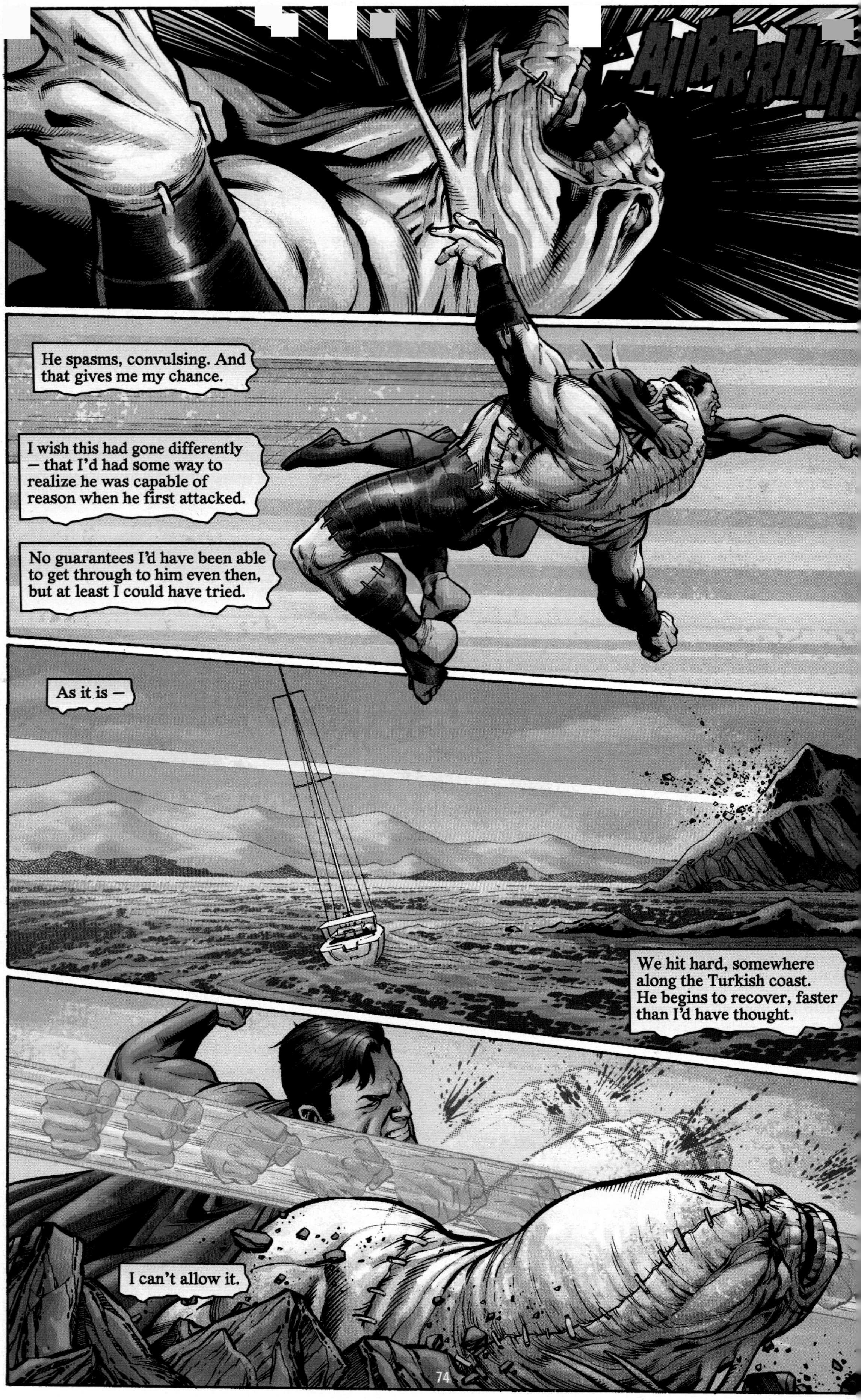
AIIRRRHHH
He spasms, convulsing. And that gives me my chance.
I wish this had gone differently — that I'd had some way to realize he was capable of reason when he first attacked.
No guarantees I'd have been able to get through to him even then, but at least I could have tried.
As it is —
We hit hard, somewhere along the Turkish coast. He begins to recover, faster than I'd have thought.
I can't allow it.

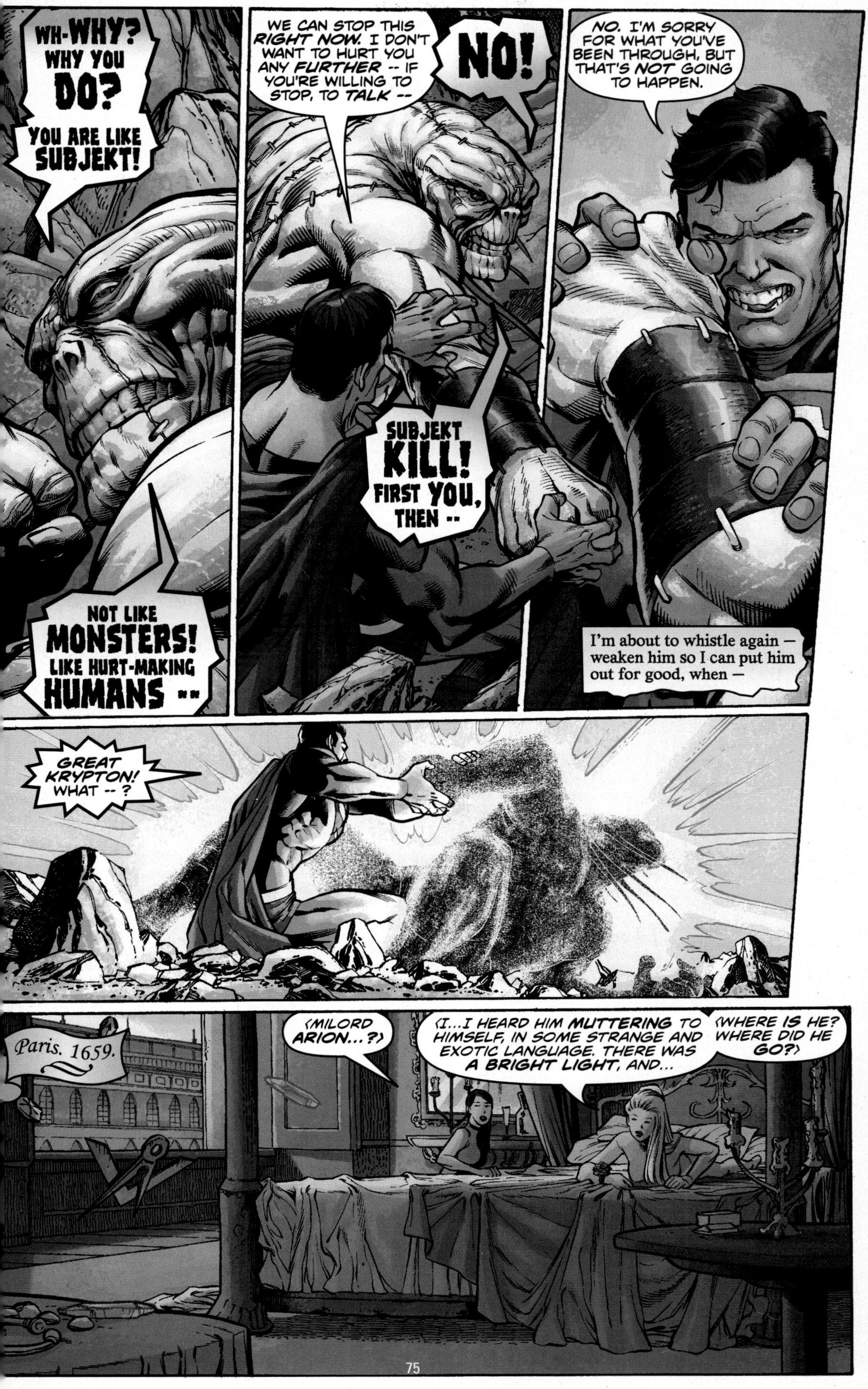
WH-WHY? WHY YOU DO? YOU ARE LIKE SUBJEKT!
NOT LIKE MONSTERS! LIKE HURT-MAKING HUMANS --
WE CAN STOP THIS RIGHT NOW. I DON'T WANT TO HURT YOU ANY FURTHER -- IF YOU'RE WILLING TO STOP, TO TALK --
NO!
SUBJEKT KILL! FIRST YOU, THEN --
NO. I'M SORRY FOR WHAT YOU'VE BEEN THROUGH, BUT THAT'S NOT GOING TO HAPPEN.
I'm about to whistle again — weaken him so I can put him out for good, when —
GREAT KRYPTON! WHAT -- ?
Paris. 1659.
‹MILORD ARION...?›
‹I...I HEARD HIM MUTTERING TO HIMSELF, IN SOME STRANGE AND EXOTIC LANGUAGE. THERE WAS A BRIGHT LIGHT, AND...
‹WHERE IS HE? WHERE DID HE GO?›

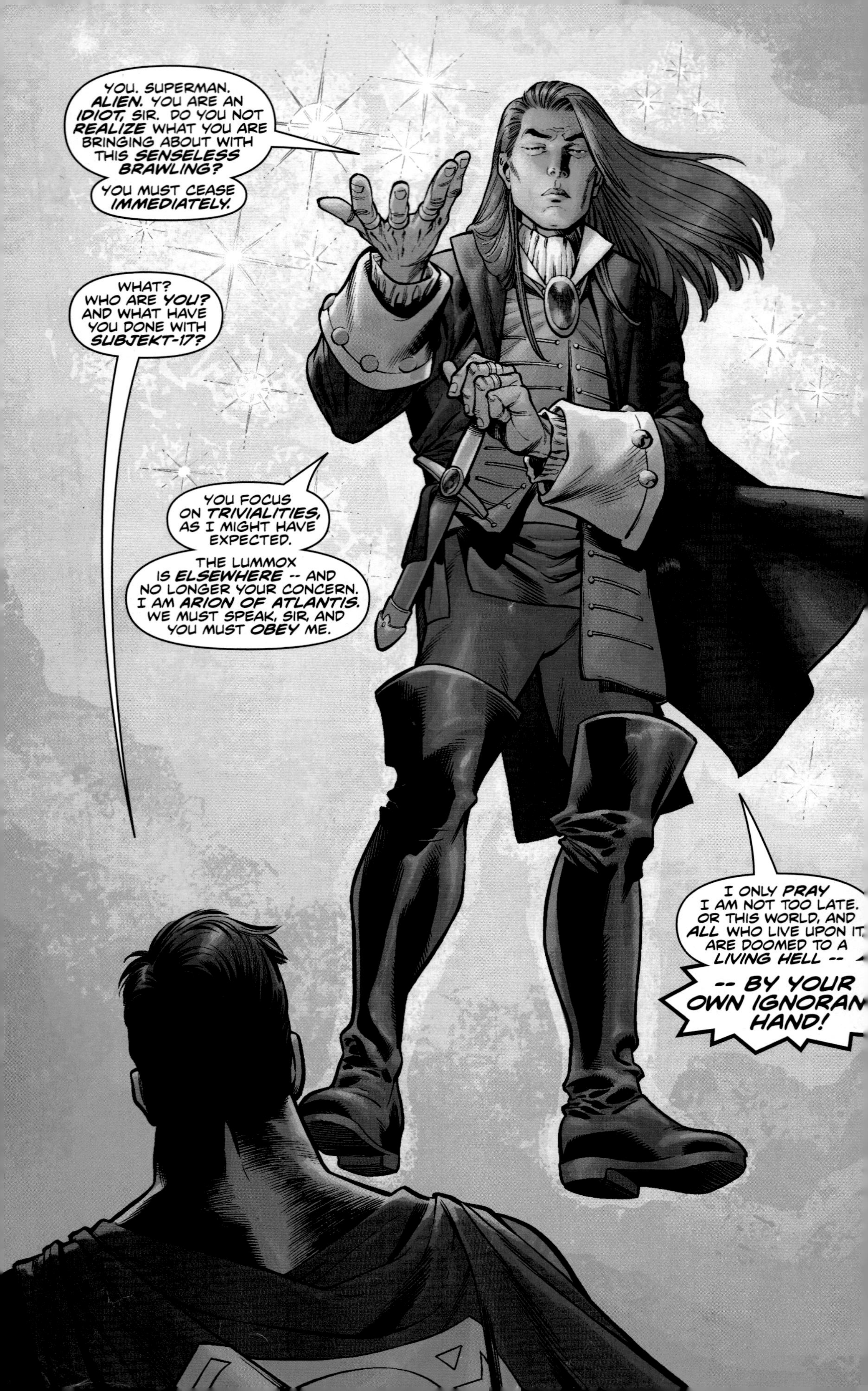
YOU. SUPERMAN. ALIEN. YOU ARE AN IDIOT, SIR. DO YOU NOT REALIZE WHAT YOU ARE BRINGING ABOUT WITH THIS SENSELESS BRAWLING?
YOU MUST CEASE IMMEDIATELY.
WHAT? WHO ARE YOU? AND WHAT HAVE YOU DONE WITH SUBJEKT-17?
YOU FOCUS ON TRIVIALITIES, AS I MIGHT HAVE EXPECTED.
THE LUMMOX IS ELSEWHERE -- AND NO LONGER YOUR CONCERN. I AM ARION OF ATLANTIS. WE MUST SPEAK, SIR, AND YOU MUST OBEY ME.
I ONLY PRAY I AM NOT TOO LATE. OR THIS WORLD, AND ALL WHO LIVE UPON IT ARE DOOMED TO A LIVING HELL --
-- BY YOUR OWN IGNORAN HAND!

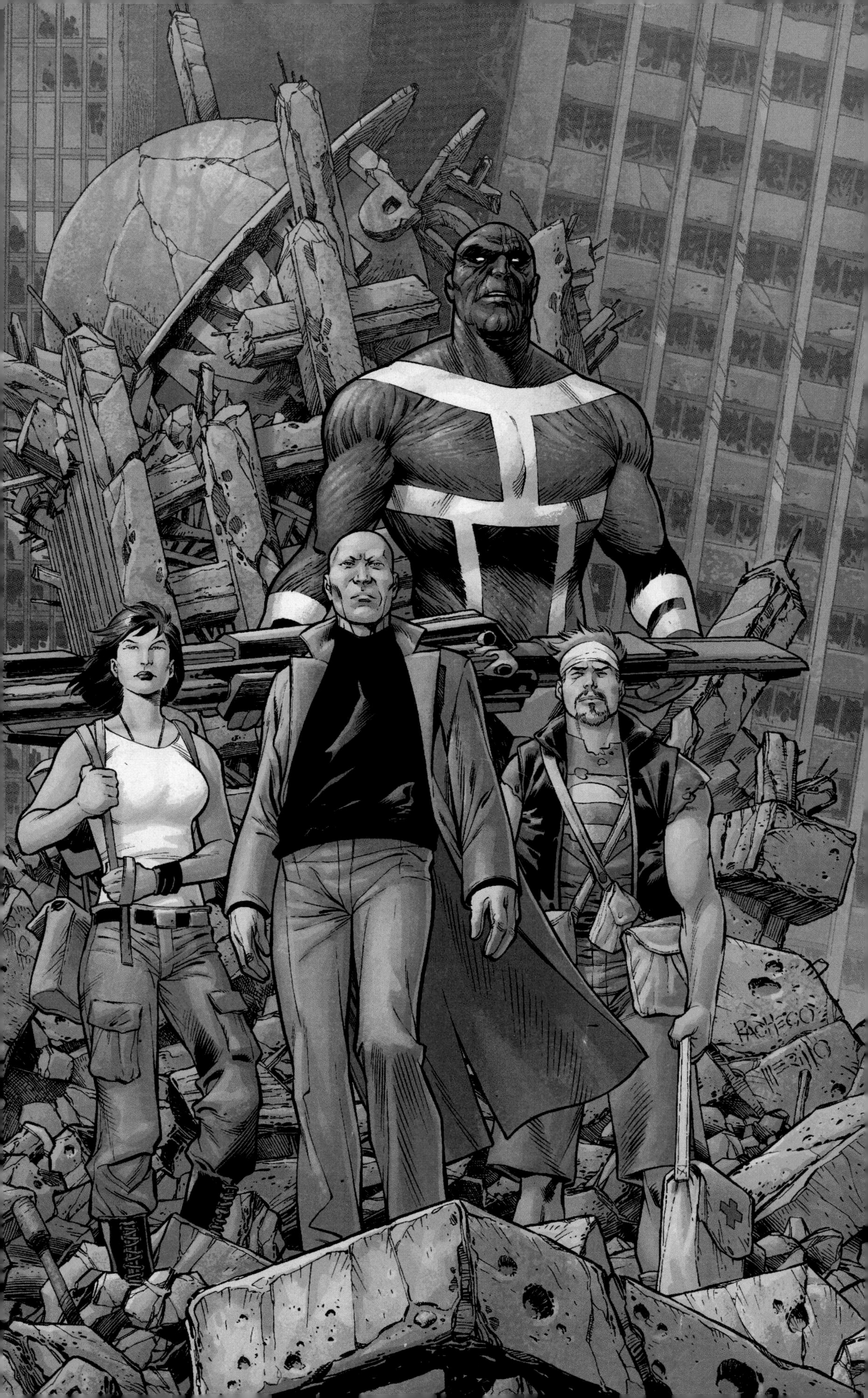
PACHECO

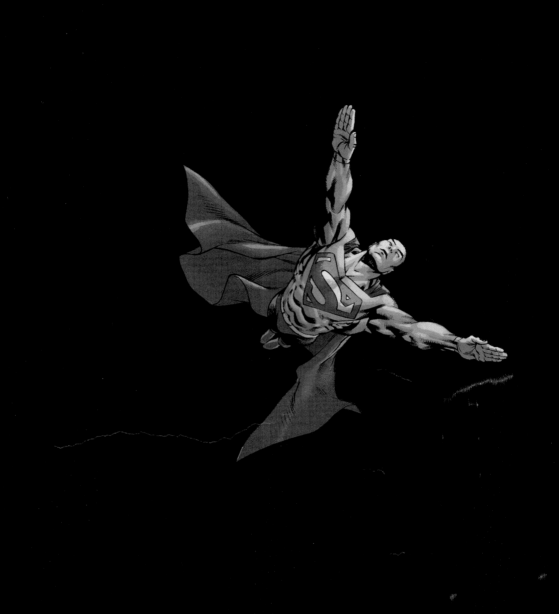

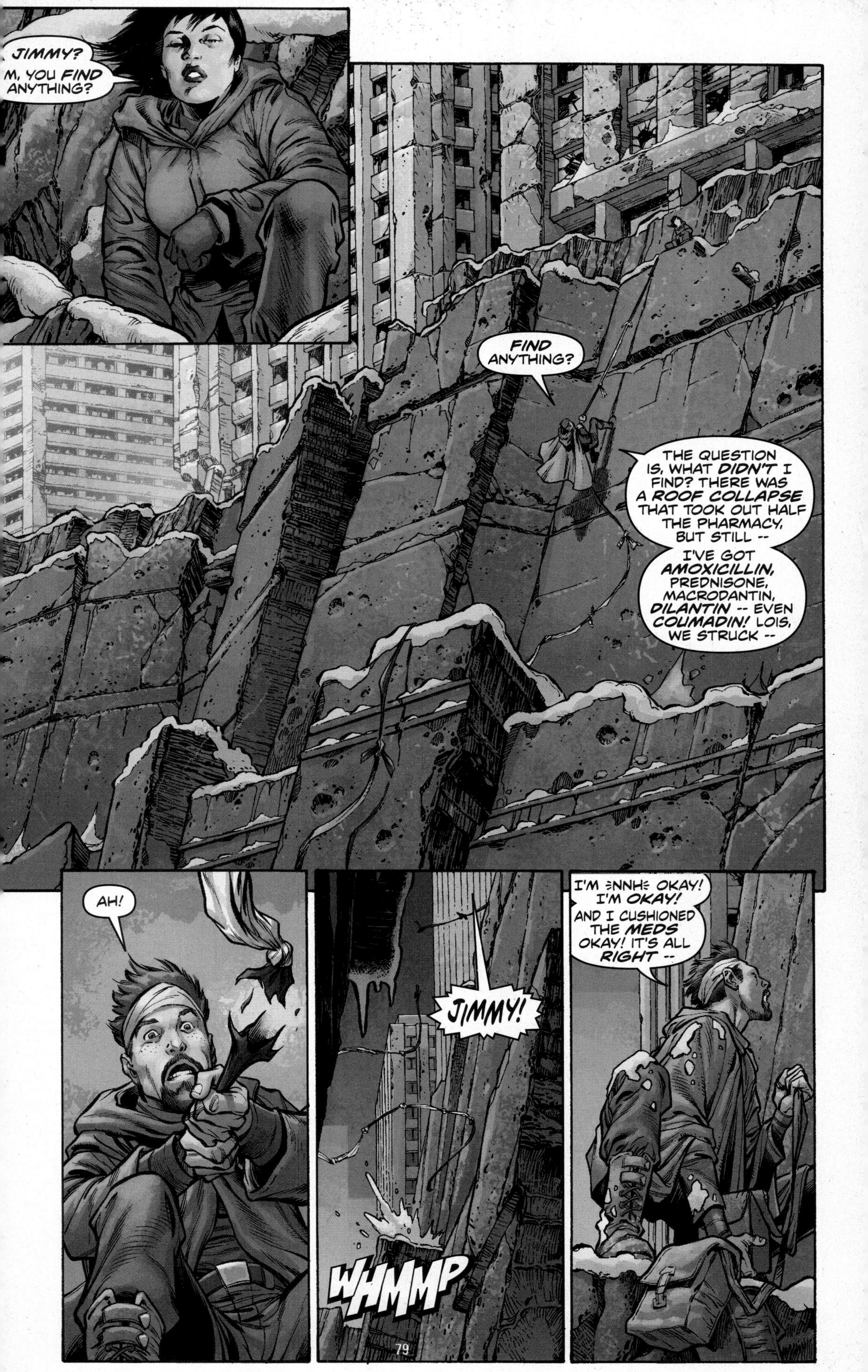
JIMMY?
M, YOU FIND ANYTHING?
FIND ANYTHING?
THE QUESTION IS, WHAT DIDN'T I FIND? THERE WAS A ROOF COLLAPSE THAT TOOK OUT HALF THE PHARMACY, BUT STILL --
I'VE GOT AMOXICILLIN, PREDNISONE, MACRODANTIN, DILANTIN -- EVEN COUMADIN! LOIS, WE STRUCK --
AH!
JIMMY!
WHMMP
I'M NNH OKAY! I'M OKAY!
AND I CUSHIONED THE MEDS OKAY! IT'S ALL RIGHT --

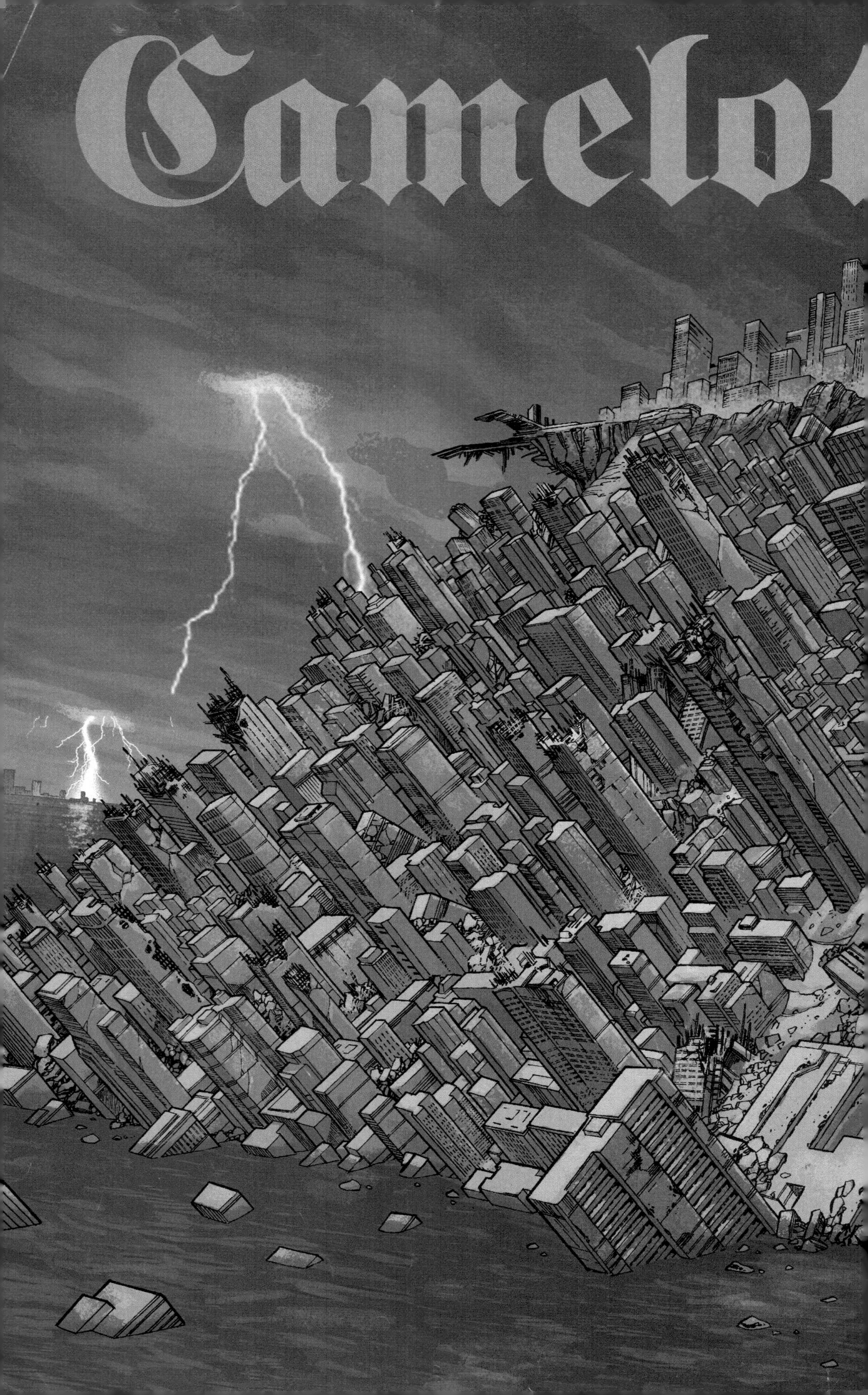
Camelo

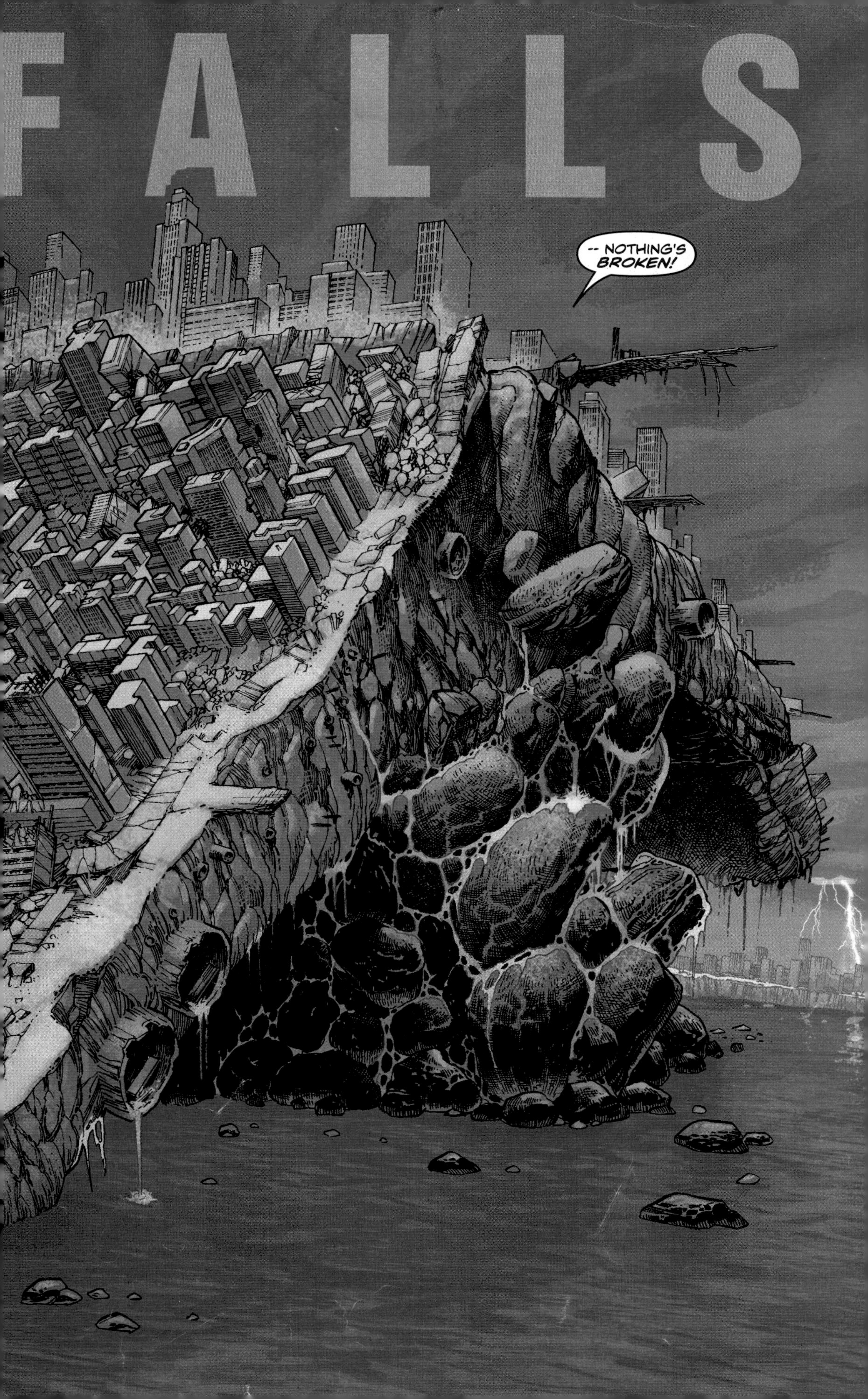
FALLS
-- NOTHING'S BROKEN!

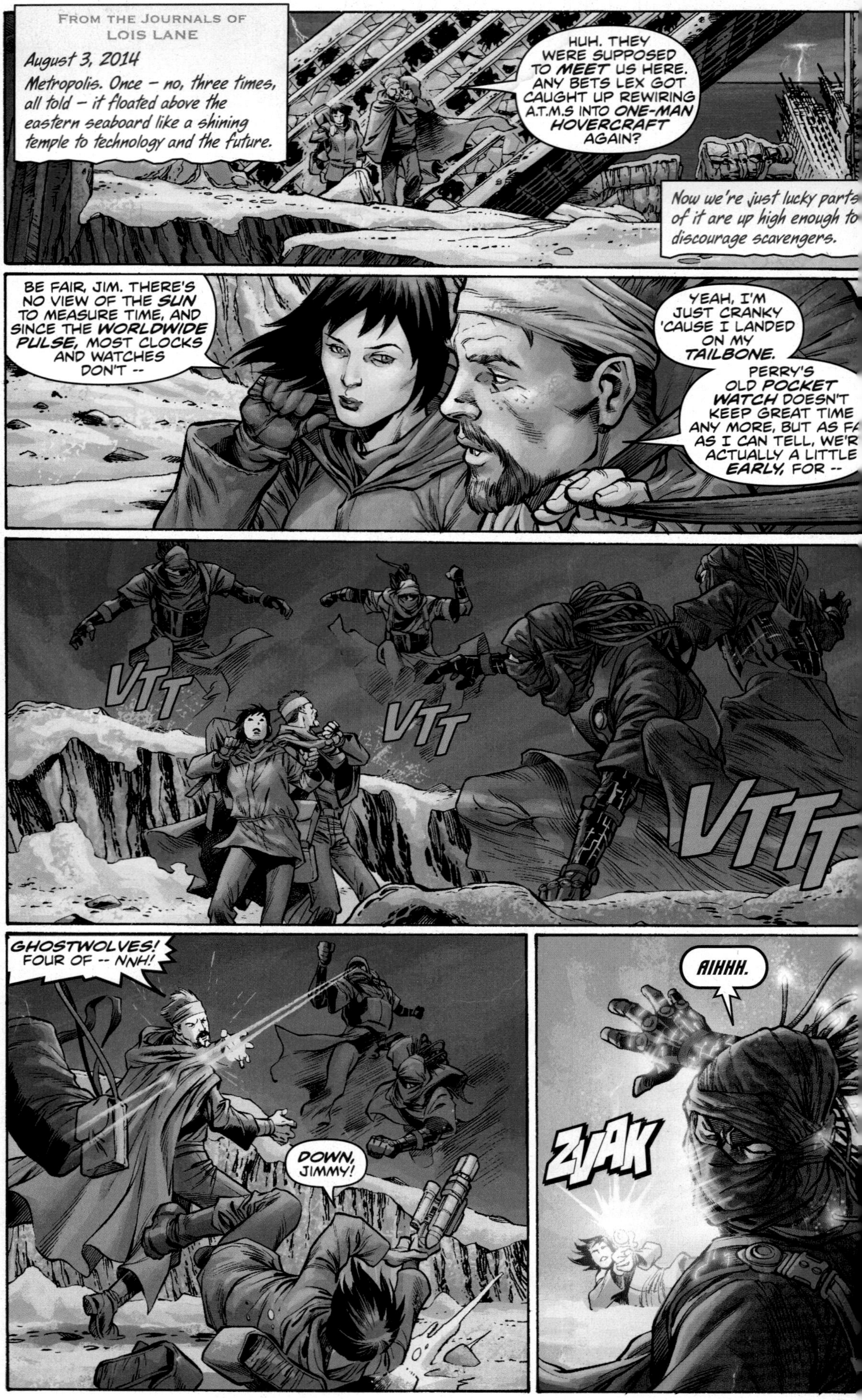
FROM THE JOURNALS OF LOIS LANE
August 3, 2014
Metropolis. Once – no, three times, all told – it floated above the eastern seaboard like a shining temple to technology and the future.
HUH. THEY WERE SUPPOSED TO MEET US HERE. ANY BETS LEX GOT CAUGHT UP REWIRING A.T.M.S INTO ONE-MAN HOVERCRAFT AGAIN?
Now we're just lucky parts of it are up high enough to discourage scavengers.
BE FAIR, JIM. THERE'S NO VIEW OF THE SUN TO MEASURE TIME, AND SINCE THE WORLDWIDE PULSE, MOST CLOCKS AND WATCHES DON'T --
YEAH, I'M JUST CRANKY 'CAUSE I LANDED ON MY TAILBONE.
PERRY'S OLD POCKET WATCH DOESN'T KEEP GREAT TIME ANY MORE, BUT AS FA AS I CAN TELL, WE'R ACTUALLY A LITTLE EARLY, FOR --
VTT
VTT
VTTT
GHOSTWOLVES! FOUR OF -- NNH!
DOWN, JIMMY!
AIHHH.
ZVAK

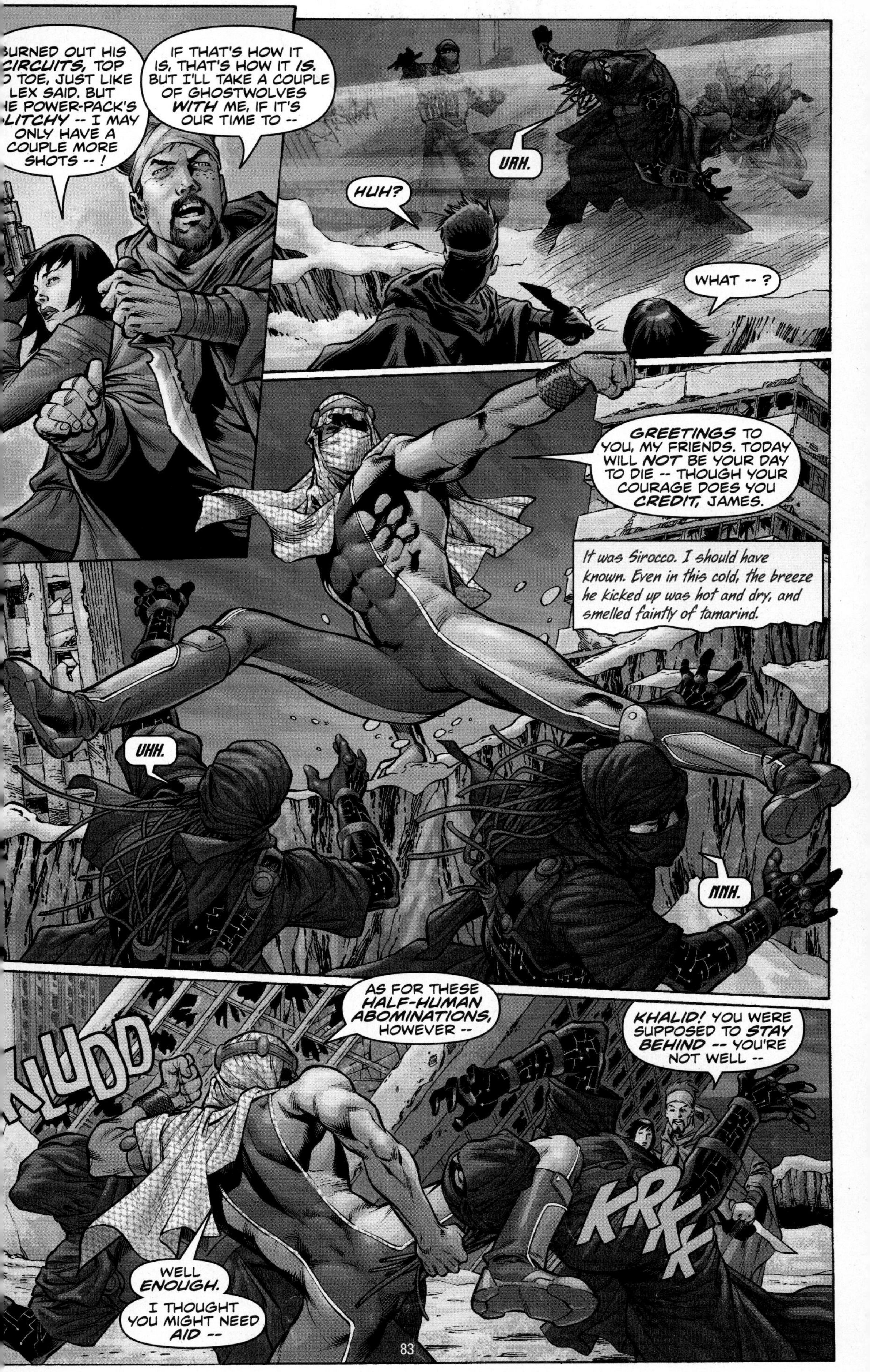

BURNED OUT HIS CIRCUITS, TOP TO TOE, JUST LIKE LEX SAID. BUT THE POWER-PACK'S GLITCHY -- I MAY ONLY HAVE A COUPLE MORE SHOTS -- !
IF THAT'S HOW IT IS, THAT'S HOW IT IS. BUT I'LL TAKE A COUPLE OF GHOSTWOLVES WITH ME, IF IT'S OUR TIME TO --
URH.
HUH?
WHAT -- ?
GREETINGS TO YOU, MY FRIENDS. TODAY WILL NOT BE YOUR DAY TO DIE -- THOUGH YOUR COURAGE DOES YOU CREDIT, JAMES.
It was Sirocco. I should have known. Even in this cold, the breeze he kicked up was hot and dry, and smelled faintly of tamarind.
UHH.
NNH.
KLUDD
AS FOR THESE HALF-HUMAN ABOMINATIONS, HOWEVER --
KHALID! YOU WERE SUPPOSED TO STAY BEHIND -- YOU'RE NOT WELL --
KRKK
WELL ENOUGH.
I THOUGHT YOU MIGHT NEED AID --

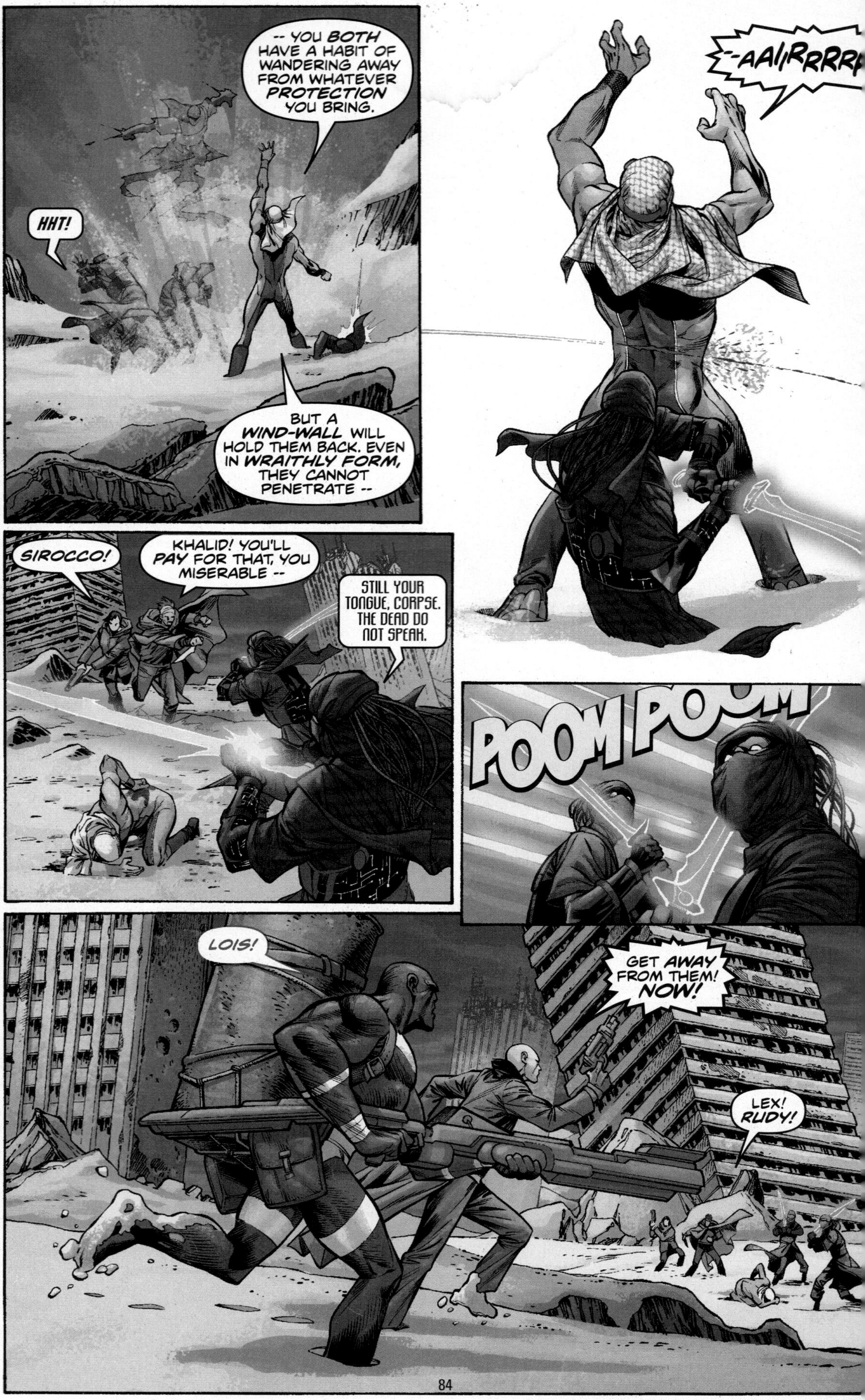
-- YOU BOTH HAVE A HABIT OF WANDERING AWAY FROM WHATEVER PROTECTION YOU BRING.
HHT!
BUT A WIND-WALL WILL HOLD THEM BACK. EVEN IN WRAITHLY FORM, THEY CANNOT PENETRATE --
-AAIIRRRR
SIROCCO!
KHALID! YOU'LL PAY FOR THAT, YOU MISERABLE --
STILL YOUR TONGUE, CORPSE. THE DEAD DO NOT SPEAK.
POOM POOM
LOIS!
GET AWAY FROM THEM! NOW!
LEX! RUDY!

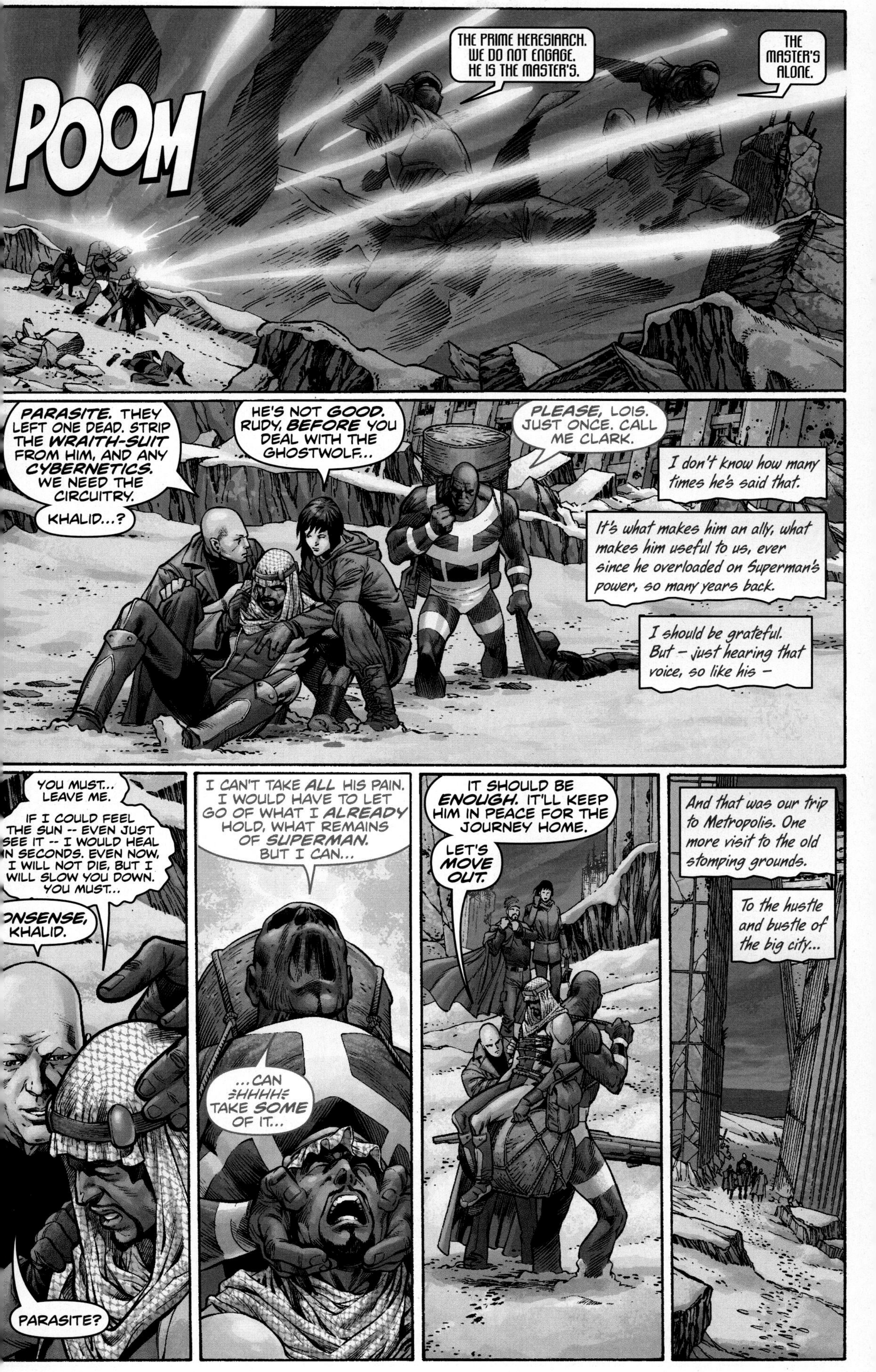
POOM
THE PRIME HERESIARCH. WE DO NOT ENGAGE. HE IS THE MASTER'S.
THE MASTER'S ALONE.
PARASITE. THEY LEFT ONE DEAD. STRIP THE WRAITH-SUIT FROM HIM, AND ANY CYBERNETICS. WE NEED THE CIRCUITRY.
KHALID...?
HE'S NOT GOOD. RUDY, BEFORE YOU DEAL WITH THE GHOSTWOLF...
PLEASE, LOIS. JUST ONCE. CALL ME CLARK.
I don't know how many times he's said that.
It's what makes him an ally, what makes him useful to us, ever since he overloaded on Superman's power, so many years back.
I should be grateful. But – just hearing that voice, so like his –
YOU MUST... LEAVE ME.
IF I COULD FEEL THE SUN -- EVEN JUST SEE IT -- I WOULD HEAL IN SECONDS. EVEN NOW, I WILL NOT DIE, BUT I WILL SLOW YOU DOWN. YOU MUST...
ONSENSE, KHALID.
PARASITE?
I CAN'T TAKE ALL HIS PAIN. I WOULD HAVE TO LET GO OF WHAT I ALREADY HOLD, WHAT REMAINS OF SUPERMAN. BUT I CAN...
...CAN HHHHH TAKE SOME OF IT...
IT SHOULD BE ENOUGH. IT'LL KEEP HIM IN PEACE FOR THE JOURNEY HOME.
LET'S MOVE OUT.
And that was our trip to Metropolis. One more visit to the old stomping grounds.
To the hustle and bustle of the big city...

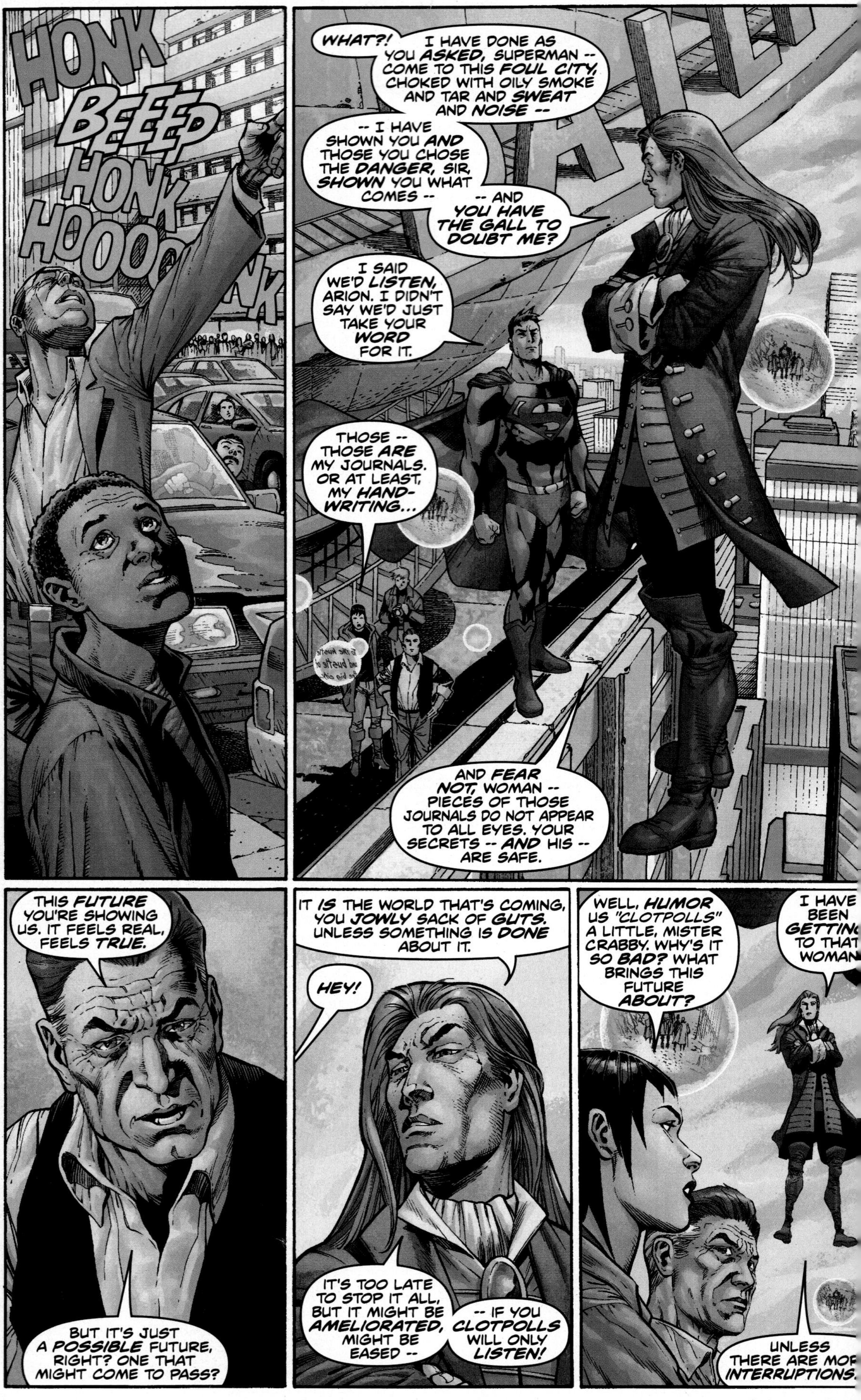
HONK
BEEEP
HONK
HOOOONK
WHAT?!
I HAVE DONE AS YOU ASKED, SUPERMAN -- COME TO THIS FOUL CITY, CHOKED WITH OILY SMOKE AND TAR AND SWEAT AND NOISE --
-- I HAVE SHOWN YOU AND THOSE YOU CHOSE THE DANGER, SIR, SHOWN YOU WHAT COMES --
-- AND YOU HAVE THE GALL TO DOUBT ME?
I SAID WE'D LISTEN, ARION. I DIDN'T SAY WE'D JUST TAKE YOUR WORD FOR IT.
THOSE -- THOSE ARE MY JOURNALS. OR AT LEAST, MY HAND-WRITING...
AND FEAR NOT, WOMAN -- PIECES OF THOSE JOURNALS DO NOT APPEAR TO ALL EYES. YOUR SECRETS -- AND HIS -- ARE SAFE.
THIS FUTURE YOU'RE SHOWING US. IT FEELS REAL, FEELS TRUE.
BUT IT'S JUST A POSSIBLE FUTURE, RIGHT? ONE THAT MIGHT COME TO PASS?
IT IS THE WORLD THAT'S COMING, YOU JOWLY SACK OF GUTS. UNLESS SOMETHING IS DONE ABOUT IT.
HEY!
IT'S TOO LATE TO STOP IT ALL, BUT IT MIGHT BE AMELIORATED, MIGHT BE EASED --
-- IF YOU CLOTPOLLS WILL ONLY LISTEN!
WELL, HUMOR US "CLOTPOLLS" A LITTLE, MISTER CRABBY. WHY'S IT SO BAD? WHAT BRINGS THIS FUTURE ABOUT?
I HAVE BEEN GETTIN TO THAT WOMAN
UNLESS THERE ARE MOR INTERRUPTIONS.

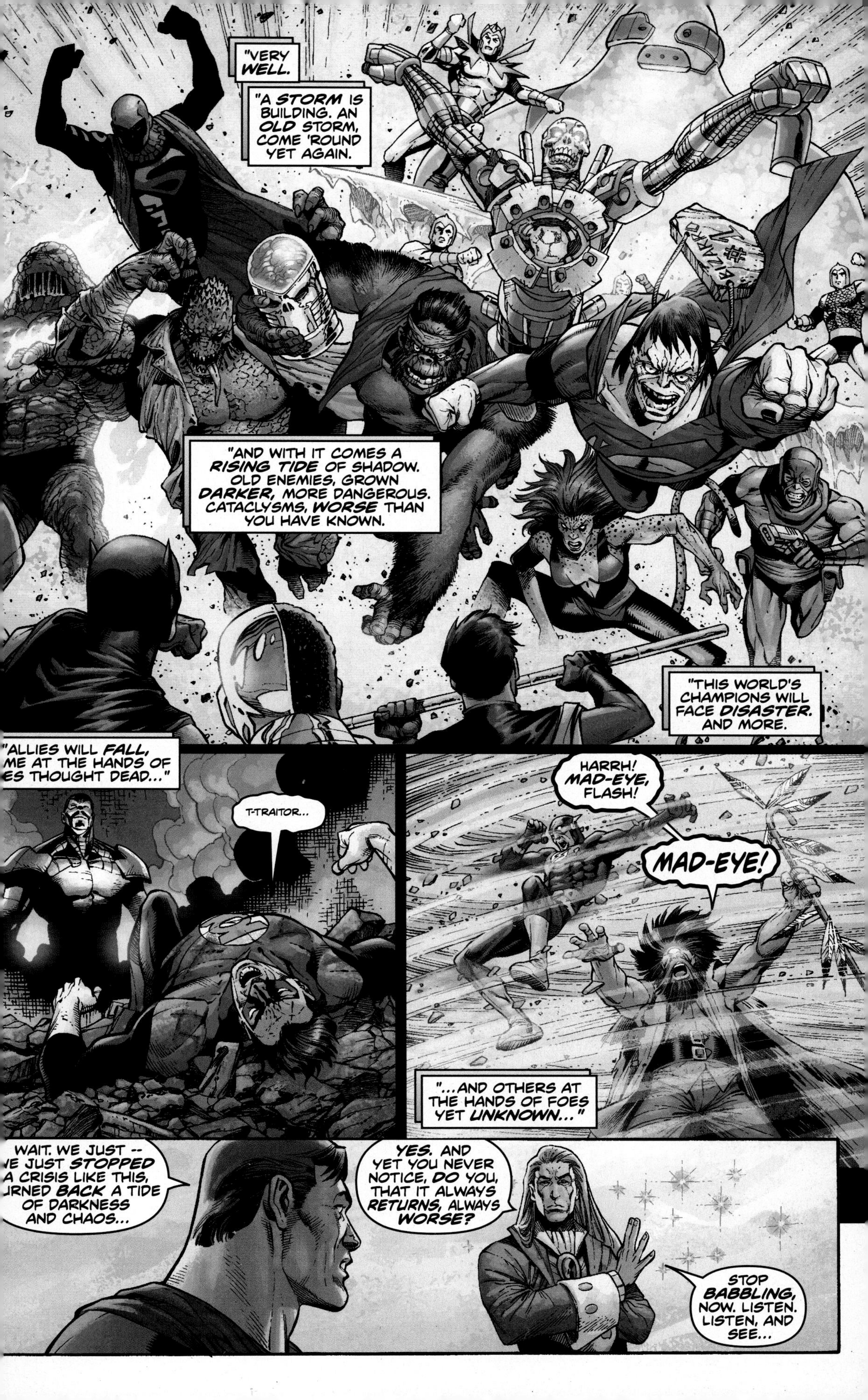
"VERY WELL.
"A STORM IS BUILDING. AN OLD STORM, COME 'ROUND YET AGAIN.
"AND WITH IT COMES A RISING TIDE OF SHADOW. OLD ENEMIES, GROWN DARKER, MORE DANGEROUS. CATACLYSMS, WORSE THAN YOU HAVE KNOWN.
"THIS WORLD'S CHAMPIONS WILL FACE DISASTER. AND MORE.
"ALLIES WILL FALL, ME AT THE HANDS OF ES THOUGHT DEAD..."
T-TRAITOR...
HARRH! MAD-EYE, FLASH!
MAD-EYE!
"...AND OTHERS AT THE HANDS OF FOES YET UNKNOWN..."
WAIT. WE JUST -- E JUST STOPPED A CRISIS LIKE THIS, URNED BACK A TIDE OF DARKNESS AND CHAOS...
YES. AND YET YOU NEVER NOTICE, DO YOU, THAT IT ALWAYS RETURNS, ALWAYS WORSE?
STOP BABBLING, NOW. LISTEN. LISTEN, AND SEE...

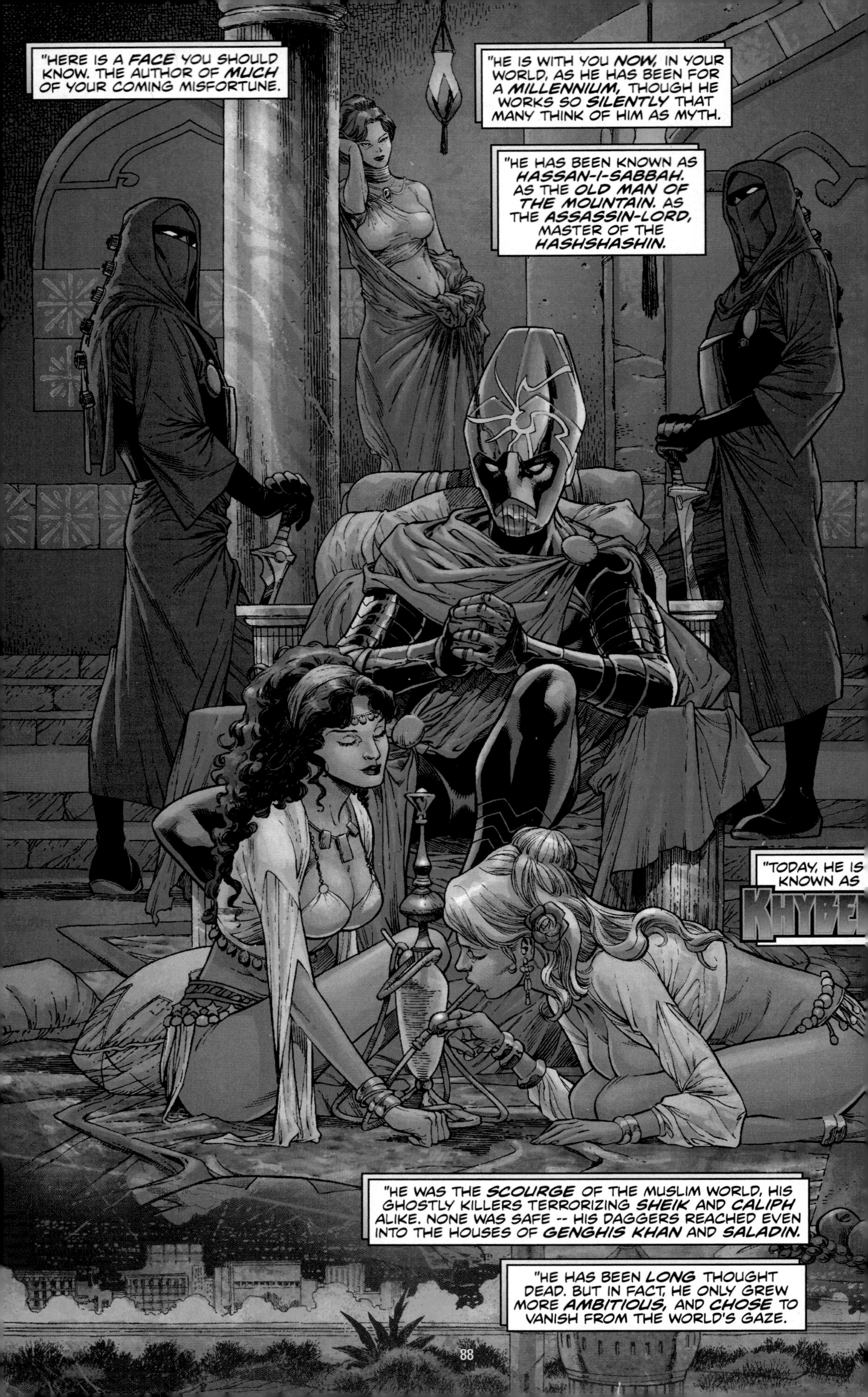
"HERE IS A FACE YOU SHOULD KNOW. THE AUTHOR OF MUCH OF YOUR COMING MISFORTUNE.
"HE IS WITH YOU NOW, IN YOUR WORLD, AS HE HAS BEEN FOR A MILLENNIUM, THOUGH HE WORKS SO SILENTLY THAT MANY THINK OF HIM AS MYTH.
"HE HAS BEEN KNOWN AS HASSAN-I-SABBAH. AS THE OLD MAN OF THE MOUNTAIN. AS THE ASSASSIN-LORD, MASTER OF THE HASHSHASHIN.
"TODAY, HE IS KNOWN AS
KHYBE
"HE WAS THE SCOURGE OF THE MUSLIM WORLD, HIS GHOSTLY KILLERS TERRORIZING SHEIK AND CALIPH ALIKE. NONE WAS SAFE -- HIS DAGGERS REACHED EVEN INTO THE HOUSES OF GENGHIS KHAN AND SALADIN.
"HE HAS BEEN LONG THOUGHT DEAD. BUT IN FACT, HE ONLY GREW MORE AMBITIOUS, AND CHOSE TO VANISH FROM THE WORLD'S GAZE.

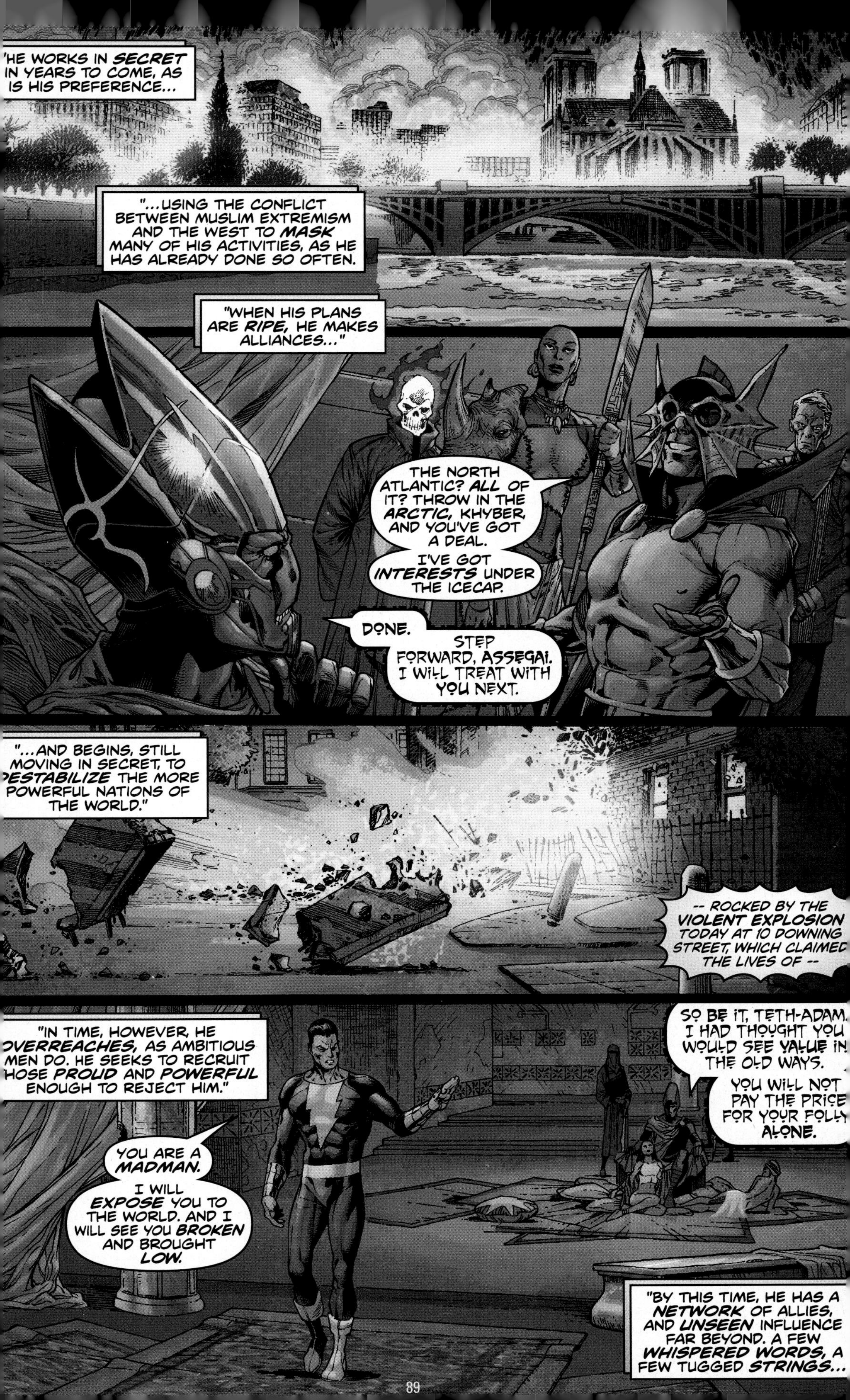

"HE WORKS IN SECRET IN YEARS TO COME, AS IS HIS PREFERENCE...
"...USING THE CONFLICT BETWEEN MUSLIM EXTREMISM AND THE WEST TO MASK MANY OF HIS ACTIVITIES, AS HE HAS ALREADY DONE SO OFTEN.
"WHEN HIS PLANS ARE RIPE, HE MAKES ALLIANCES..."
THE NORTH ATLANTIC? ALL OF IT? THROW IN THE ARCTIC, KHYBER, AND YOU'VE GOT A DEAL.
I'VE GOT INTERESTS UNDER THE ICECAP.
DONE.
STEP FORWARD, ASSEGAI. I WILL TREAT WITH YOU NEXT.
"...AND BEGINS, STILL MOVING IN SECRET, TO DESTABILIZE THE MORE POWERFUL NATIONS OF THE WORLD."
-- ROCKED BY THE VIOLENT EXPLOSION TODAY AT 10 DOWNING STREET, WHICH CLAIMED THE LIVES OF --
"IN TIME, HOWEVER, HE OVERREACHES, AS AMBITIOUS MEN DO. HE SEEKS TO RECRUIT THOSE PROUD AND POWERFUL ENOUGH TO REJECT HIM."
YOU ARE A MADMAN.
I WILL EXPOSE YOU TO THE WORLD. AND I WILL SEE YOU BROKEN AND BROUGHT LOW.
SO BE IT, TETH-ADAM. I HAD THOUGHT YOU WOULD SEE VALUE IN THE OLD WAYS.
YOU WILL NOT PAY THE PRICE FOR YOUR FOLLY ALONE.
"BY THIS TIME, HE HAS A NETWORK OF ALLIES, AND UNSEEN INFLUENCE FAR BEYOND. A FEW WHISPERED WORDS, A FEW TUGGED STRINGS...

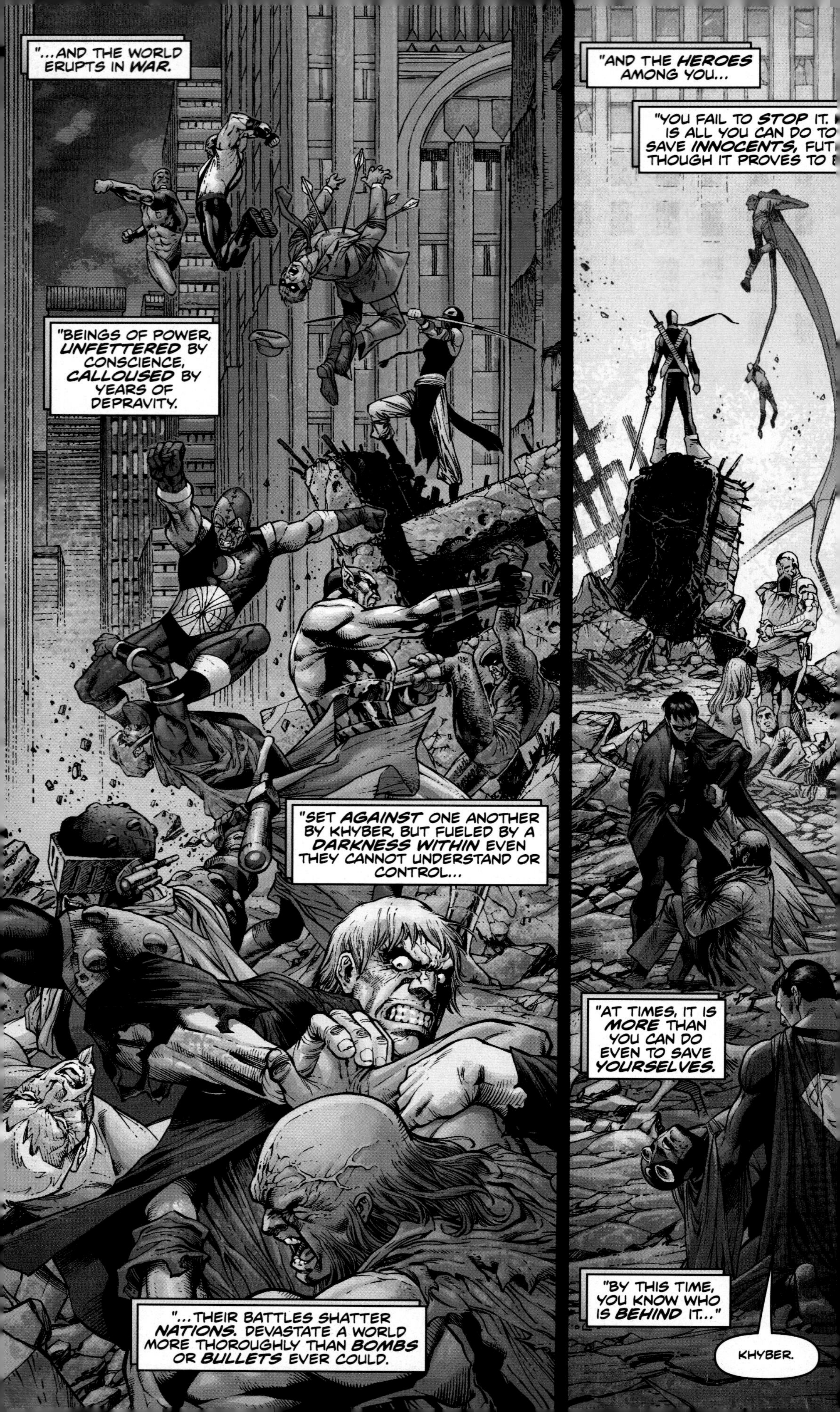
"...AND THE WORLD ERUPTS IN WAR.
"BEINGS OF POWER, UNFETTERED BY CONSCIENCE, CALLOUSED BY YEARS OF DEPRAVITY.
"SET AGAINST ONE ANOTHER BY KHYBER, BUT FUELED BY A DARKNESS WITHIN EVEN THEY CANNOT UNDERSTAND OR CONTROL...
"...THEIR BATTLES SHATTER NATIONS. DEVASTATE A WORLD MORE THOROUGHLY THAN BOMBS OR BULLETS EVER COULD.
"AND THE HEROES AMONG YOU...
"YOU FAIL TO STOP IT.
IS ALL YOU CAN DO TO
SAVE INNOCENTS, FUT
THOUGH IT PROVES TO
"AT TIMES, IT IS MORE THAN YOU CAN DO EVEN TO SAVE YOURSELVES.
"BY THIS TIME, YOU KNOW WHO IS BEHIND IT..."
KHYBER.

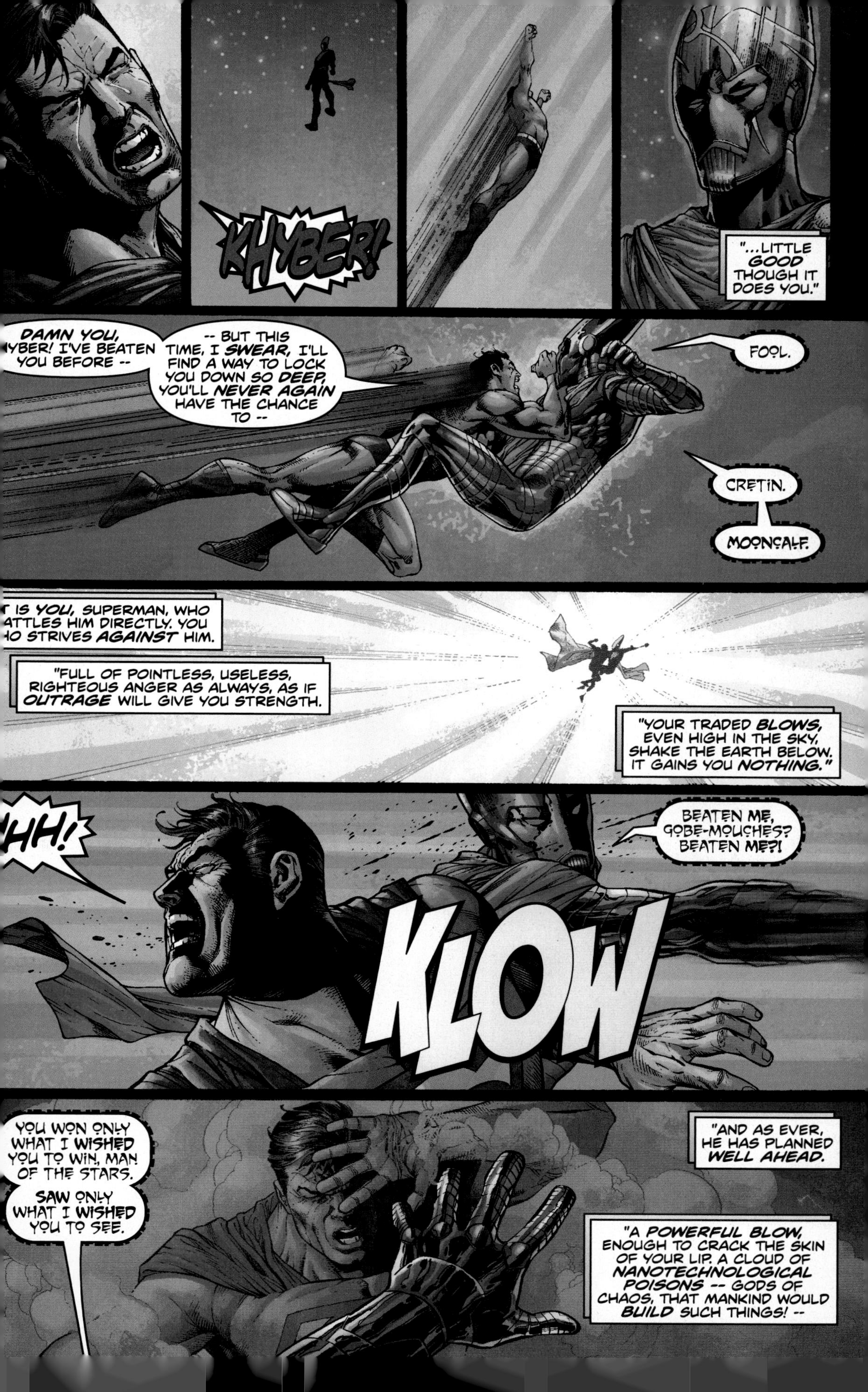
KHYBER!
"...LITTLE GOOD THOUGH IT DOES YOU."
DAMN YOU, KHYBER! I'VE BEATEN YOU BEFORE --
-- BUT THIS TIME, I SWEAR, I'LL FIND A WAY TO LOCK YOU DOWN SO DEEP, YOU'LL NEVER AGAIN HAVE THE CHANCE TO --
FOOL.
CRETIN.
MOONCALF.
IT IS YOU, SUPERMAN, WHO BATTLES HIM DIRECTLY. YOU WHO STRIVES AGAINST HIM.
"FULL OF POINTLESS, USELESS, RIGHTEOUS ANGER AS ALWAYS, AS IF OUTRAGE WILL GIVE YOU STRENGTH.
"YOUR TRADED BLOWS, EVEN HIGH IN THE SKY, SHAKE THE EARTH BELOW. IT GAINS YOU NOTHING."
HH!
BEATEN ME, GOBE-MOUCHES? BEATEN ME?!
KLOW
YOU WON ONLY WHAT I WISHED YOU TO WIN, MAN OF THE STARS.
SAW ONLY WHAT I WISHED YOU TO SEE.
"AND AS EVER, HE HAS PLANNED WELL AHEAD.
"A POWERFUL BLOW, ENOUGH TO CRACK THE SKIN OF YOUR LIP. A CLOUD OF NANOTECHNOLOGICAL POISONS -- GODS OF CHAOS, THAT MANKIND WOULD BUILD SUCH THINGS! --

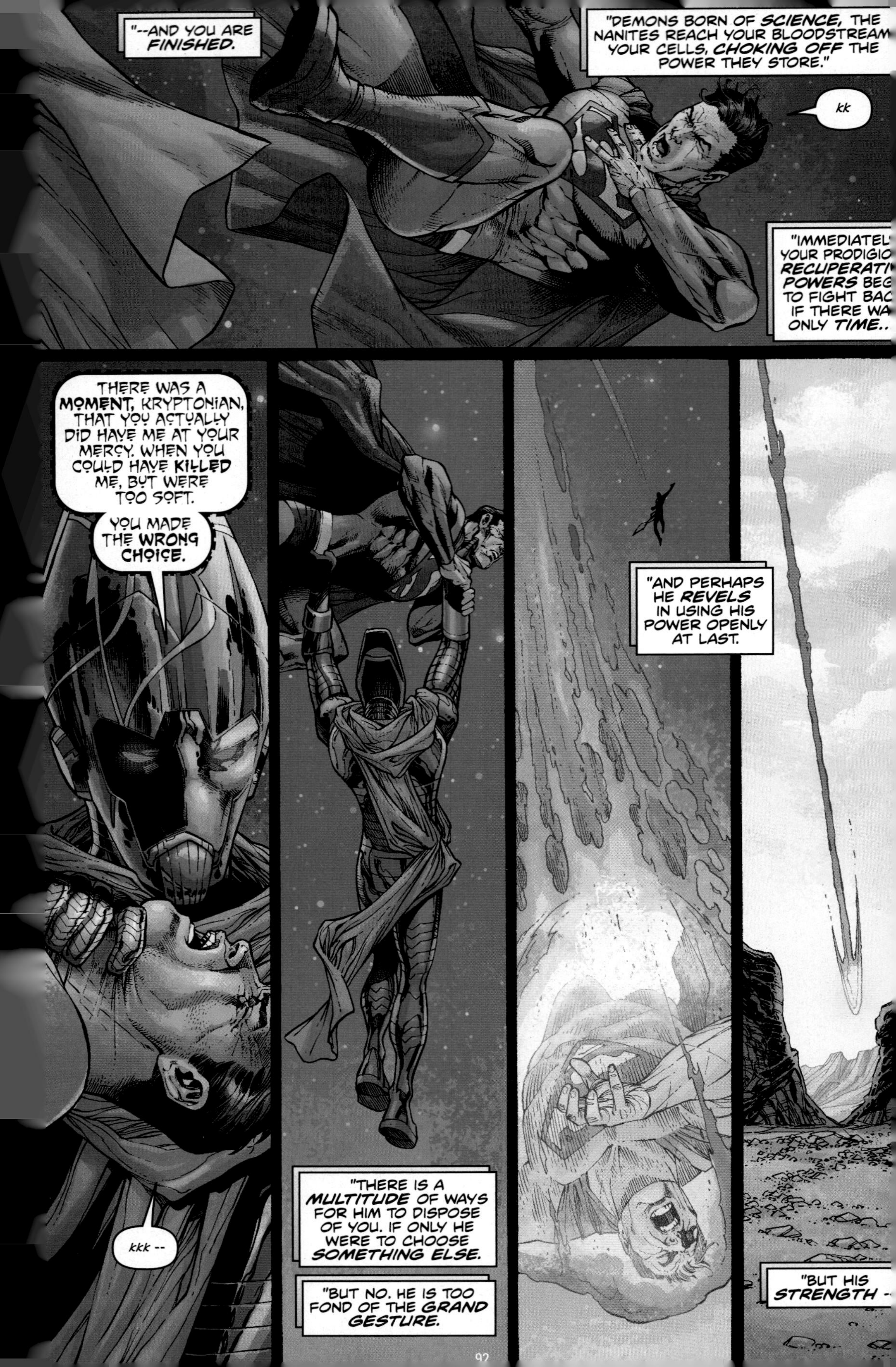
"--AND YOU ARE FINISHED.
"DEMONS BORN OF SCIENCE, THE NANITES REACH YOUR BLOODSTREAM YOUR CELLS, CHOKING OFF THE POWER THEY STORE."
kk
"IMMEDIATEL YOUR PRODIGIO RECUPERATI POWERS BEG TO FIGHT BAC IF THERE WA ONLY TIME..
THERE WAS A MOMENT, KRYPTONIAN, THAT YOU ACTUALLY DID HAVE ME AT YOUR MERCY. WHEN YOU COULD HAVE KILLED ME, BUT WERE TOO SOFT.
YOU MADE THE WRONG CHOICE.
kkk --
"THERE IS A MULTITUDE OF WAYS FOR HIM TO DISPOSE OF YOU. IF ONLY HE WERE TO CHOOSE SOMETHING ELSE.
"BUT NO. HE IS TOO FOND OF THE GRAND GESTURE.
"AND PERHAPS HE REVELS IN USING HIS POWER OPENLY AT LAST.
"BUT HIS STRENGTH --

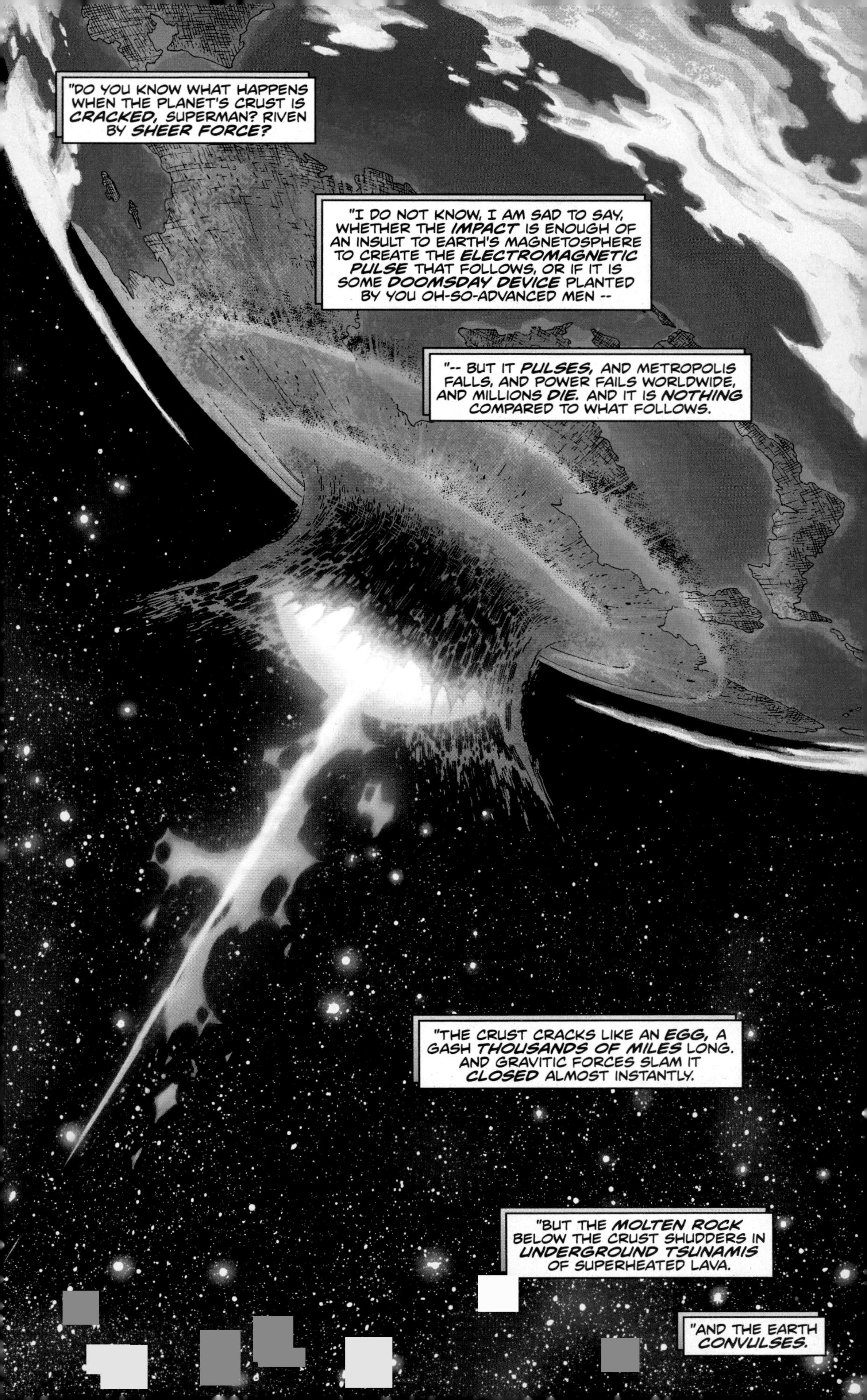
"DO YOU KNOW WHAT HAPPENS WHEN THE PLANET'S CRUST IS CRACKED, SUPERMAN? RIVEN BY SHEER FORCE?
"I DO NOT KNOW, I AM SAD TO SAY, WHETHER THE IMPACT IS ENOUGH OF AN INSULT TO EARTH'S MAGNETOSPHERE TO CREATE THE ELECTROMAGNETIC PULSE THAT FOLLOWS, OR IF IT IS SOME DOOMSDAY DEVICE PLANTED BY YOU OH-SO-ADVANCED MEN --
"-- BUT IT PULSES, AND METROPOLIS FALLS, AND POWER FAILS WORLDWIDE, AND MILLIONS DIE. AND IT IS NOTHING COMPARED TO WHAT FOLLOWS.
"THE CRUST CRACKS LIKE AN EGG, A GASH THOUSANDS OF MILES LONG. AND GRAVITIC FORCES SLAM IT CLOSED ALMOST INSTANTLY.
"BUT THE MOLTEN ROCK BELOW THE CRUST SHUDDERS IN UNDERGROUND TSUNAMIS OF SUPERHEATED LAVA.
"AND THE EARTH CONVULSES.

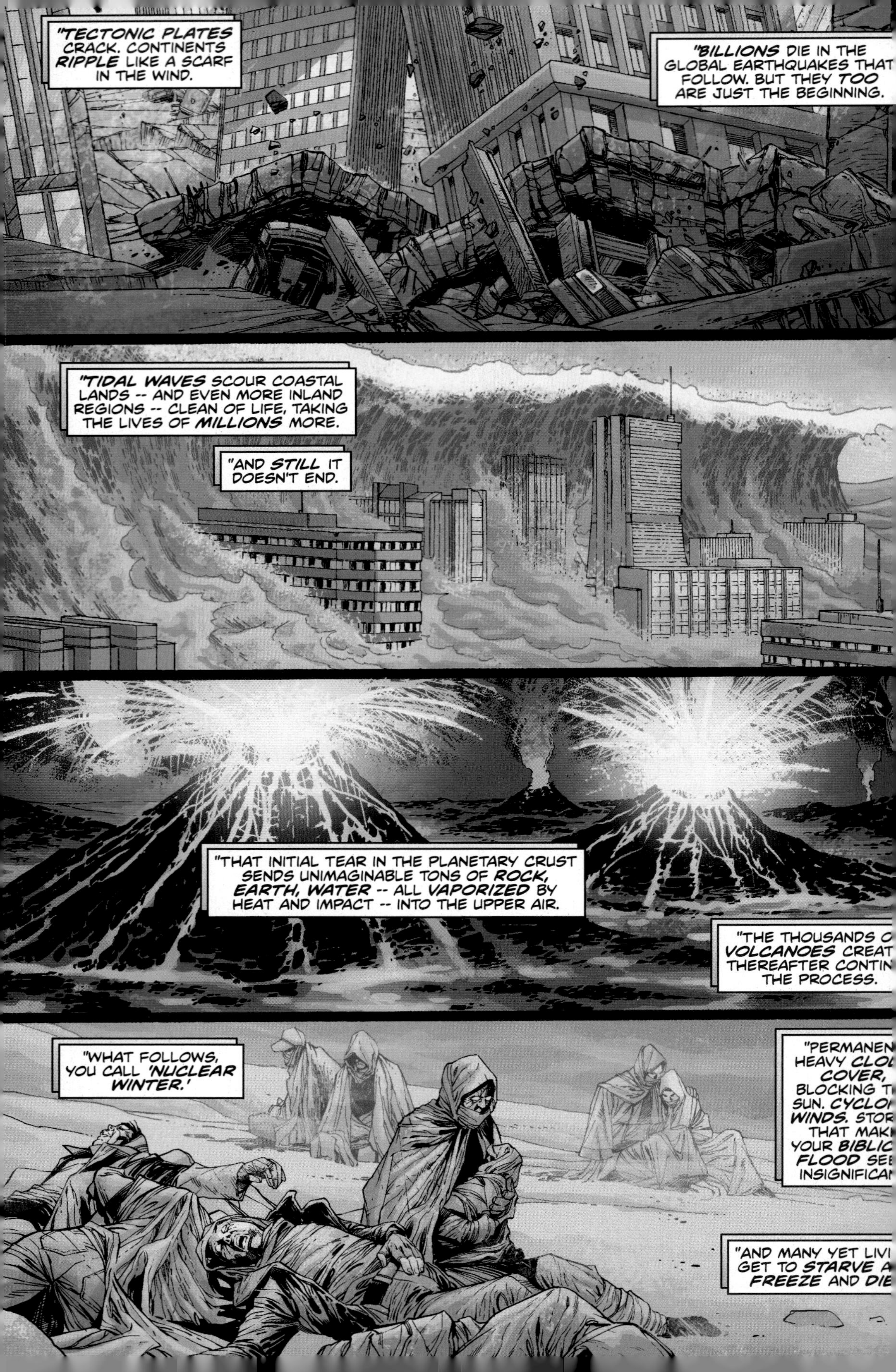
"TECTONIC PLATES CRACK. CONTINENTS RIPPLE LIKE A SCARF IN THE WIND.
"BILLIONS DIE IN THE GLOBAL EARTHQUAKES THAT FOLLOW. BUT THEY TOO ARE JUST THE BEGINNING.
"TIDAL WAVES SCOUR COASTAL LANDS -- AND EVEN MORE INLAND REGIONS -- CLEAN OF LIFE, TAKING THE LIVES OF MILLIONS MORE.
"AND STILL IT DOESN'T END.
"THAT INITIAL TEAR IN THE PLANETARY CRUST SENDS UNIMAGINABLE TONS OF ROCK, EARTH, WATER -- ALL VAPORIZED BY HEAT AND IMPACT -- INTO THE UPPER AIR.
"THE THOUSANDS O VOLCANOES CREAT THEREAFTER CONTIN THE PROCESS.
"WHAT FOLLOWS, YOU CALL 'NUCLEAR WINTER.'
"PERMANEN HEAVY CLO COVER, BLOCKING T SUN. CYCLO WINDS. STOR THAT MAK YOUR BIBLIC FLOOD SE INSIGNIFICA
"AND MANY YET LIVI GET TO STARVE A FREEZE AND DIE

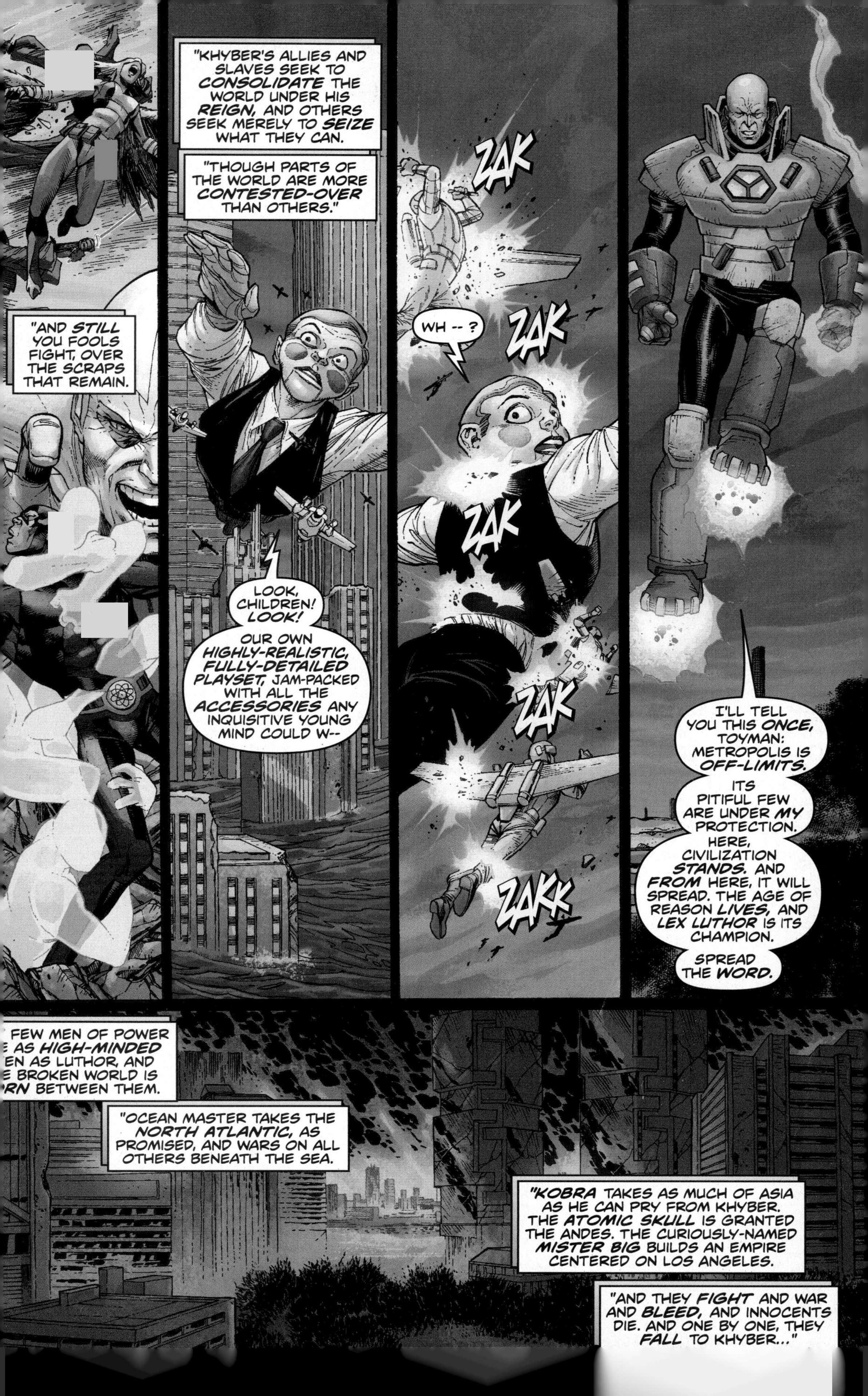
"AND STILL YOU FOOLS FIGHT, OVER THE SCRAPS THAT REMAIN.
"KHYBER'S ALLIES AND SLAVES SEEK TO CONSOLIDATE THE WORLD UNDER HIS REIGN, AND OTHERS SEEK MERELY TO SEIZE WHAT THEY CAN.
"THOUGH PARTS OF THE WORLD ARE MORE CONTESTED-OVER THAN OTHERS."
LOOK, CHILDREN! LOOK!
OUR OWN HIGHLY-REALISTIC, FULLY-DETAILED PLAYSET, JAM-PACKED WITH ALL THE ACCESSORIES ANY INQUISITIVE YOUNG MIND COULD W--
ZAK
WH -- ?
ZAK
ZAK
ZAK
ZAKK
I'LL TELL YOU THIS ONCE, TOYMAN: METROPOLIS IS OFF-LIMITS.
ITS PITIFUL FEW ARE UNDER MY PROTECTION. HERE, CIVILIZATION STANDS. AND FROM HERE, IT WILL SPREAD. THE AGE OF REASON LIVES, AND LEX LUTHOR IS ITS CHAMPION.
SPREAD THE WORD.
FEW MEN OF POWER E AS HIGH-MINDED EN AS LUTHOR, AND E BROKEN WORLD IS RN BETWEEN THEM.
"OCEAN MASTER TAKES THE NORTH ATLANTIC, AS PROMISED, AND WARS ON ALL OTHERS BENEATH THE SEA.
"KOBRA TAKES AS MUCH OF ASIA AS HE CAN PRY FROM KHYBER. THE ATOMIC SKULL IS GRANTED THE ANDES. THE CURIOUSLY-NAMED MISTER BIG BUILDS AN EMPIRE CENTERED ON LOS ANGELES.
"AND THEY FIGHT AND WAR AND BLEED, AND INNOCENTS DIE. AND ONE BY ONE, THEY FALL TO KHYBER..."

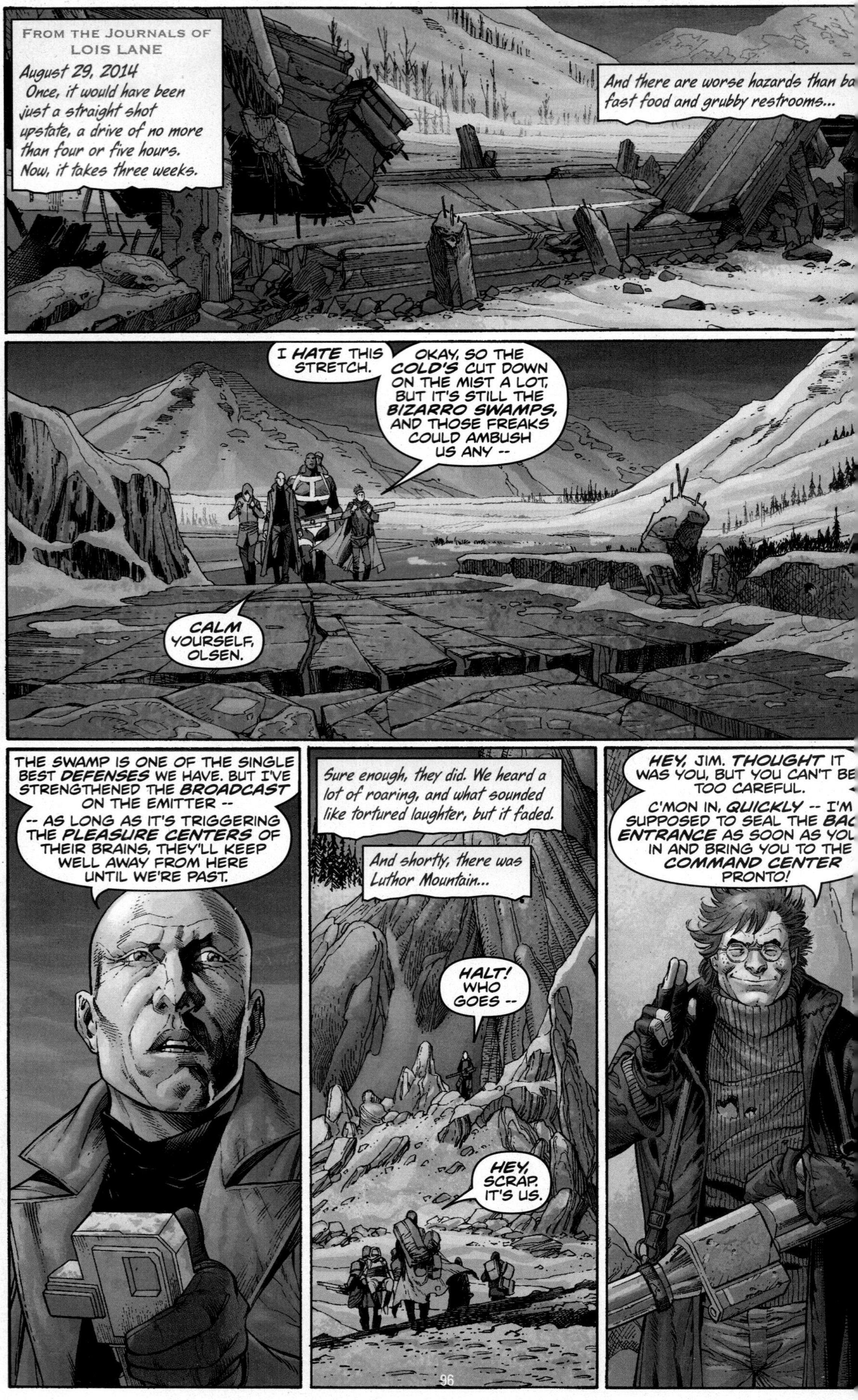

From the Journals of Lois Lane
August 29, 2014 Once, it would have been just a straight shot upstate, a drive of no more than four or five hours. Now, it takes three weeks.
And there are worse hazards than ba fast food and grubby restrooms...
I HATE THIS STRETCH.
OKAY, SO THE COLD'S CUT DOWN ON THE MIST A LOT, BUT IT'S STILL THE BIZARRO SWAMPS, AND THOSE FREAKS COULD AMBUSH US ANY --
CALM YOURSELF, OLSEN.
THE SWAMP IS ONE OF THE SINGLE BEST DEFENSES WE HAVE. BUT I'VE STRENGTHENED THE BROADCAST ON THE EMITTER --
-- AS LONG AS IT'S TRIGGERING THE PLEASURE CENTERS OF THEIR BRAINS, THEY'LL KEEP WELL AWAY FROM HERE UNTIL WE'RE PAST.
Sure enough, they did. We heard a lot of roaring, and what sounded like tortured laughter, but it faded.
And shortly, there was Luthor Mountain...
HALT! WHO GOES --
HEY, SCRAP. IT'S US.
HEY, JIM. THOUGHT IT WAS YOU, BUT YOU CAN'T BE TOO CAREFUL.
C'MON IN, QUICKLY -- I'M SUPPOSED TO SEAL THE BAC ENTRANCE AS SOON AS YOU IN AND BRING YOU TO THE COMMAND CENTER PRONTO!

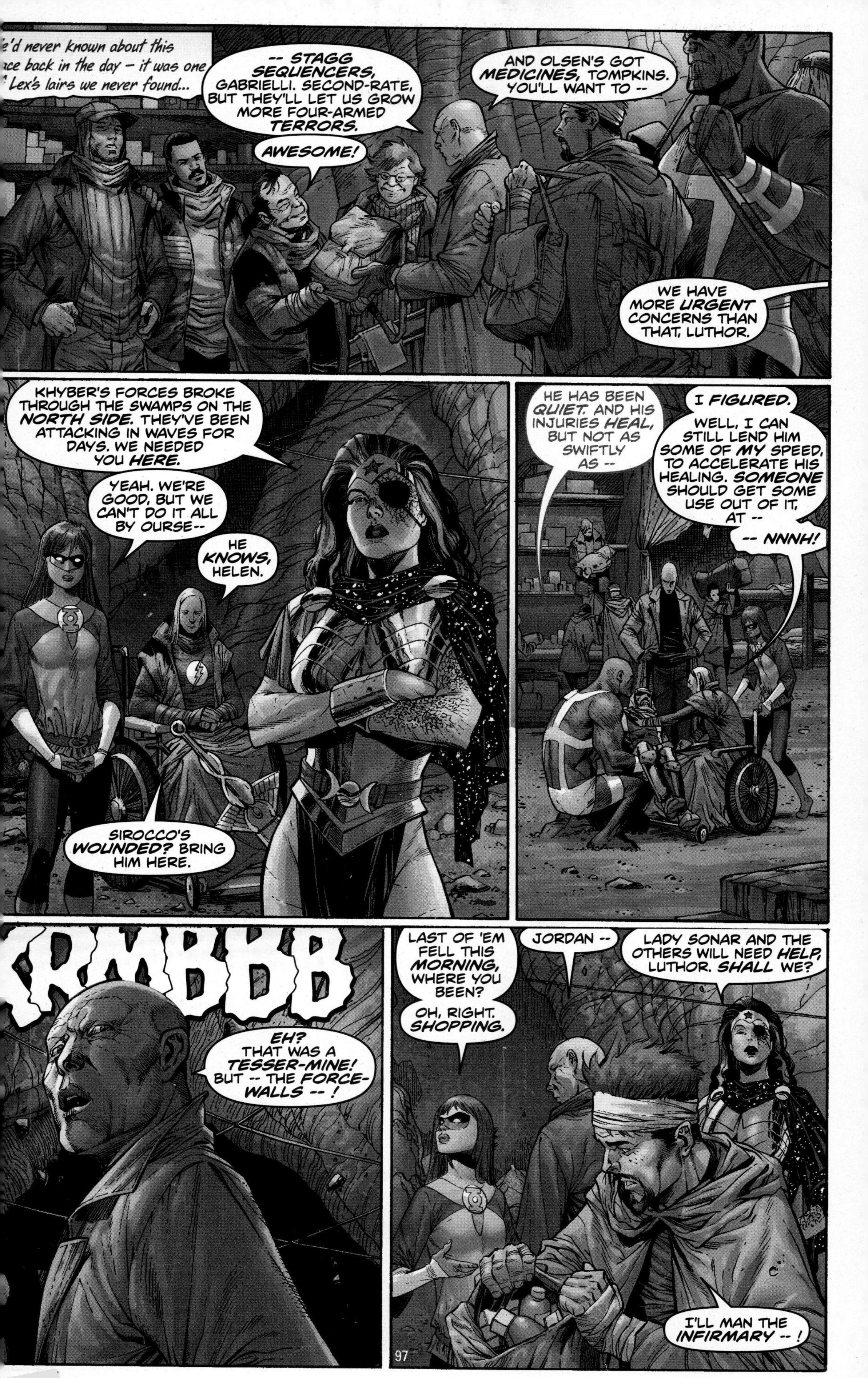

e'd never known about this
ace back in the day – it was one
Lex's lairs we never found...
-- STAGG SEQUENCERS, GABRIELLI. SECOND-RATE, BUT THEY'LL LET US GROW MORE FOUR-ARMED TERRORS.
AWESOME!
AND OLSEN'S GOT MEDICINES, TOMPKINS. YOU'LL WANT TO --
WE HAVE MORE URGENT CONCERNS THAN THAT, LUTHOR.
KHYBER'S FORCES BROKE THROUGH THE SWAMPS ON THE NORTH SIDE. THEY'VE BEEN ATTACKING IN WAVES FOR DAYS. WE NEEDED YOU HERE.
YEAH. WE'RE GOOD, BUT WE CAN'T DO IT ALL BY OURSE--
HE KNOWS, HELEN.
SIROCCO'S WOUNDED? BRING HIM HERE.
HE HAS BEEN QUIET. AND HIS INJURIES HEAL, BUT NOT AS SWIFTLY AS --
I FIGURED.
WELL, I CAN STILL LEND HIM SOME OF MY SPEED, TO ACCELERATE HIS HEALING. SOMEONE SHOULD GET SOME USE OUT OF IT, AT --
-- NNNH!
RMBBB
EH? THAT WAS A TESSER-MINE! BUT -- THE FORCE-WALLS -- !
LAST OF 'EM FELL THIS MORNING, WHERE YOU BEEN?
OH, RIGHT. SHOPPING.
JORDAN --
LADY SONAR AND THE OTHERS WILL NEED HELP, LUTHOR. SHALL WE?
I'LL MAN THE INFIRMARY -- !

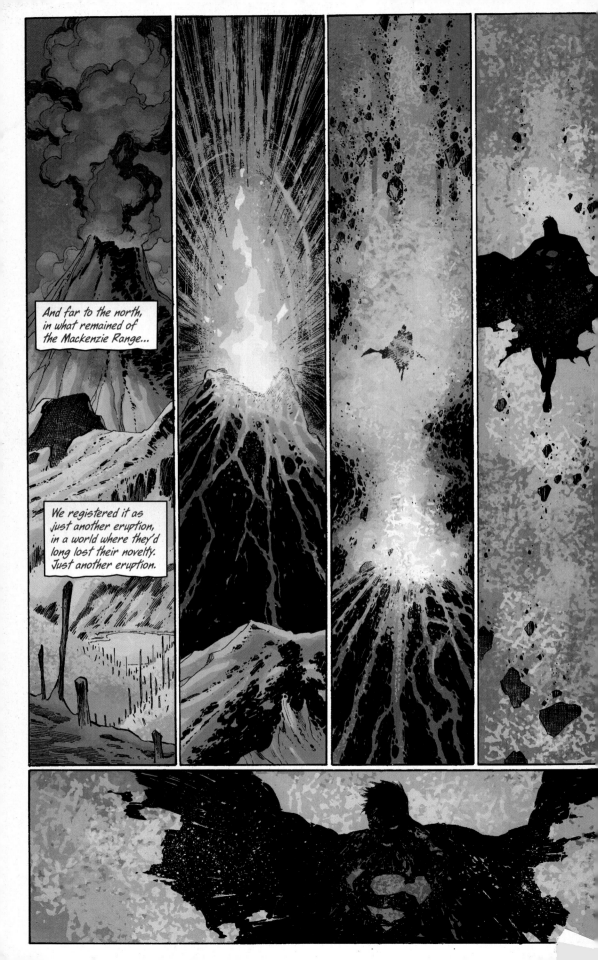

And far to the north, in what remained of the Mackenzie Range...

We registered it as just another eruption, in a world where they'd long lost their novelty. Just another eruption.

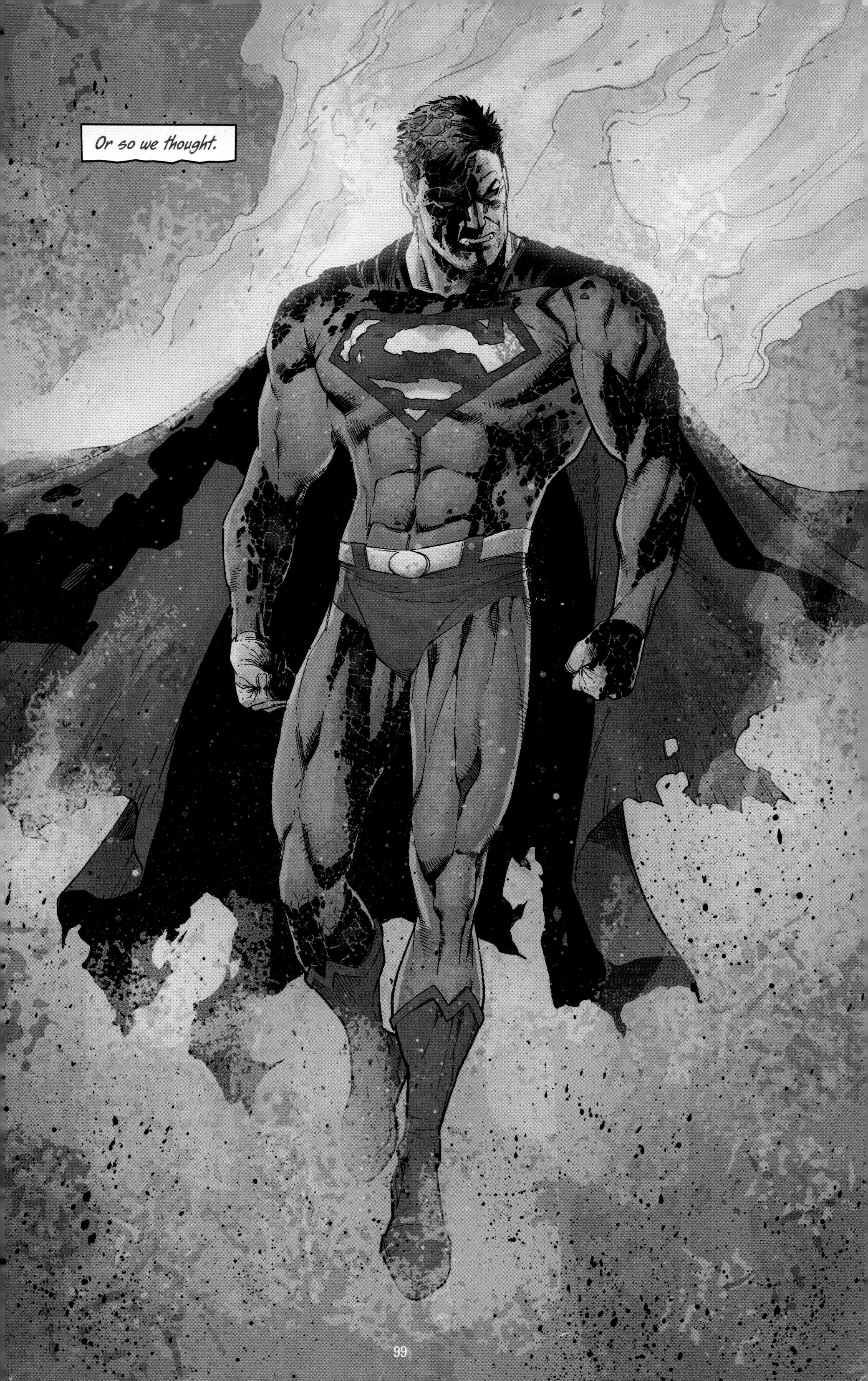
Or so we thought.

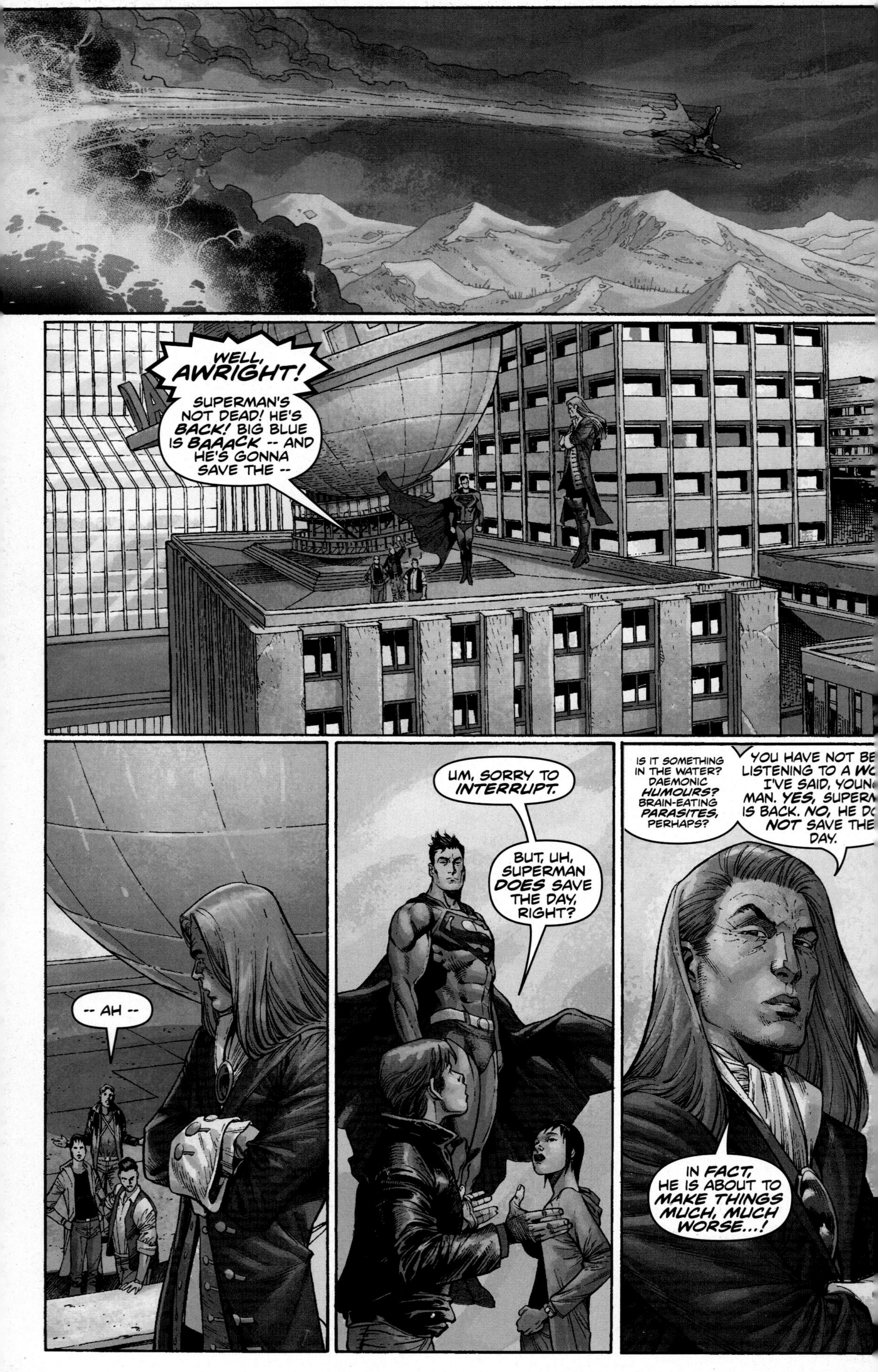
WELL, AWRIGHT!
SUPERMAN'S NOT DEAD! HE'S BACK! BIG BLUE IS BAAACK -- AND HE'S GONNA SAVE THE --
-- AH --
UM, SORRY TO INTERRUPT.
BUT, UH, SUPERMAN DOES SAVE THE DAY, RIGHT?
IS IT SOMETHING IN THE WATER? DAEMONIC HUMOURS? BRAIN-EATING PARASITES, PERHAPS?
YOU HAVE NOT BE LISTENING TO A WO I'VE SAID, YOUN MAN. YES, SUPERM IS BACK. NO, HE DO NOT SAVE THE DAY.
IN FACT, HE IS ABOUT TO MAKE THINGS MUCH, MUCH WORSE...!

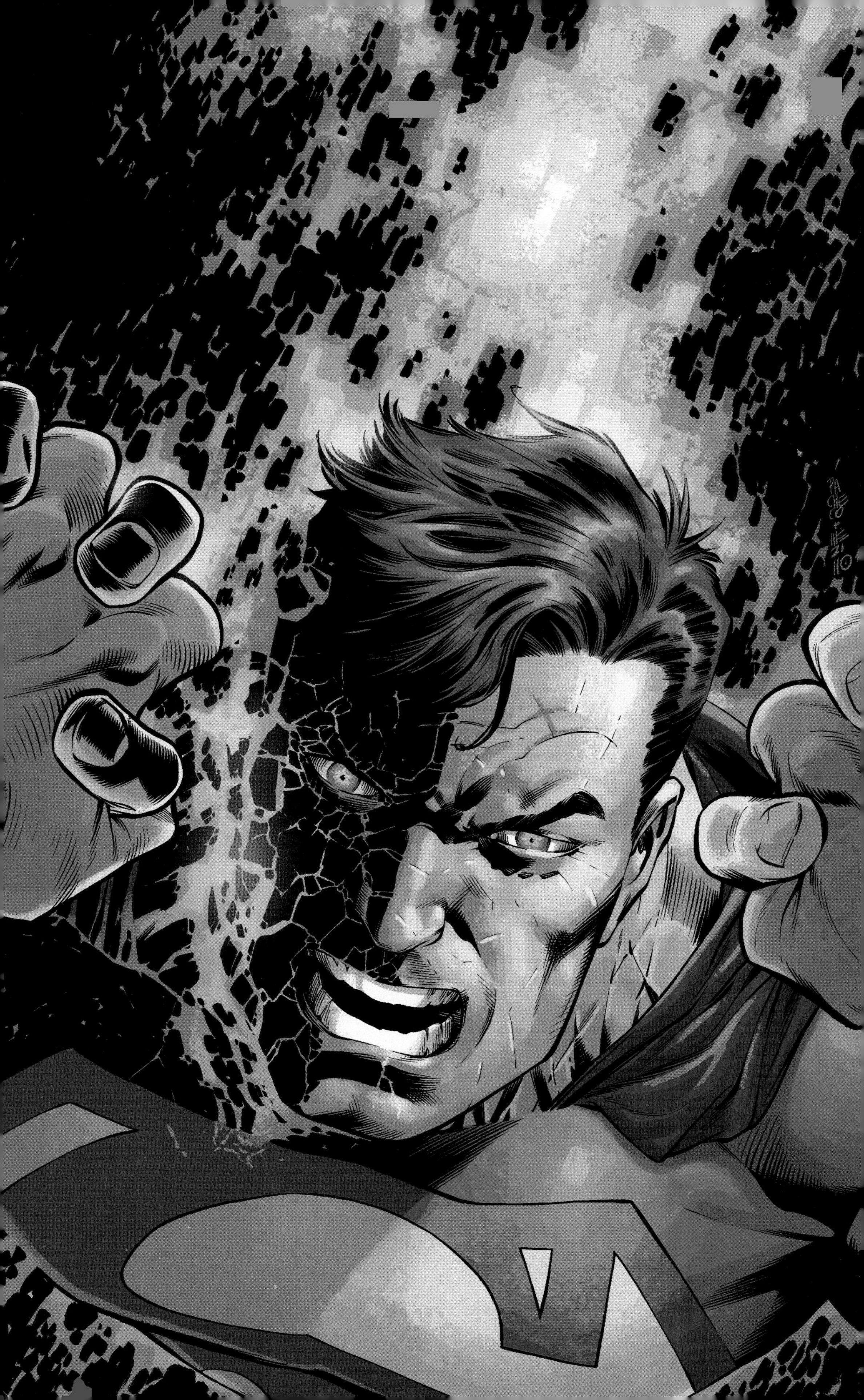

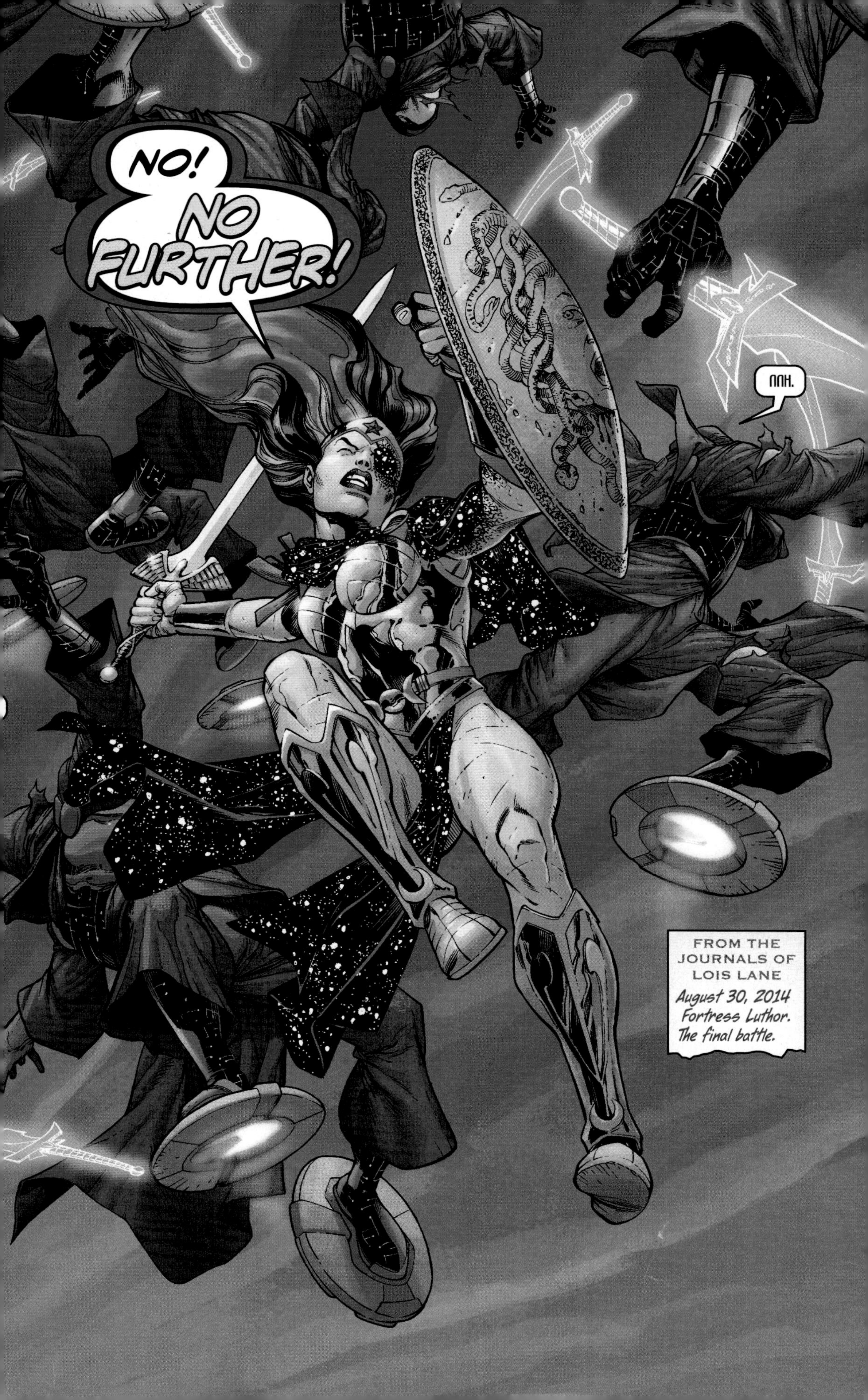
NO! NO FURTHER!
NNH.
FROM THE JOURNALS OF LOIS LANE
August 30, 2014
Fortress Luthor.
The final battle.

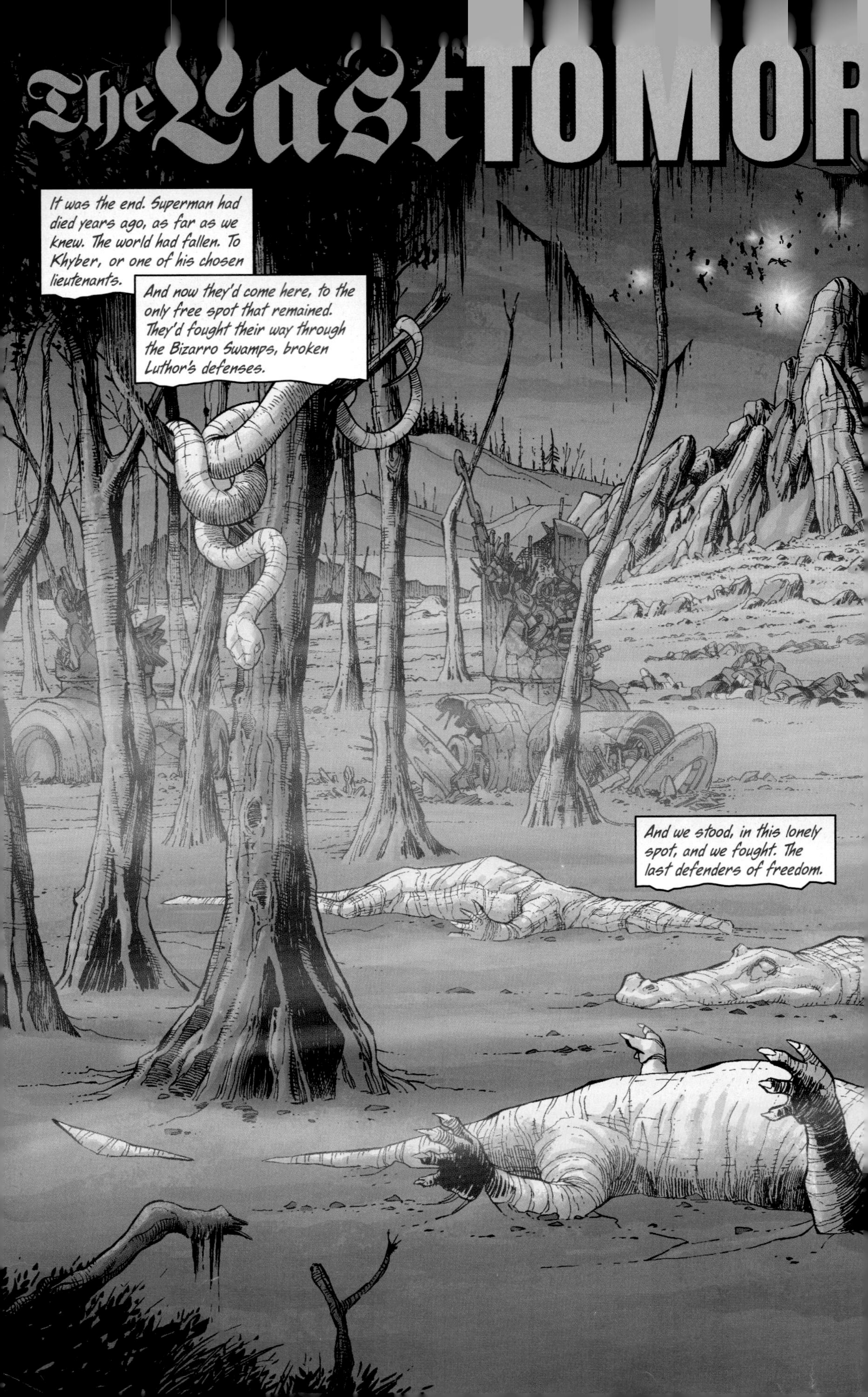
The Last TOMOR
It was the end. Superman had died years ago, as far as we knew. The world had fallen. To Khyber, or one of his chosen lieutenants.
And now they'd come here, to the only free spot that remained. They'd fought their way through the Bizarro Swamps, broken Luthor's defenses.
And we stood, in this lonely spot, and we fought. The last defenders of freedom.

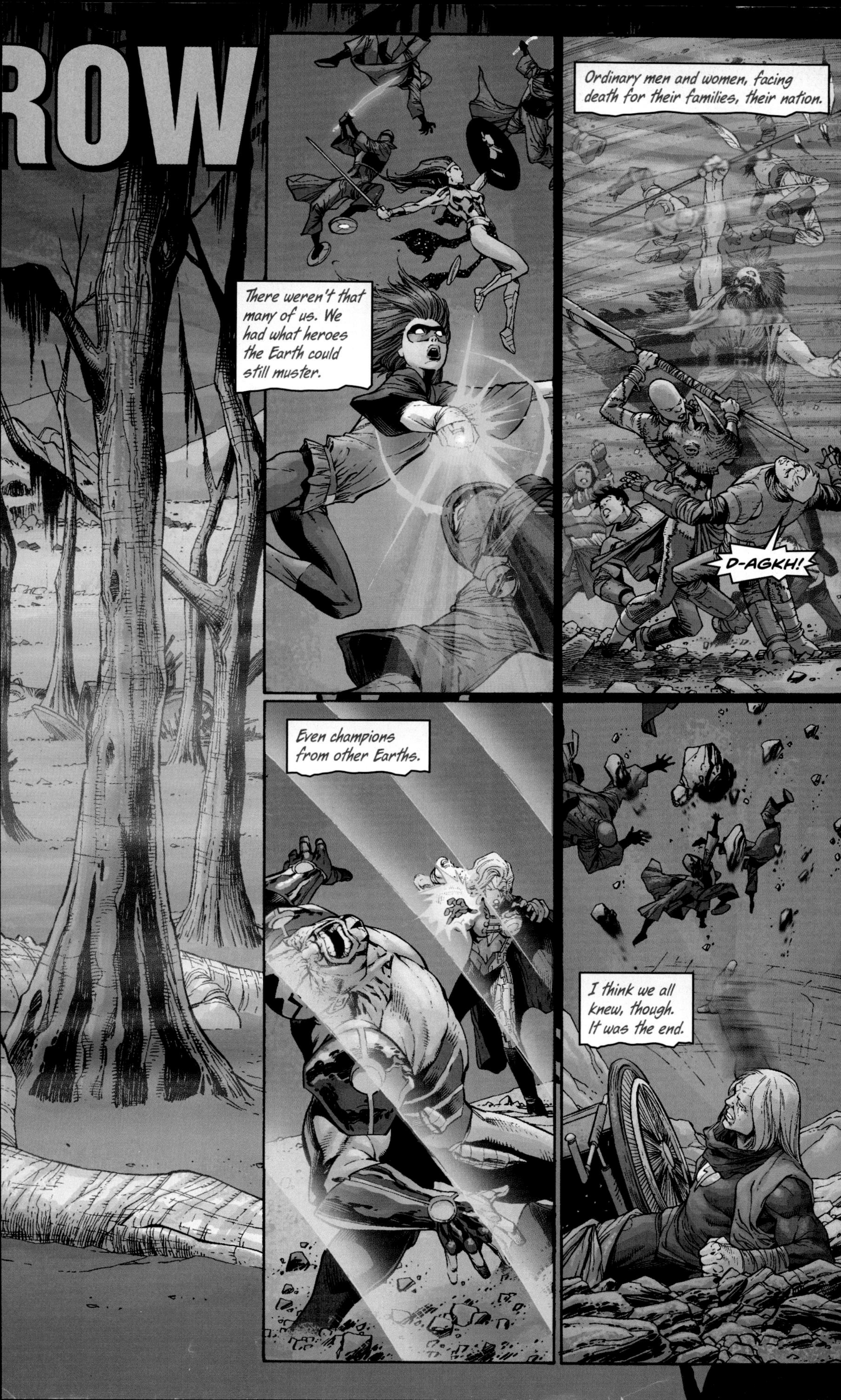
ROW
There weren't that many of us. We had what heroes the Earth could still muster.
Ordinary men and women, facing death for their families, their nation.
D-AGKH!
Even champions from other Earths.
I think we all knew, though. It was the end.

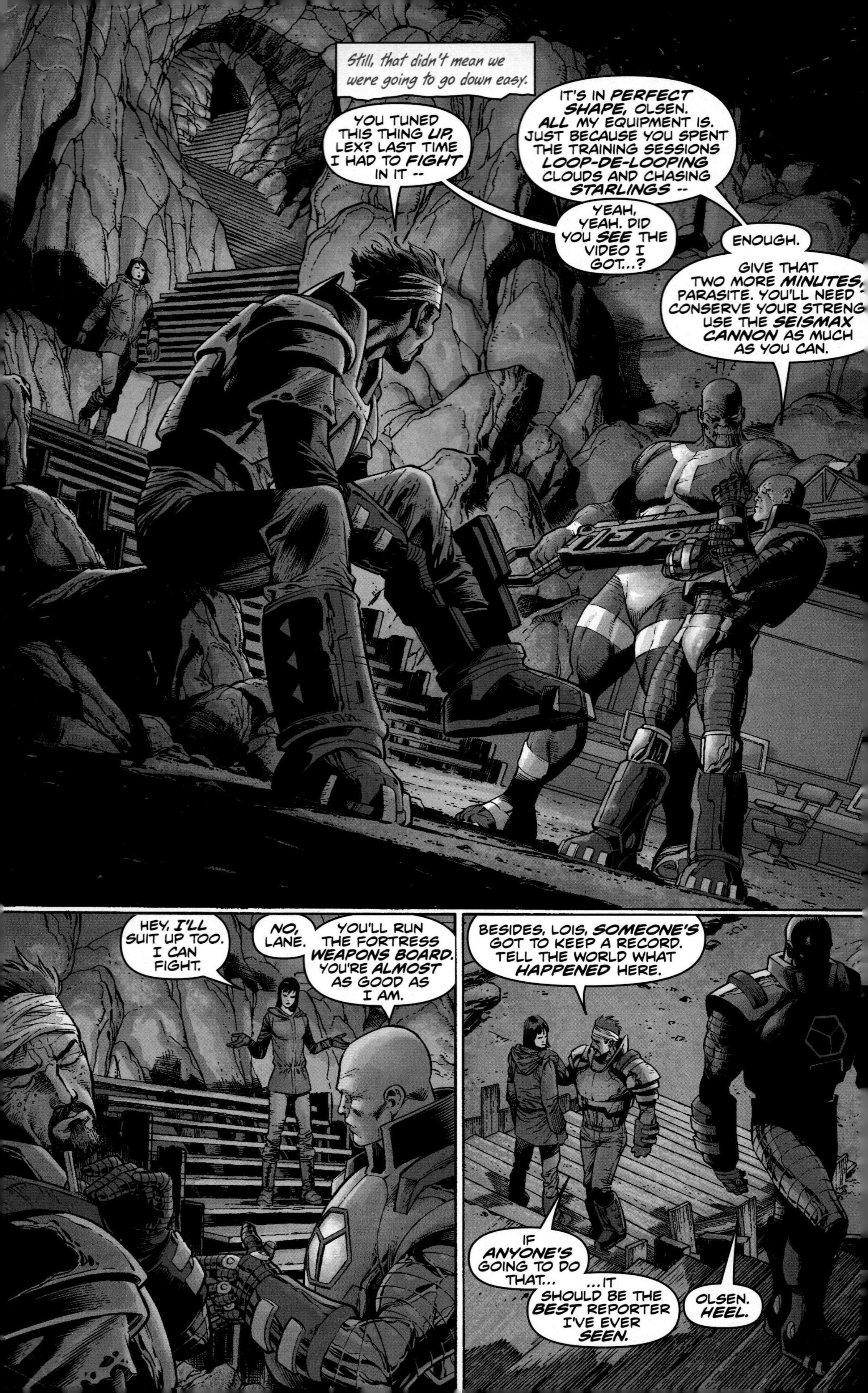
Still, that didn't mean we were going to go down easy.
YOU TUNED THIS THING UP, LEX? LAST TIME I HAD TO FIGHT IN IT --
IT'S IN PERFECT SHAPE, OLSEN. ALL MY EQUIPMENT IS. JUST BECAUSE YOU SPENT THE TRAINING SESSIONS LOOP-DE-LOOPING CLOUDS AND CHASING STARLINGS --
YEAH, YEAH. DID YOU SEE THE VIDEO I GOT...?
ENOUGH.
GIVE THAT TWO MORE MINUTES, PARASITE. YOU'LL NEED CONSERVE YOUR STRENG USE THE SEISMAX CANNON AS MUCH AS YOU CAN.
HEY, I'LL SUIT UP TOO. I CAN FIGHT.
NO, LANE.
YOU'LL RUN THE FORTRESS WEAPONS BOARD. YOU'RE ALMOST AS GOOD AS I AM.
BESIDES, LOIS, SOMEONE'S GOT TO KEEP A RECORD. TELL THE WORLD WHAT HAPPENED HERE.
IF ANYONE'S GOING TO DO THAT...
...IT SHOULD BE THE BEST REPORTER I'VE EVER SEEN.
OLSEN. HEEL.

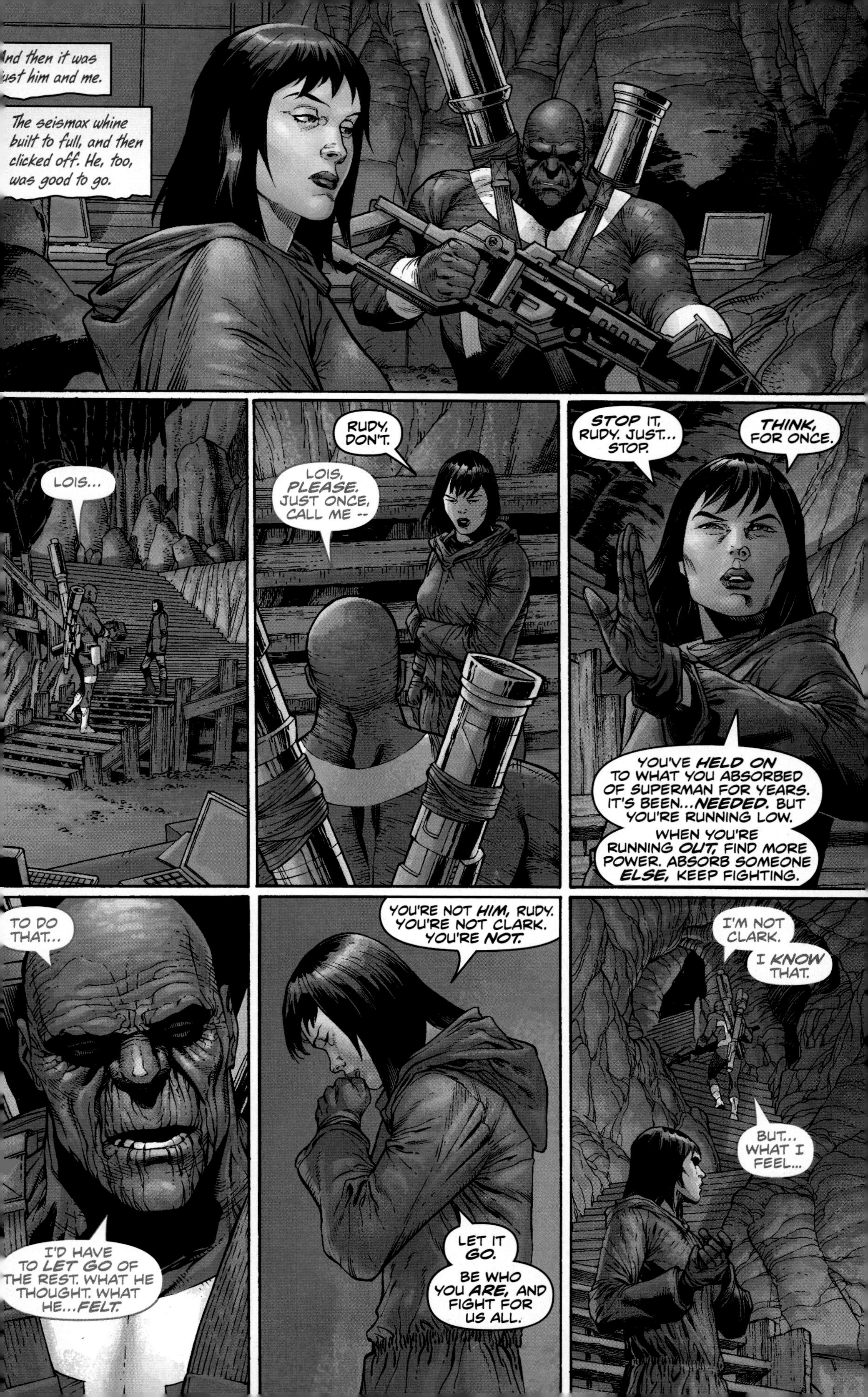
And then it was just him and me.
The seismax whine built to full, and then clicked off. He, too, was good to go.
LOIS...
RUDY, DON'T.
LOIS, PLEASE. JUST ONCE, CALL ME --
STOP IT, RUDY. JUST... STOP.
THINK, FOR ONCE.
YOU'VE HELD ON TO WHAT YOU ABSORBED OF SUPERMAN FOR YEARS. IT'S BEEN...NEEDED. BUT YOU'RE RUNNING LOW.
WHEN YOU'RE RUNNING OUT, FIND MORE POWER. ABSORB SOMEONE ELSE, KEEP FIGHTING.
TO DO THAT...
I'D HAVE TO LET GO OF THE REST. WHAT HE THOUGHT. WHAT HE...FELT.
YOU'RE NOT HIM, RUDY. YOU'RE NOT CLARK. YOU'RE NOT.
LET IT GO.
BE WHO YOU ARE, AND FIGHT FOR US ALL.
I'M NOT CLARK.
I KNOW THAT.
BUT... WHAT I FEEL...

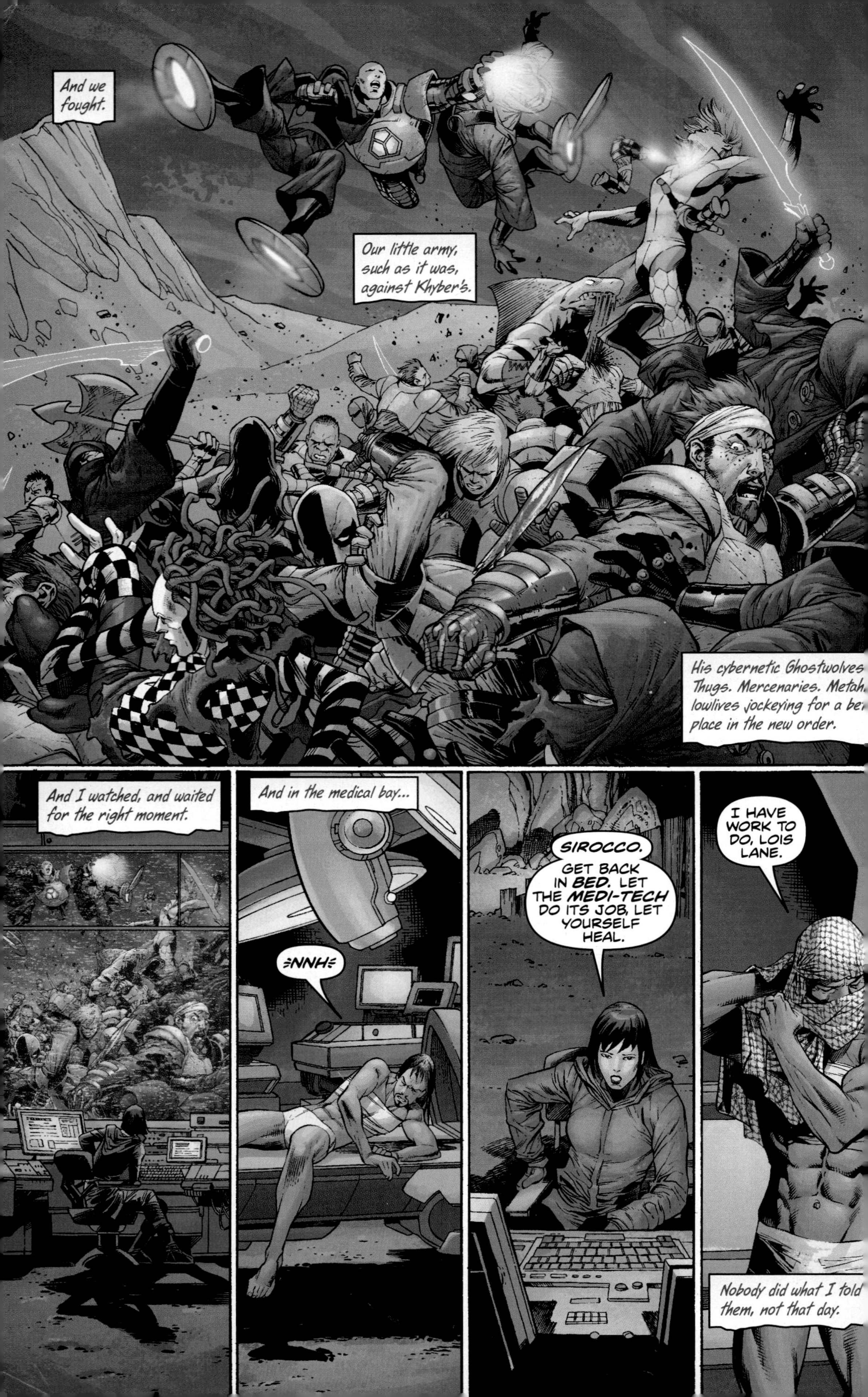
And we fought.
Our little army, such as it was, against Khyber's.
His cybernetic Ghostwolves. Thugs. Mercenaries. Metah
lowlives jockeying for a be
place in the new order.
And I watched, and waited for the right moment.
And in the medical bay...
NNH
SIROCCO.
GET BACK IN BED. LET THE MEDI-TECH DO ITS JOB, LET YOURSELF HEAL.
I HAVE WORK TO DO, LOIS LANE.
Nobody did what I told them, not that day.

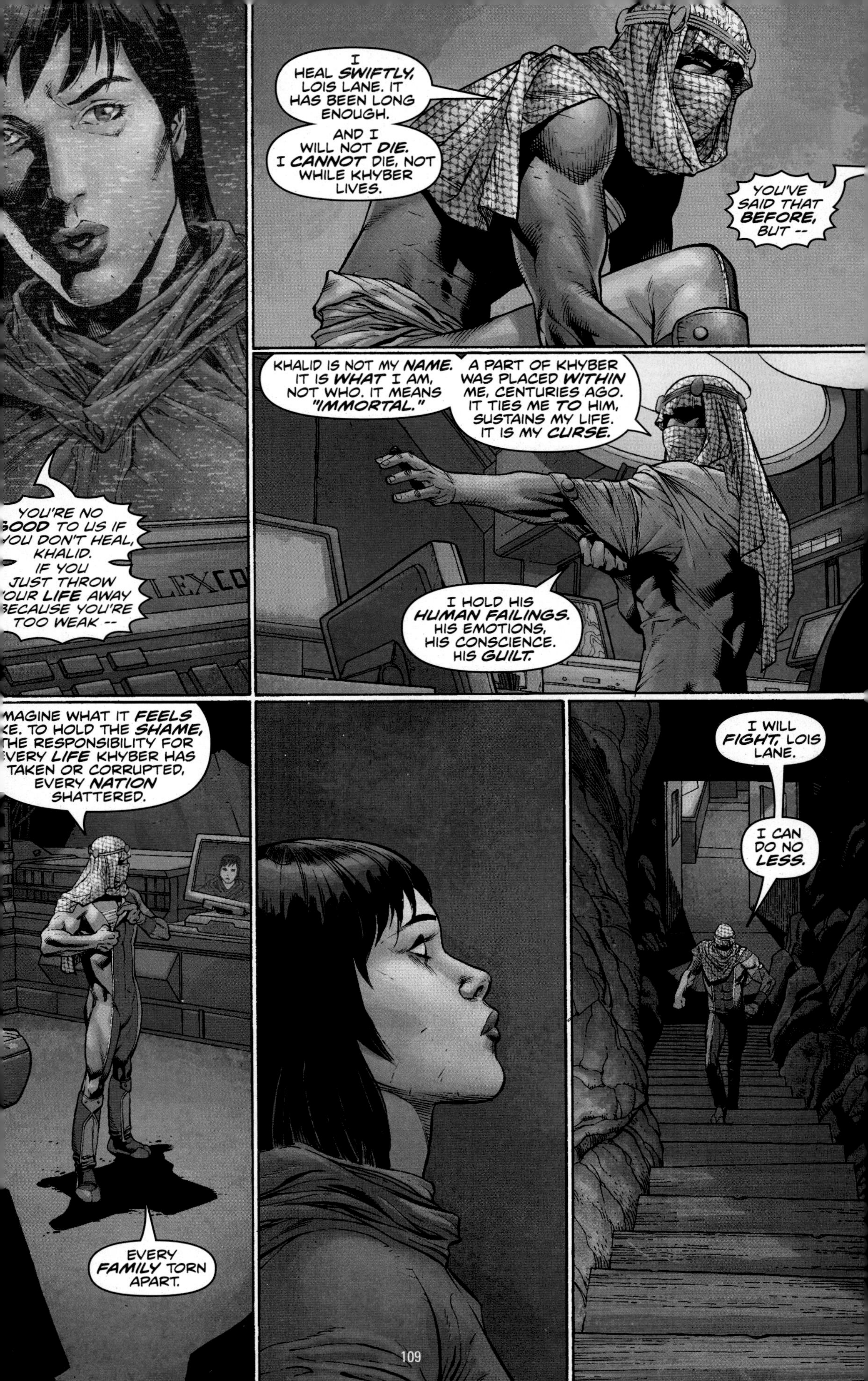

I HEAL SWIFTLY, LOIS LANE. IT HAS BEEN LONG ENOUGH.
AND I WILL NOT DIE. I CANNOT DIE, NOT WHILE KHYBER LIVES.
YOU'VE SAID THAT BEFORE, BUT --
YOU'RE NO GOOD TO US IF YOU DON'T HEAL, KHALID. IF YOU JUST THROW YOUR LIFE AWAY BECAUSE YOU'RE TOO WEAK --
LEXCO
KHALID IS NOT MY NAME. IT IS WHAT I AM, NOT WHO. IT MEANS "IMMORTAL."
A PART OF KHYBER WAS PLACED WITHIN ME, CENTURIES AGO. IT TIES ME TO HIM, SUSTAINS MY LIFE. IT IS MY CURSE.
I HOLD HIS HUMAN FAILINGS. HIS EMOTIONS, HIS CONSCIENCE. HIS GUILT.
MAGINE WHAT IT FEELS KE. TO HOLD THE SHAME, THE RESPONSIBILITY FOR EVERY LIFE KHYBER HAS TAKEN OR CORRUPTED, EVERY NATION SHATTERED.
EVERY FAMILY TORN APART.
I WILL FIGHT, LOIS LANE.
I CAN DO NO LESS.

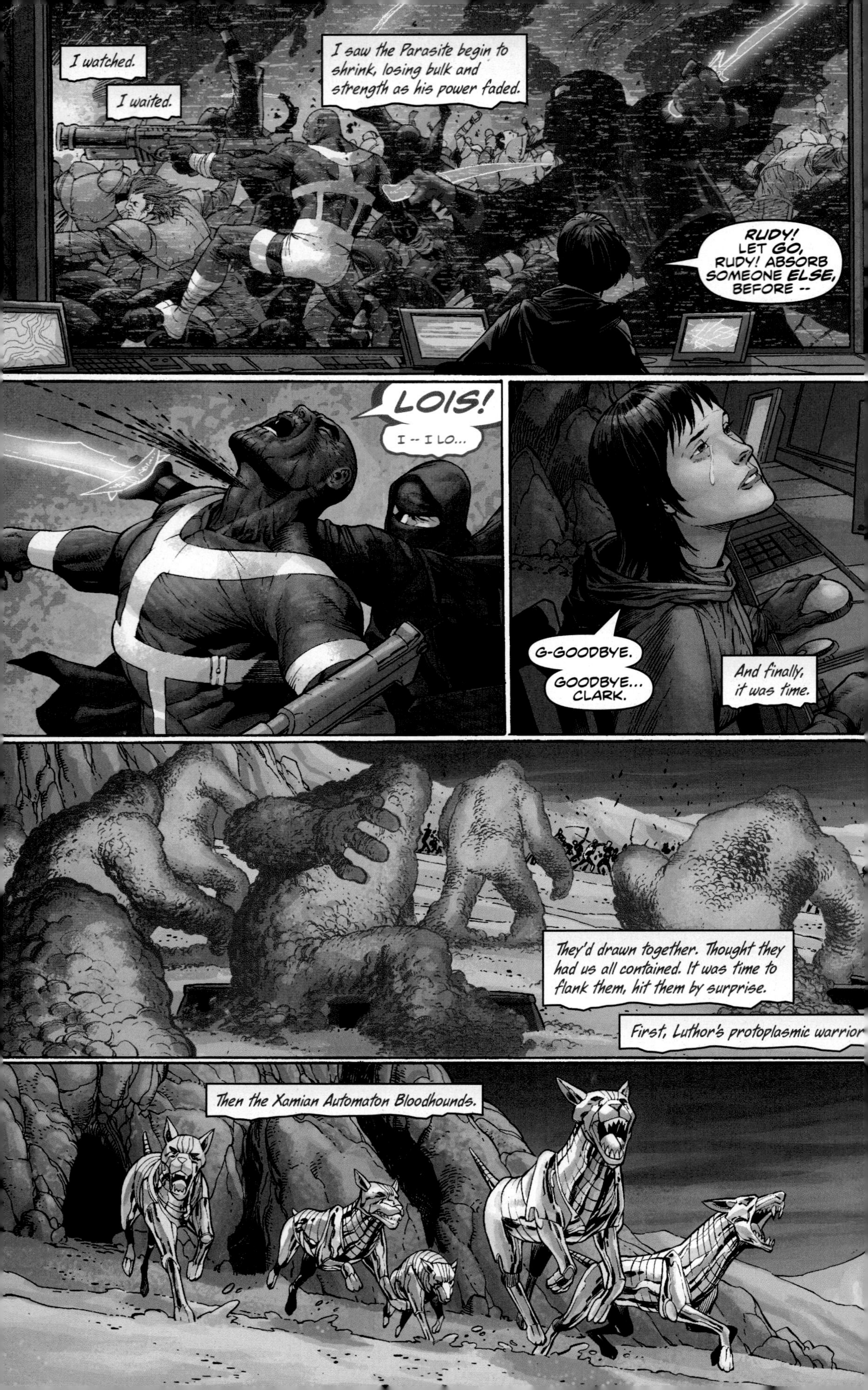

I watched.
I waited.
I saw the Parasite begin to shrink, losing bulk and strength as his power faded.
RUDY! LET GO, RUDY! ABSORB SOMEONE ELSE, BEFORE --
LOIS!
I -- I LO...
G-GOODBYE.
GOODBYE... CLARK.
And finally, it was time.
They'd drawn together. Thought they had us all contained. It was time to flank them, hit them by surprise.
First, Luthor's protoplasmic warrior
Then the Xamian Automaton Bloodhounds.

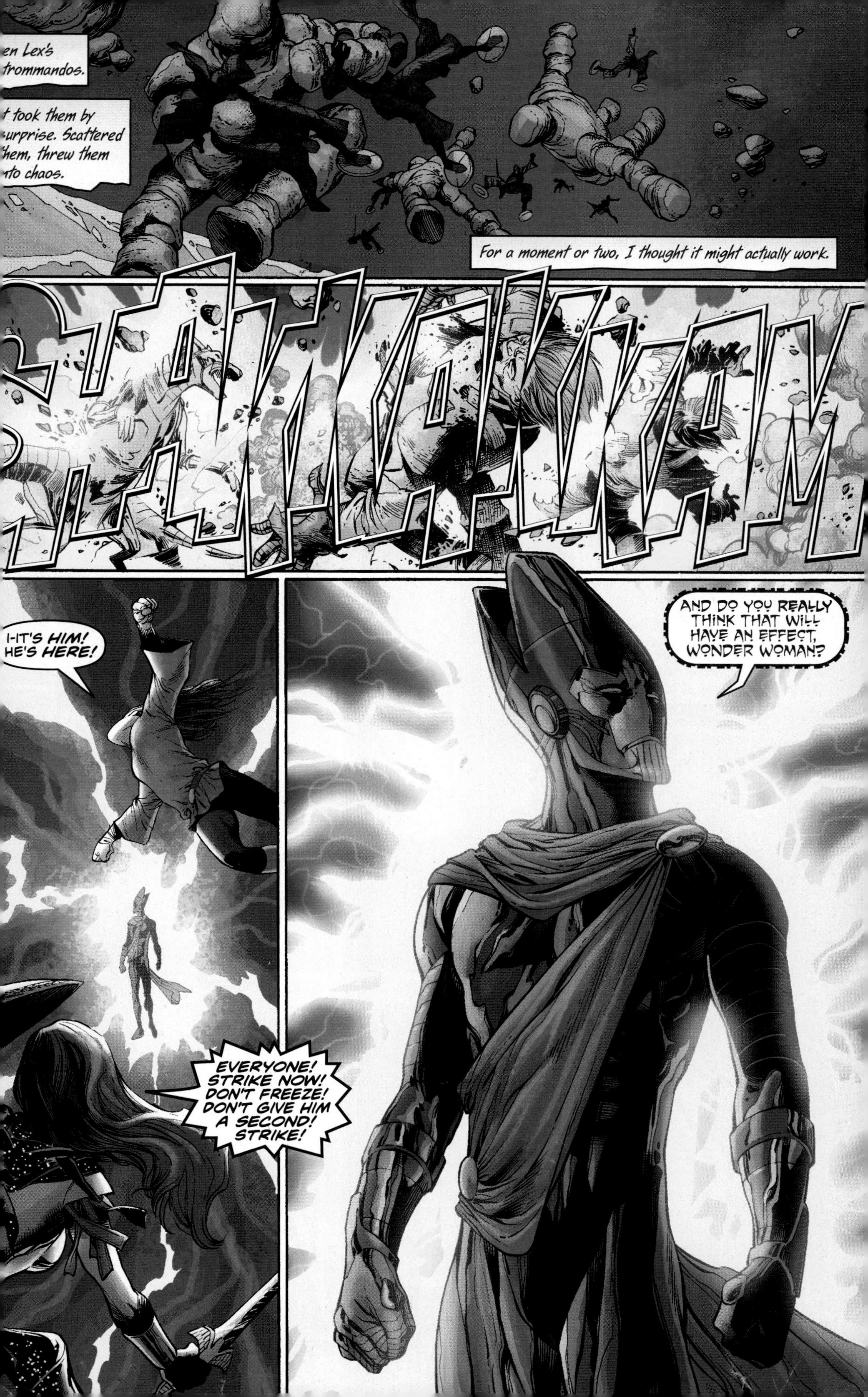
en Lex's
trommandos.
t took them by
surprise. Scattered
them, threw them
nto chaos.
For a moment or two, I thought it might actually work.
I-IT'S HIM! HE'S HERE!
AND DO YOU REALLY THINK THAT WILL HAVE AN EFFECT, WONDER WOMAN?
EVERYONE! STRIKE NOW! DON'T FREEZE! DON'T GIVE HIM A SECOND! STRIKE!

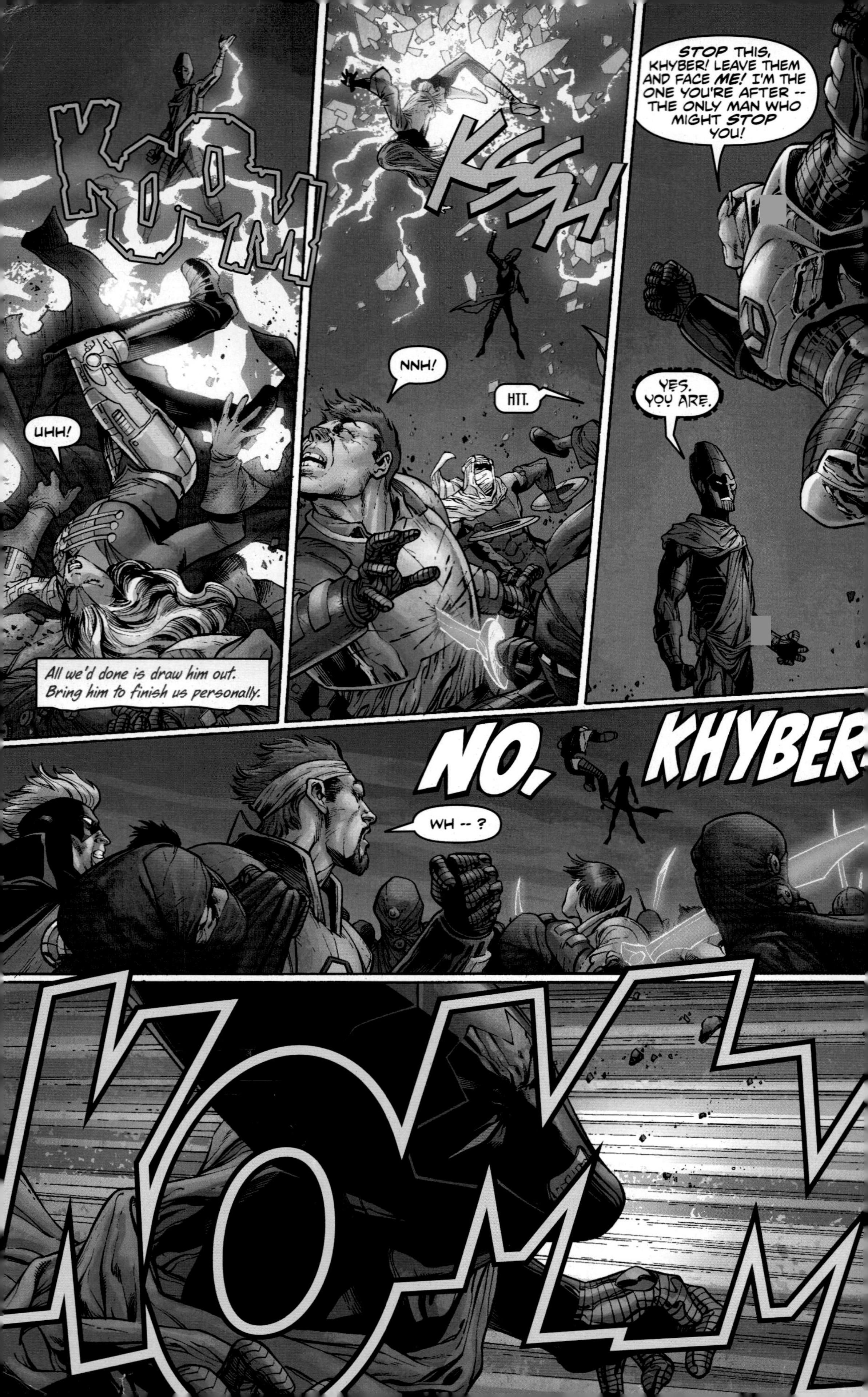
KOOOM
UHH!
All we'd done is draw him out. Bring him to finish us personally.
KSSH
NNH!
HTT.
STOP THIS, KHYBER! LEAVE THEM AND FACE ME! I'M THE ONE YOU'RE AFTER -- THE ONLY MAN WHO MIGHT STOP YOU!
YES. YOU ARE.
NO, KHYBER
WH -- ?
KOOOM

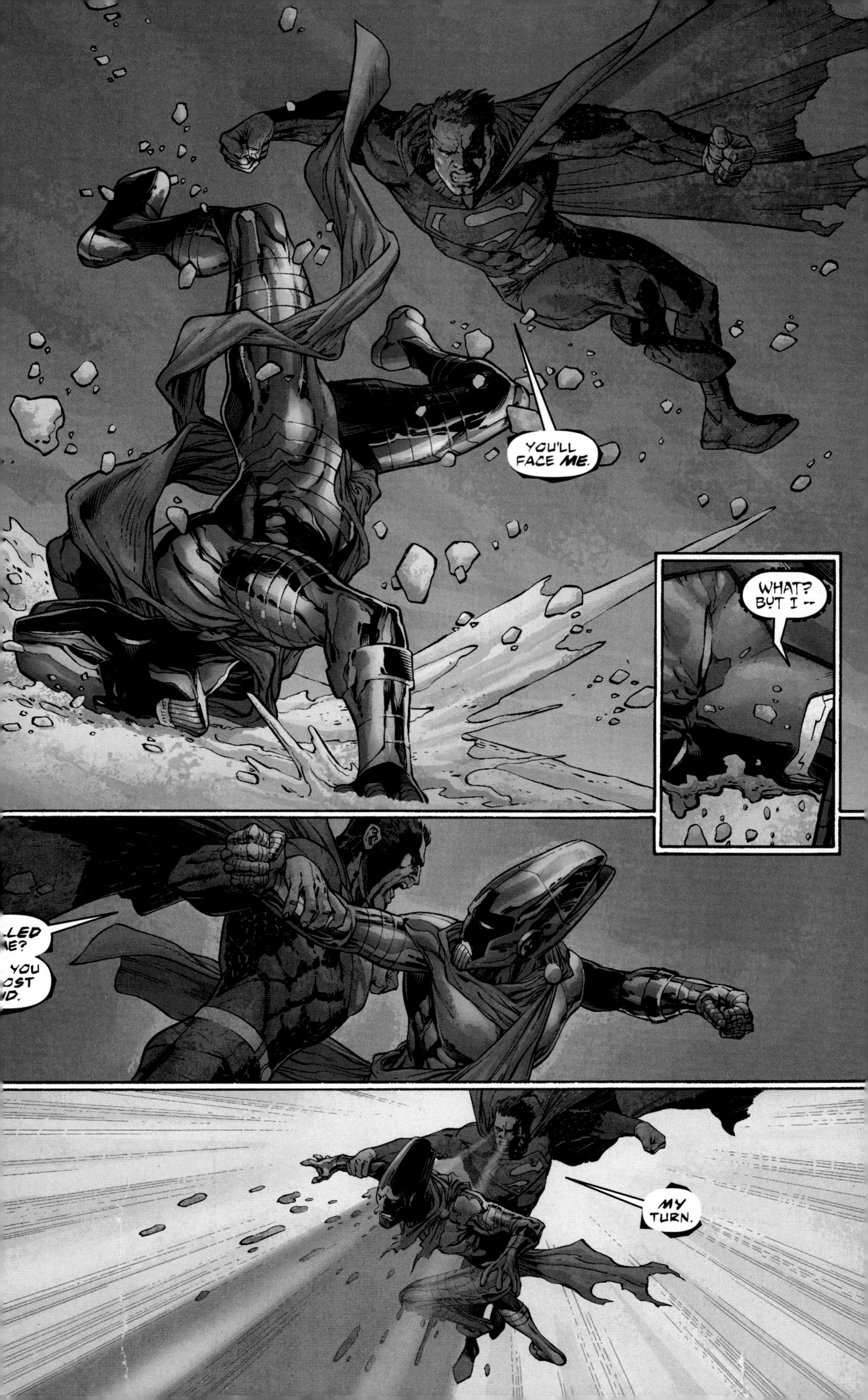
YOU'LL FACE *ME*.
WHAT? BUT I --
...LED ...E? ... YOU ...OST ...D.
MY TURN.

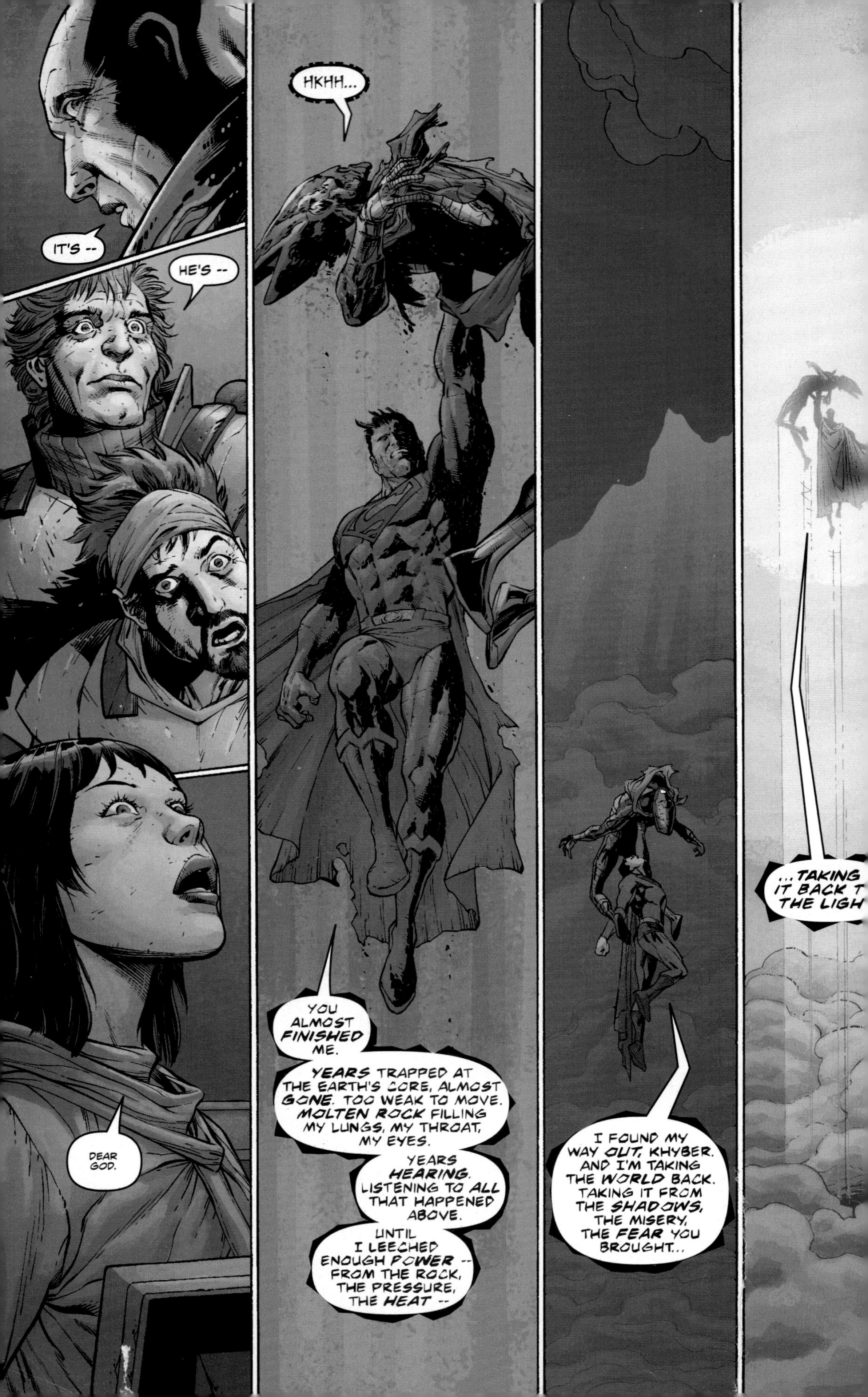

IT'S --
HE'S --
DEAR GOD.
HKHH...
YOU ALMOST FINISHED ME.
YEARS TRAPPED AT THE EARTH'S CORE, ALMOST GONE. TOO WEAK TO MOVE. MOLTEN ROCK FILLING MY LUNGS, MY THROAT, MY EYES.
YEARS HEARING. LISTENING TO ALL THAT HAPPENED ABOVE.
UNTIL I LEECHED ENOUGH POWER -- FROM THE ROCK, THE PRESSURE, THE HEAT --
I FOUND MY WAY OUT, KHYBER. AND I'M TAKING THE WORLD BACK. TAKING IT FROM THE SHADOWS, THE MISERY, THE FEAR YOU BROUGHT...
...TAKING IT BACK T THE LIGH

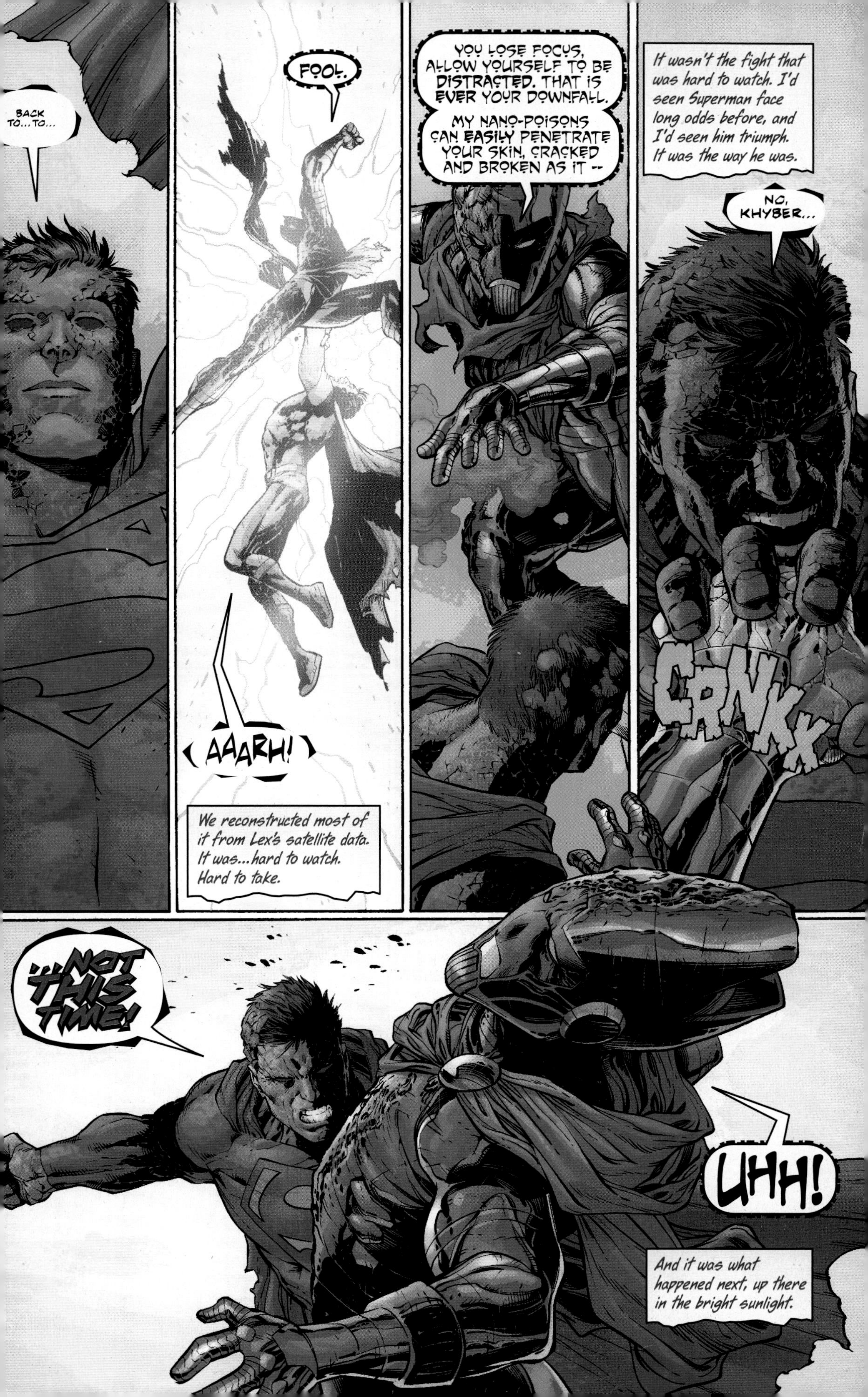
BACK TO... TO...
FOOL.
AAARH!
We reconstructed most of it from Lex's satellite data. It was...hard to watch. Hard to take.
YOU LOSE FOCUS, ALLOW YOURSELF TO BE DISTRACTED. THAT IS EVER YOUR DOWNFALL.
MY NANO-POISONS CAN EASILY PENETRATE YOUR SKIN, CRACKED AND BROKEN AS IT --
It wasn't the fight that was hard to watch. I'd seen Superman face long odds before, and I'd seen him triumph. It was the way he was.
NO, KHYBER...
CRNKK
...NOT THIS TIME!
UHH!
And it was what happened next, up there in the bright sunlight.

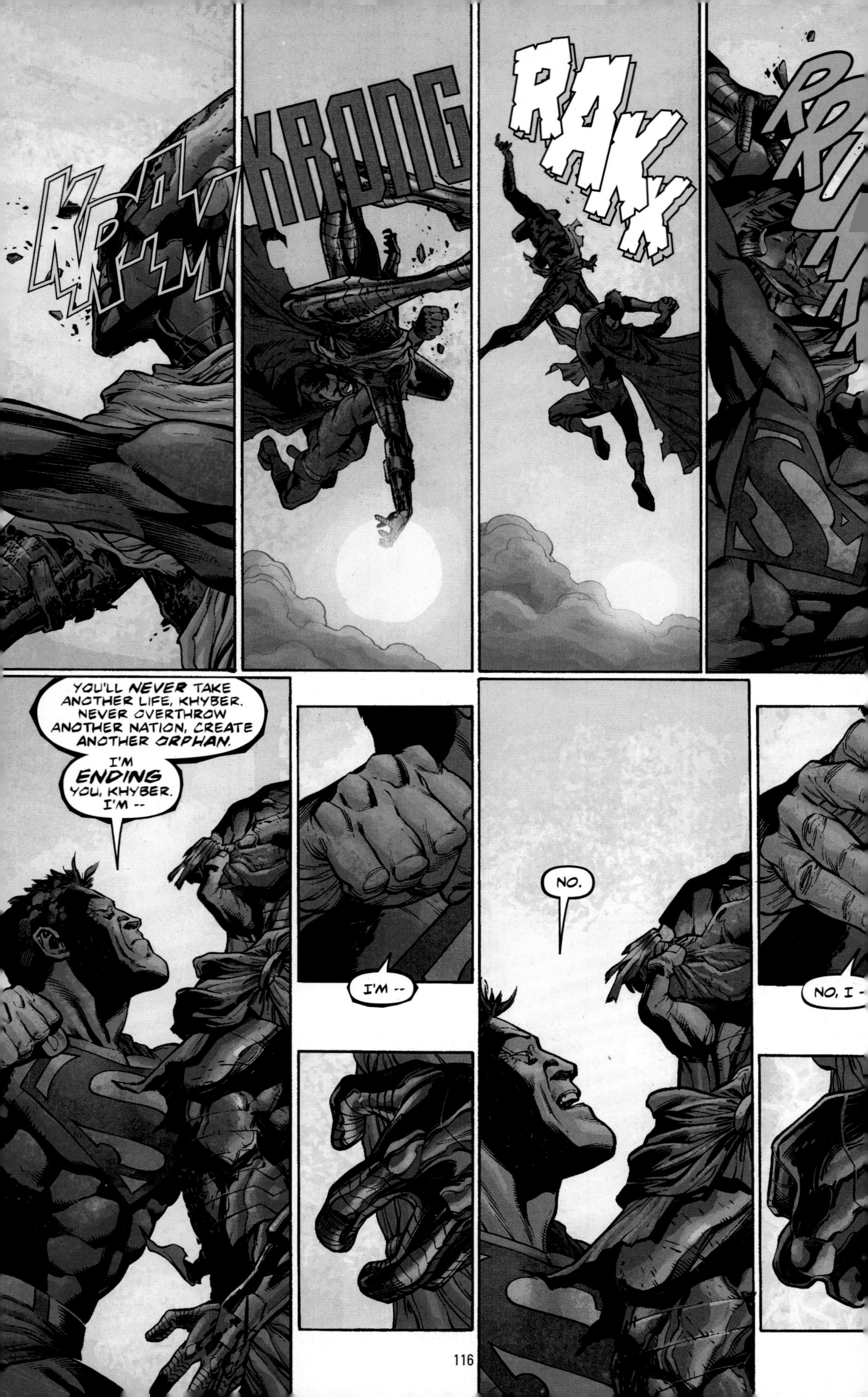
KRAM
KRONG
RAKK
YOU'LL NEVER TAKE ANOTHER LIFE, KHYBER. NEVER OVERTHROW ANOTHER NATION, CREATE ANOTHER ORPHAN.
I'M ENDING YOU, KHYBER. I'M --
I'M --
NO.
NO, I -

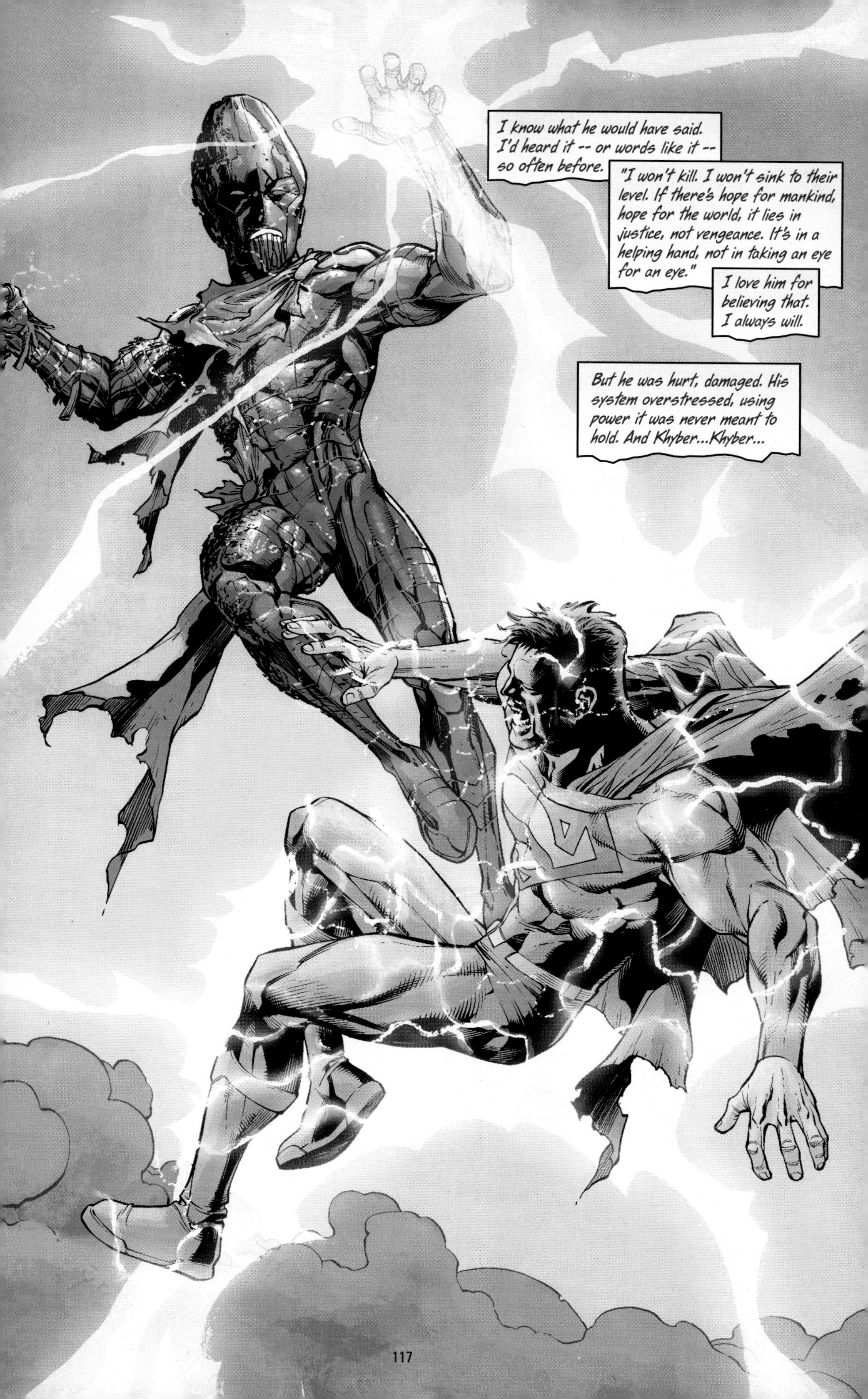
I know what he would have said. I'd heard it -- or words like it -- so often before.
"I won't kill. I won't sink to their level. If there's hope for mankind, hope for the world, it lies in justice, not vengeance. It's in a helping hand, not in taking an eye for an eye."
I love him for believing that. I always will.
But he was hurt, damaged. His system overstressed, using power it was never meant to hold. And Khyber...Khyber...

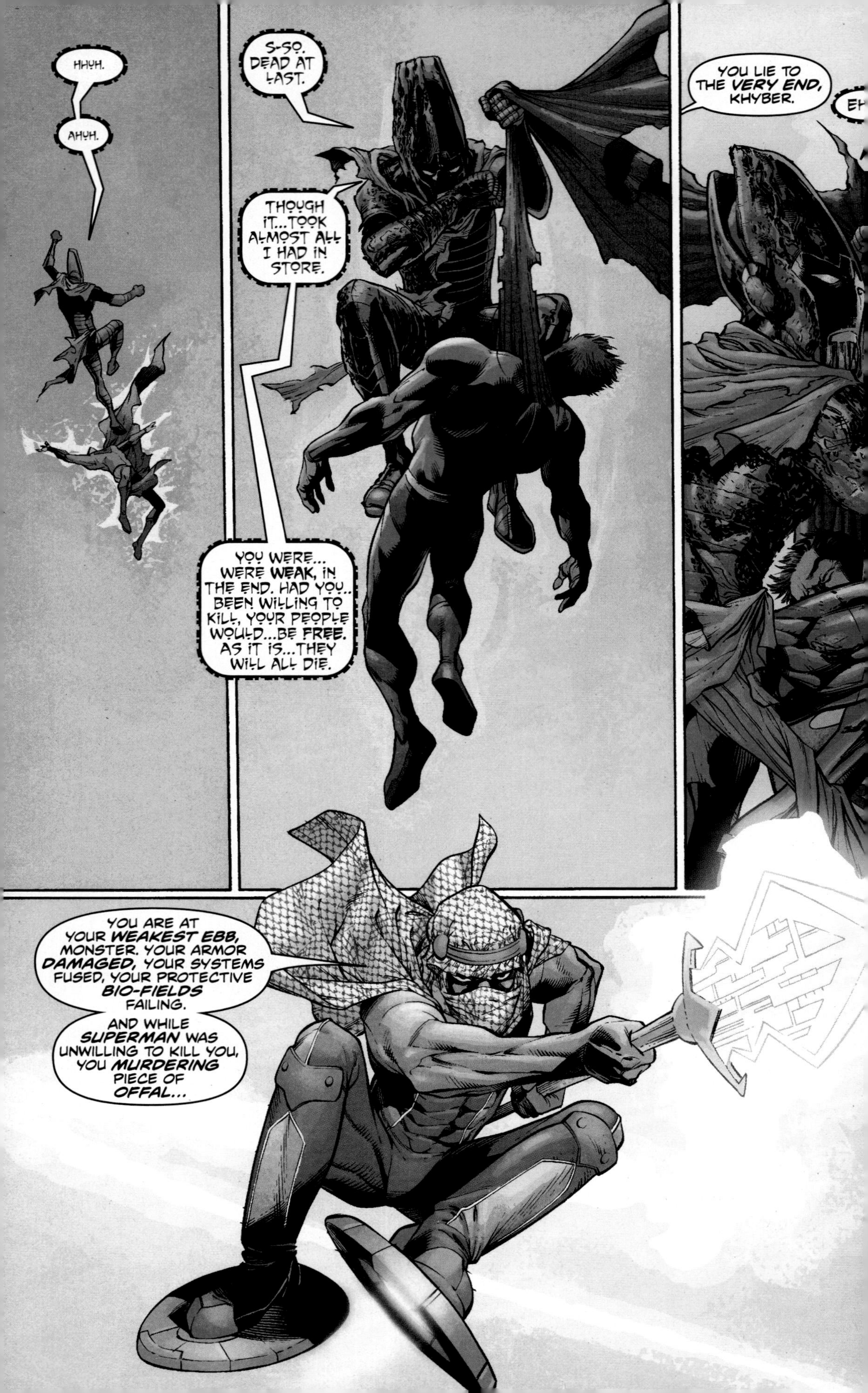
HHUH.
AHUH.
S-SO. DEAD AT LAST.
THOUGH IT...TOOK ALMOST ALL I HAD IN STORE.
YOU WERE... WERE WEAK, IN THE END. HAD YOU... BEEN WILLING TO KILL, YOUR PEOPLE WOULD...BE FREE. AS IT IS...THEY WILL ALL DIE.
YOU LIE TO THE VERY END, KHYBER.
YOU ARE AT YOUR WEAKEST EBB, MONSTER. YOUR ARMOR DAMAGED, YOUR SYSTEMS FUSED, YOUR PROTECTIVE BIO-FIELDS FAILING.
AND WHILE SUPERMAN WAS UNWILLING TO KILL YOU, YOU MURDERING PIECE OF OFFAL...

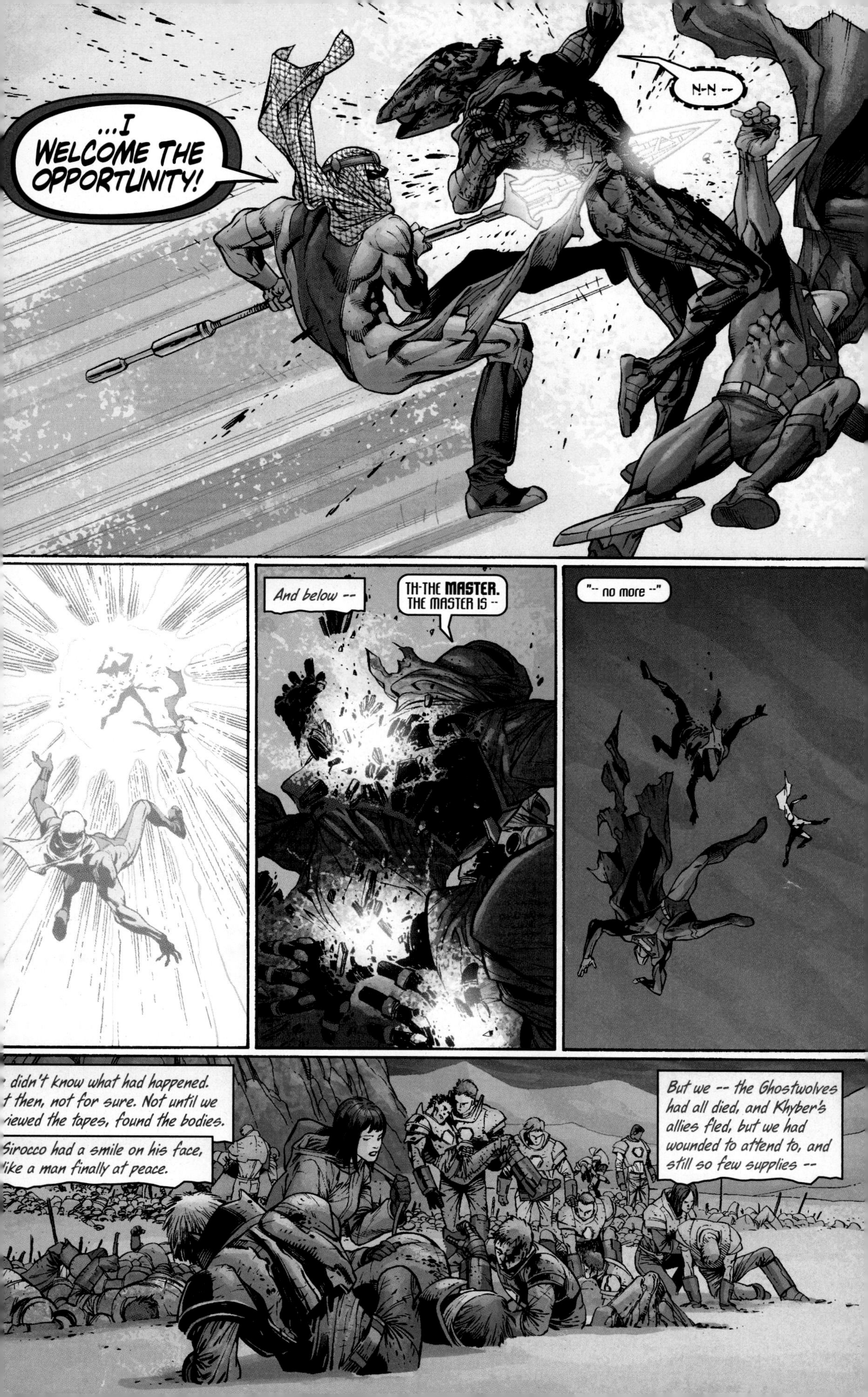
...I WELCOME THE OPPORTUNITY!
N-N! --
And below --
TH-THE **MASTER.** THE MASTER IS --
"-- no more --"
didn't know what had happened. t then, not for sure. Not until we viewed the tapes, found the bodies.
Sirocco had a smile on his face, like a man finally at peace.
But we -- the Ghostwolves had all died, and Khyber's allies fled, but we had wounded to attend to, and still so few supplies --

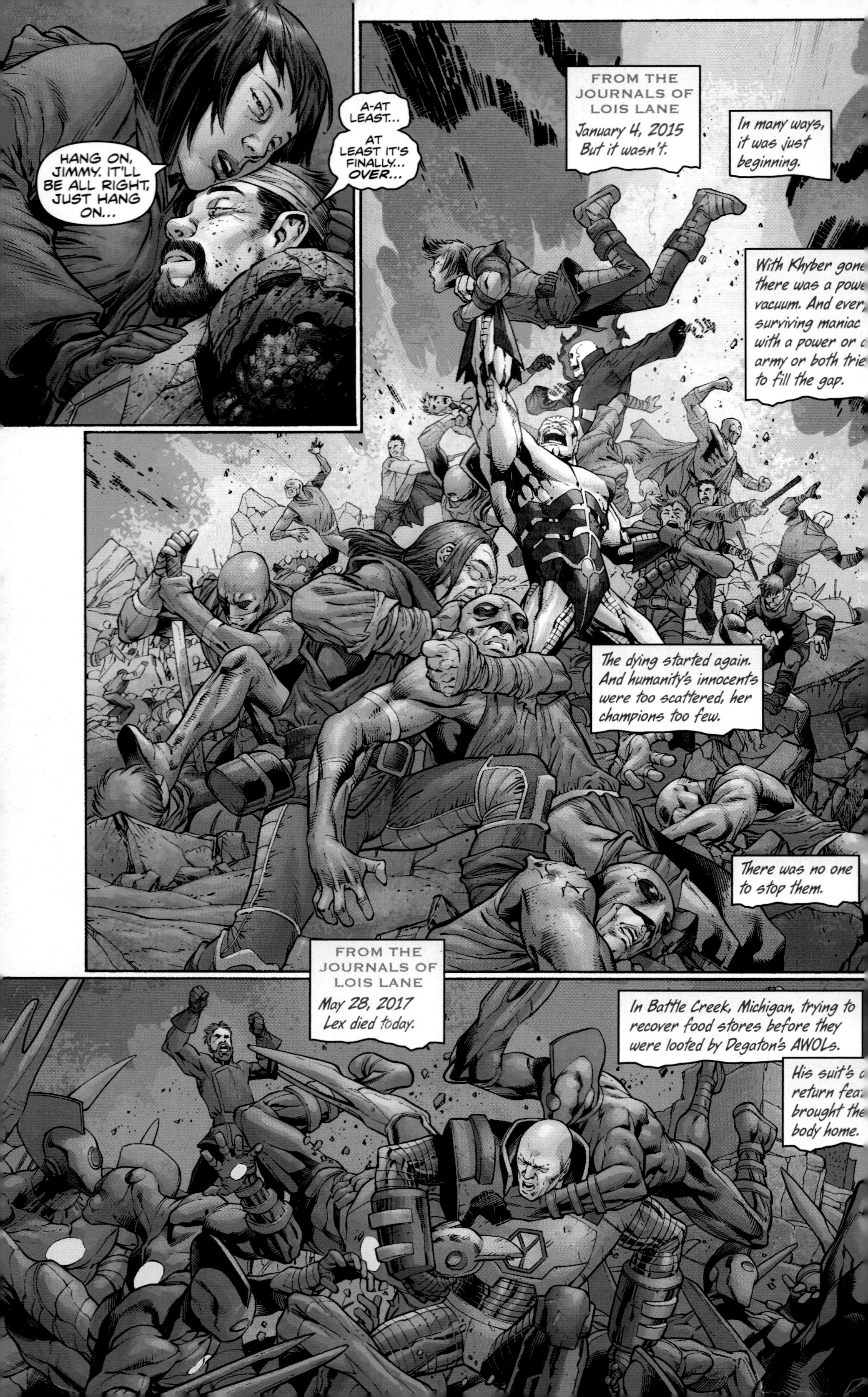
HANG ON, JIMMY. IT'LL BE ALL RIGHT, JUST HANG ON...
A-AT LEAST...
AT LEAST IT'S FINALLY... OVER...
FROM THE JOURNALS OF LOIS LANE
January 4, 2015
But it wasn't.
In many ways, it was just beginning.
With Khyber gone there was a power vacuum. And every surviving maniac with a power or an army or both tried to fill the gap.
The dying started again. And humanity's innocents were too scattered, her champions too few.
There was no one to stop them.
FROM THE JOURNALS OF LOIS LANE
May 28, 2017
Lex died today.
In Battle Creek, Michigan, trying to recover food stores before they were looted by Degaton's AWOLs.
His suit's return fea brought the body home.

We buried him next to Superman.

I don't know if either of them would have wanted it that way, but it seemed appropriate.

FROM THE JOURNALS OF LOIS LANE
September 9, 2020
We've been in the Cascade Mountains a full year now. The stores Luthor had in his lair here should last us a generation or more.

But it's been a bad year. The Flash's damaged metabolism finally took him, younger than me and dead of old age.

Green Lantern left Earth in February, seeking help. She said she'd be back in three weeks. And Wonder Woman...nobody knows.

FROM THE JOURNALS OF LOIS LANE
September 7, 2032
The MacGuire twins turned six today. They're happy. They've never known a different life.

But we don't have the population to survive as a community. We need to find other survivors. Other people.

FROM THE JOURNALS OF LOIS LANE
January 3, 2039
No word from the group that headed for the coast, to check into those lights. I hope they stayed because they found something good.

At least the sun finally came back.

FROM THE JOURNALS OF ~~LOIS LANE~~ James Olsen
March 13, 2045
Sorry, Lois. I guess the sun came back too late.

At least I brought you home. At least I'm still strong enough for that.

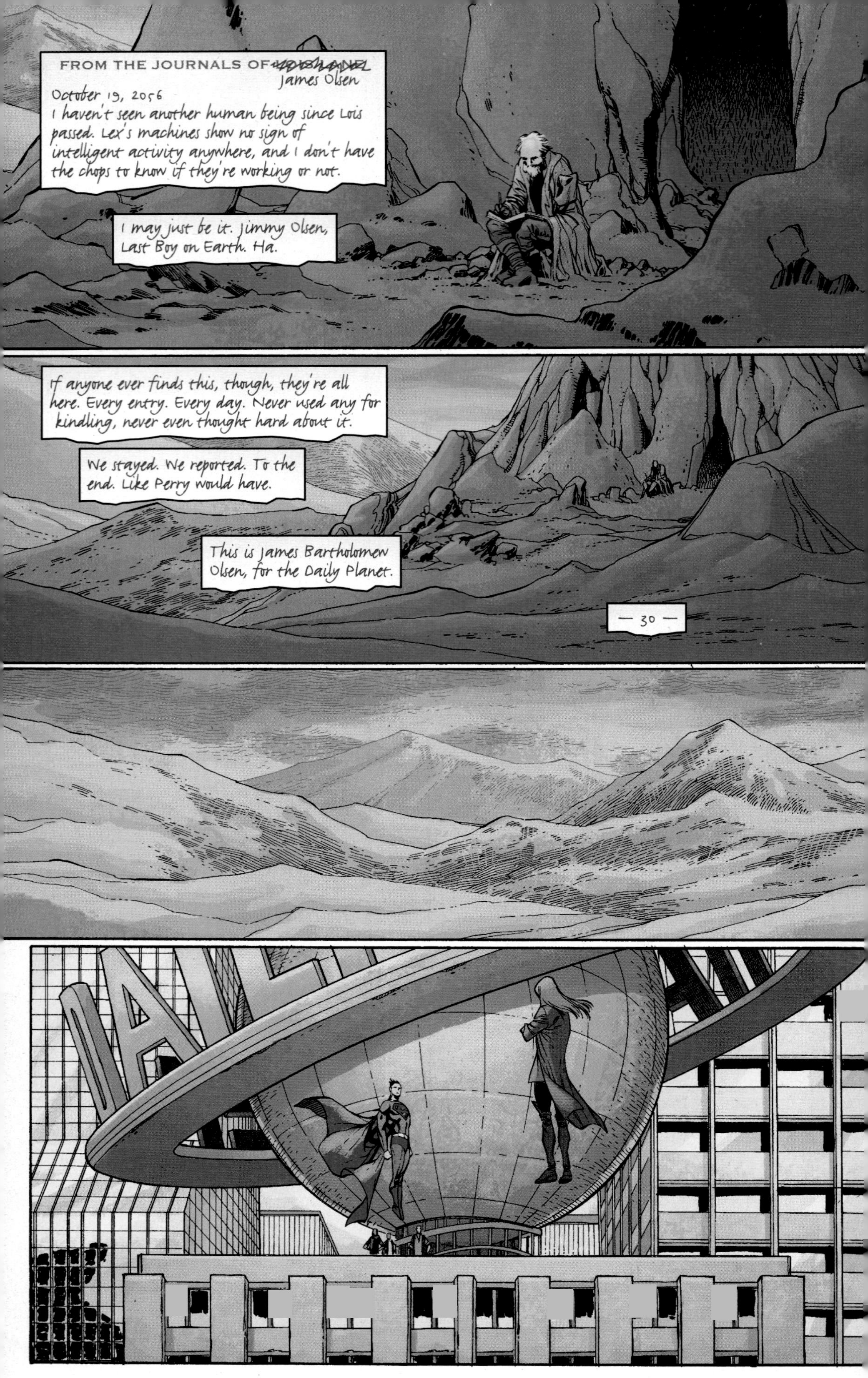
FROM THE JOURNALS OF ~~LOIS LANE~~ James Olsen
October 19, 2056
I haven't seen another human being since Lois passed. Lex's machines show no sign of intelligent activity anywhere, and I don't have the chops to know if they're working or not.
I may just be it. Jimmy Olsen, Last Boy on Earth. Ha.
If anyone ever finds this, though, they're all here. Every entry. Every day. Never used any for kindling, never even thought hard about it.
We stayed. We reported. To the end. Like Perry would have.
This is James Bartholomew Olsen, for the Daily Planet.
— 30 —

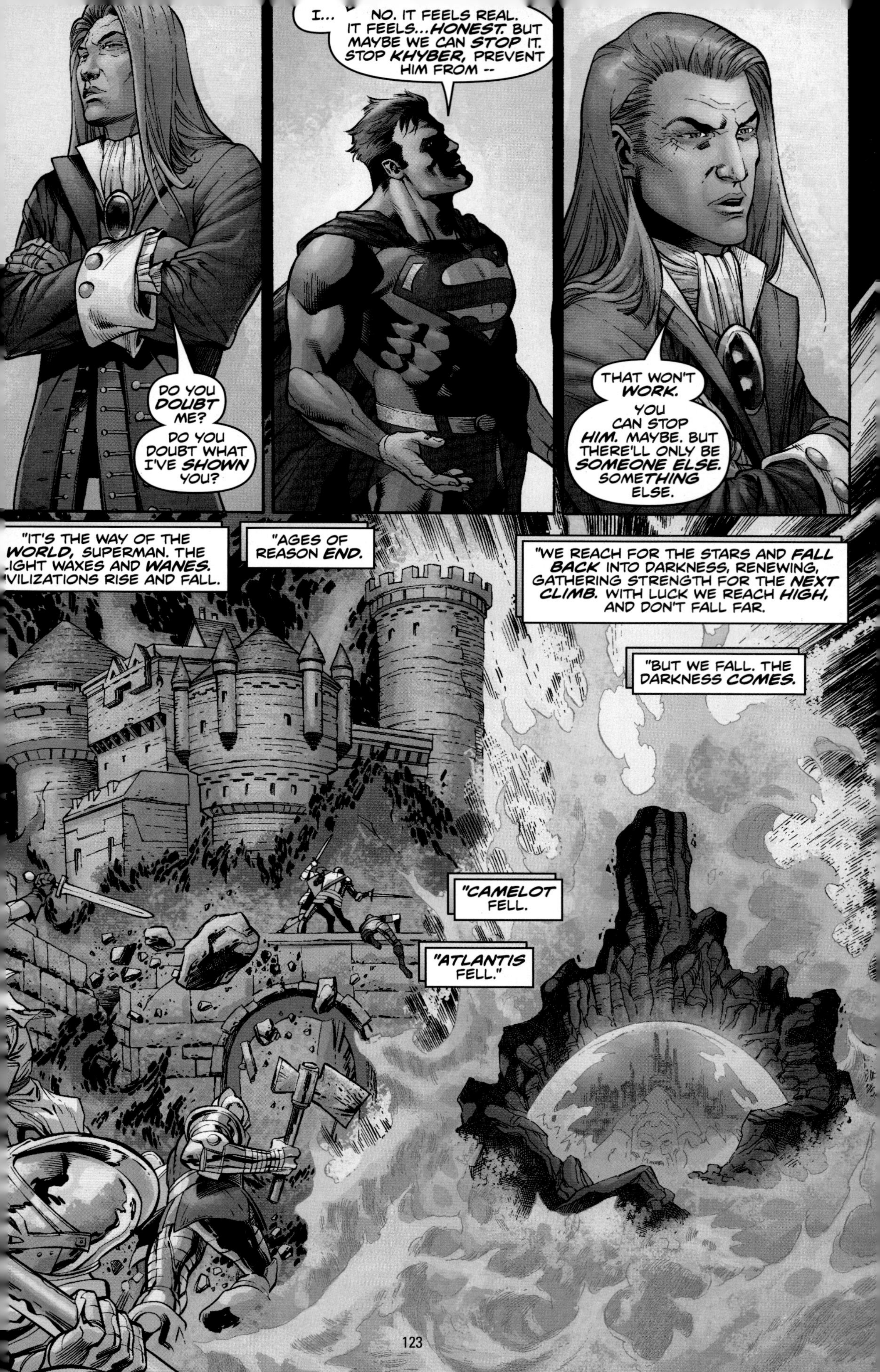
I...
NO. IT FEELS REAL. IT FEELS... HONEST. BUT MAYBE WE CAN STOP IT. STOP KHYBER, PREVENT HIM FROM --
DO YOU DOUBT ME?
DO YOU DOUBT WHAT I'VE SHOWN YOU?
THAT WON'T WORK.
YOU CAN STOP HIM. MAYBE. BUT THERE'LL ONLY BE SOMEONE ELSE. SOMETHING ELSE.
"IT'S THE WAY OF THE WORLD, SUPERMAN. THE LIGHT WAXES AND WANES. CIVILIZATIONS RISE AND FALL.
"AGES OF REASON END.
"WE REACH FOR THE STARS AND FALL BACK INTO DARKNESS, RENEWING, GATHERING STRENGTH FOR THE NEXT CLIMB. WITH LUCK WE REACH HIGH, AND DON'T FALL FAR.
"BUT WE FALL. THE DARKNESS COMES.
"CAMELOT FELL.
"ATLANTIS FELL."

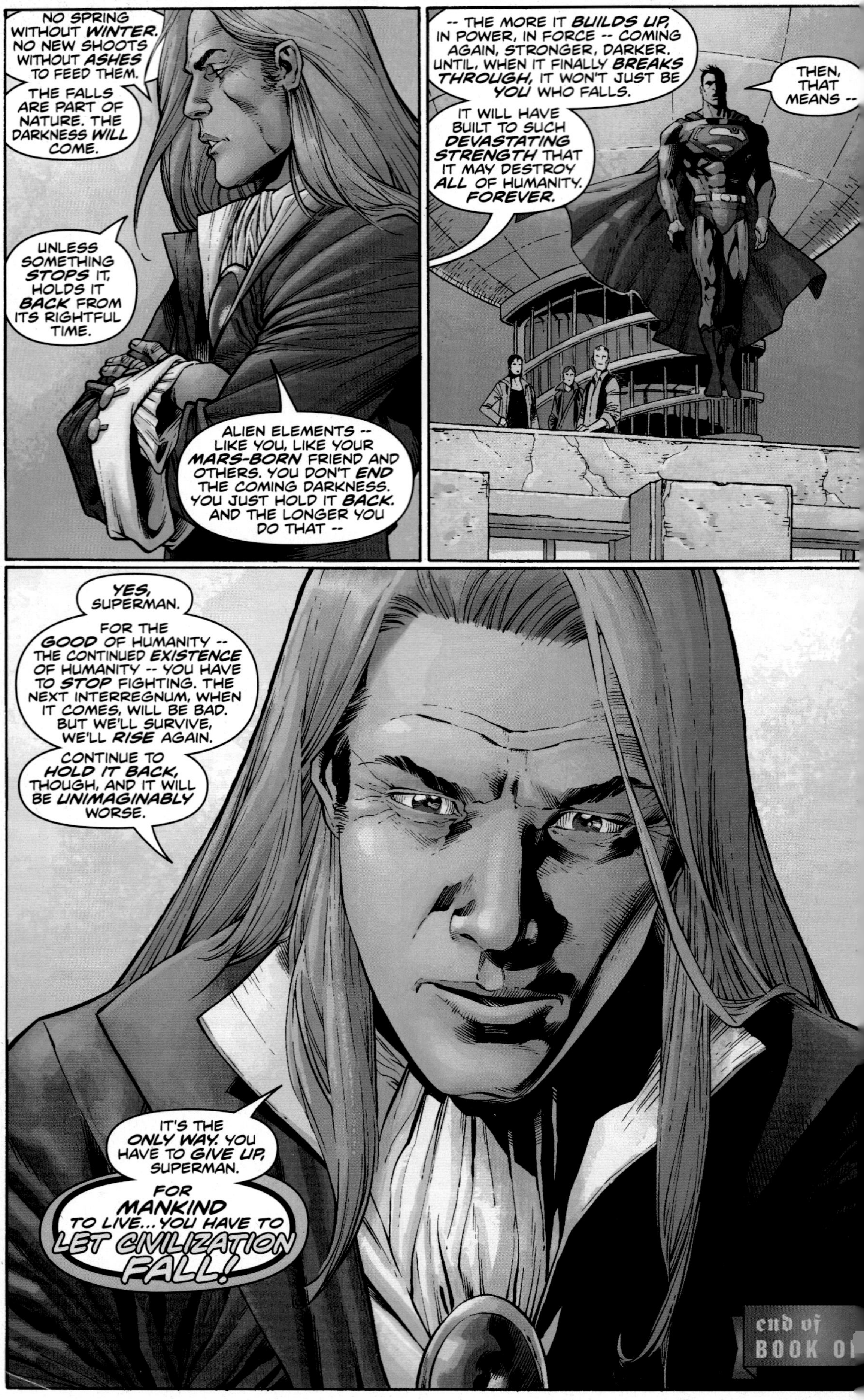
NO SPRING WITHOUT WINTER. NO NEW SHOOTS WITHOUT ASHES TO FEED THEM.
THE FALLS ARE PART OF NATURE. THE DARKNESS WILL COME.
UNLESS SOMETHING STOPS IT, HOLDS IT BACK FROM ITS RIGHTFUL TIME.
ALIEN ELEMENTS -- LIKE YOU, LIKE YOUR MARS-BORN FRIEND AND OTHERS. YOU DON'T END THE COMING DARKNESS. YOU JUST HOLD IT BACK. AND THE LONGER YOU DO THAT --
-- THE MORE IT BUILDS UP, IN POWER, IN FORCE -- COMING AGAIN, STRONGER, DARKER. UNTIL, WHEN IT FINALLY BREAKS THROUGH, IT WON'T JUST BE YOU WHO FALLS.
IT WILL HAVE BUILT TO SUCH DEVASTATING STRENGTH THAT IT MAY DESTROY ALL OF HUMANITY. FOREVER.
THEN, THAT MEANS --
YES, SUPERMAN.
FOR THE GOOD OF HUMANITY -- THE CONTINUED EXISTENCE OF HUMANITY -- YOU HAVE TO STOP FIGHTING. THE NEXT INTERREGNUM, WHEN IT COMES, WILL BE BAD. BUT WE'LL SURVIVE, WE'LL RISE AGAIN.
CONTINUE TO HOLD IT BACK, THOUGH, AND IT WILL BE UNIMAGINABLY WORSE.
IT'S THE ONLY WAY. YOU HAVE TO GIVE UP, SUPERMAN.
FOR MANKIND TO LIVE... YOU HAVE TO LET CIVILIZATION FALL!
end of BOOK O

CARLOS PACHECO SKETCHES

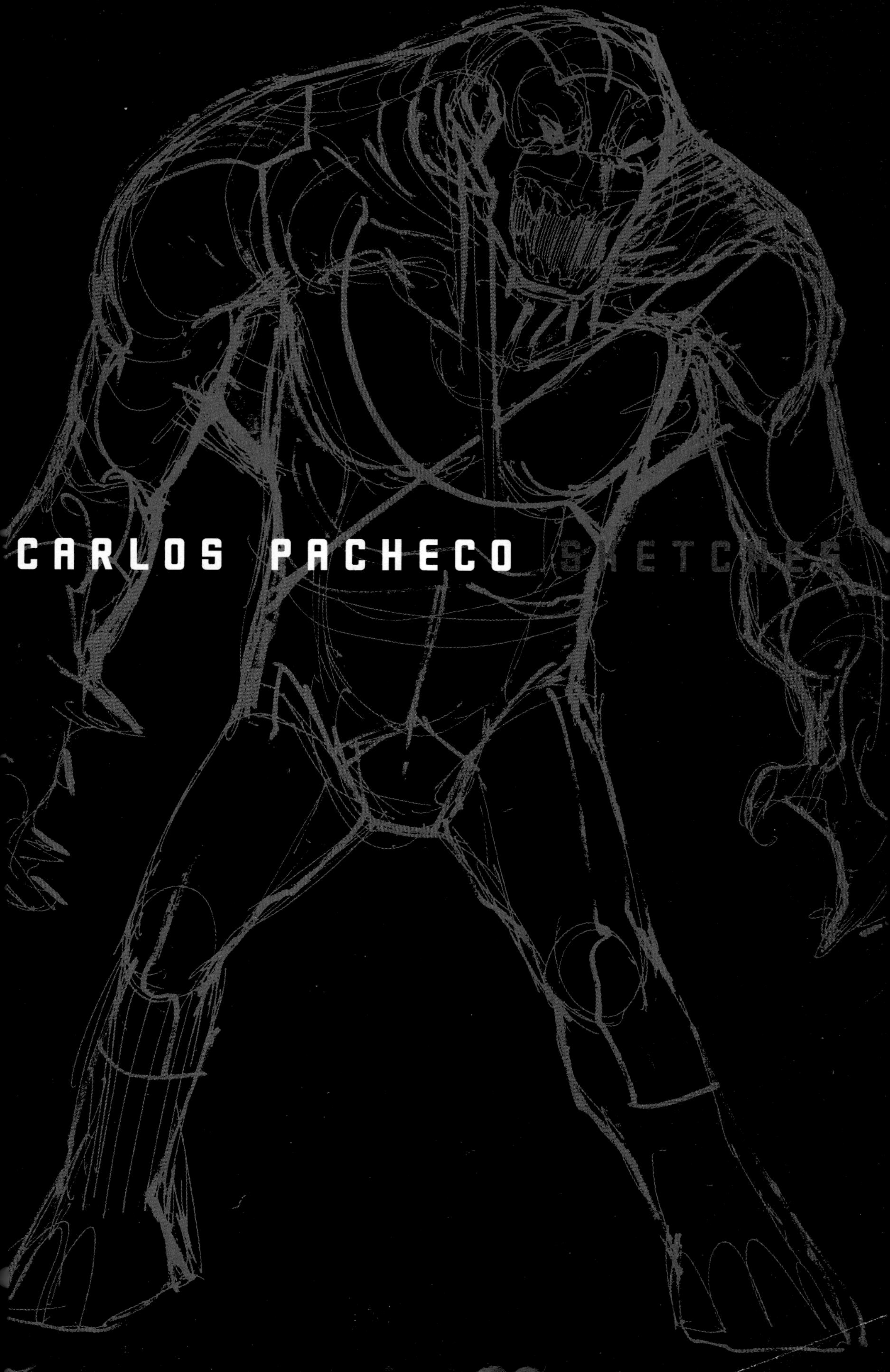

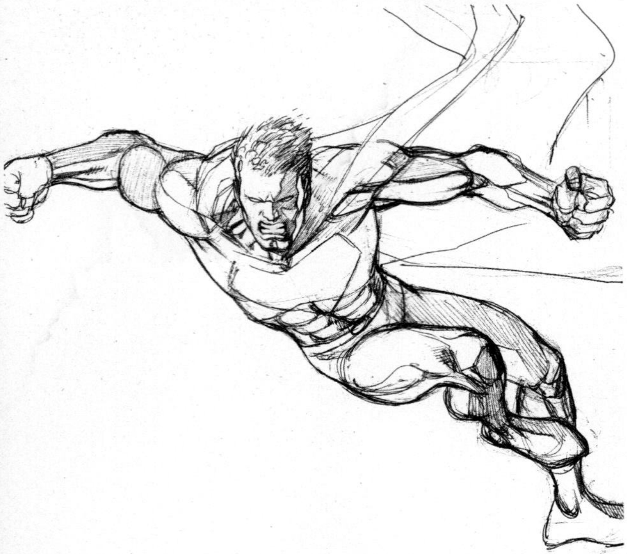

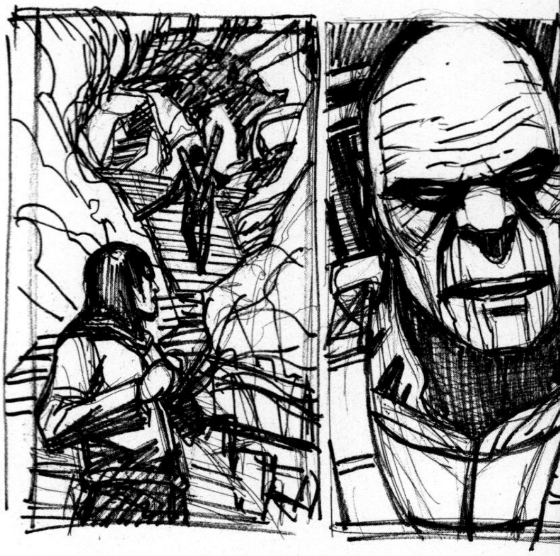

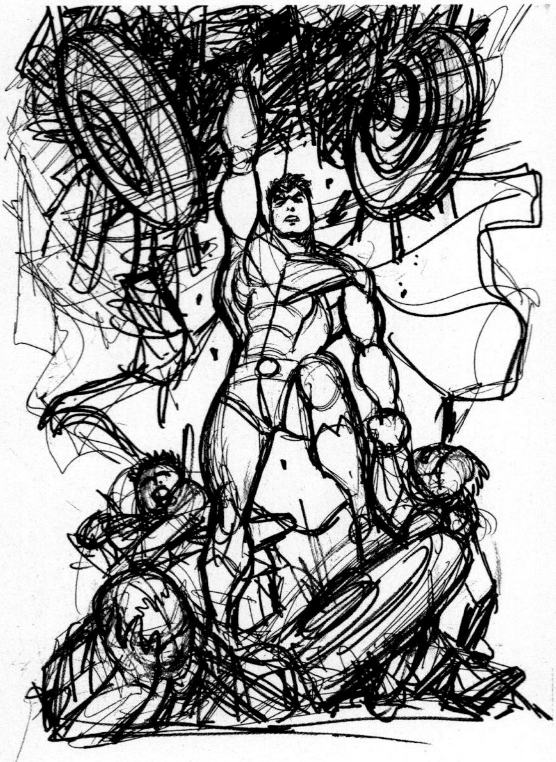

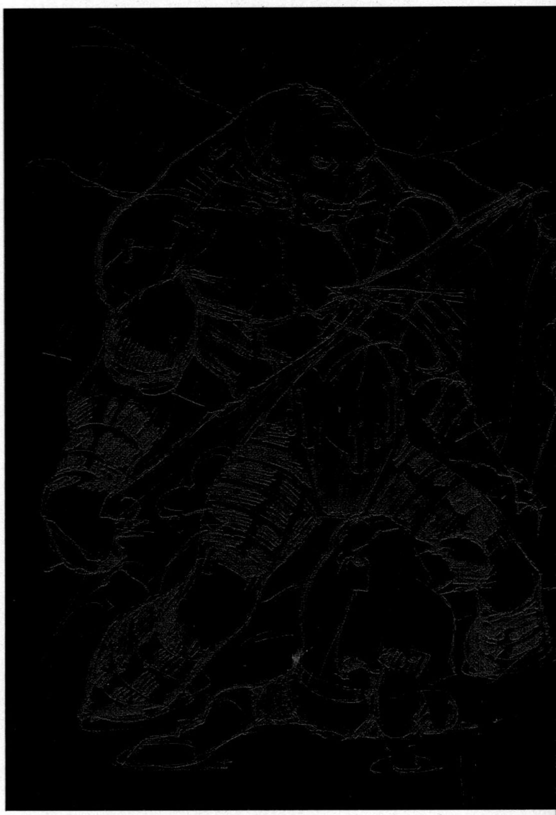

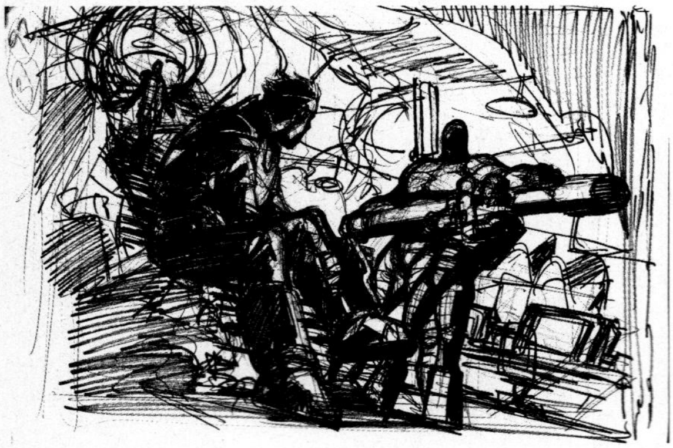

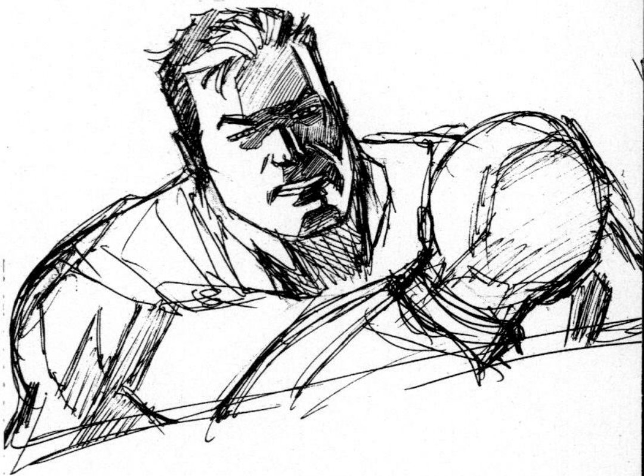

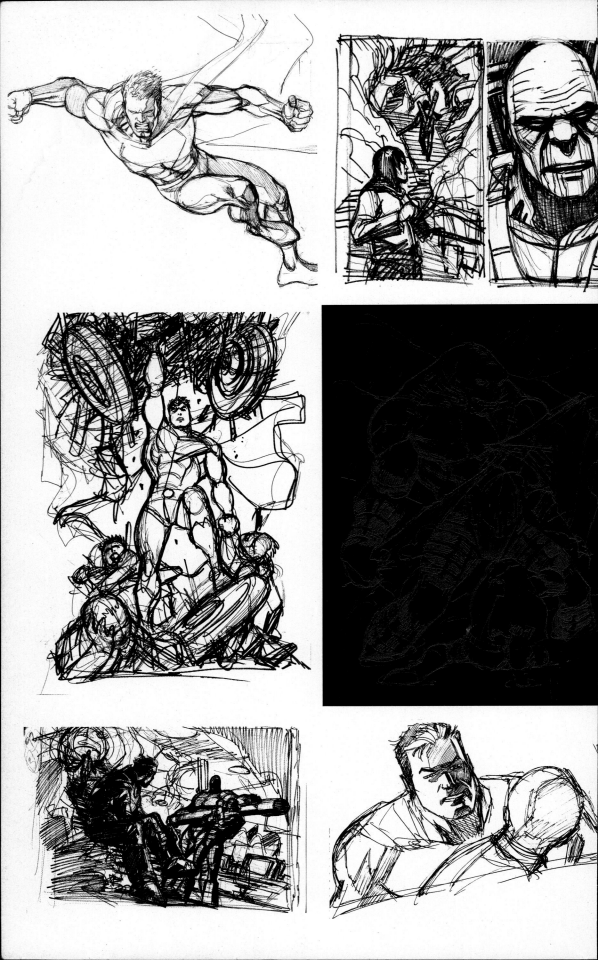

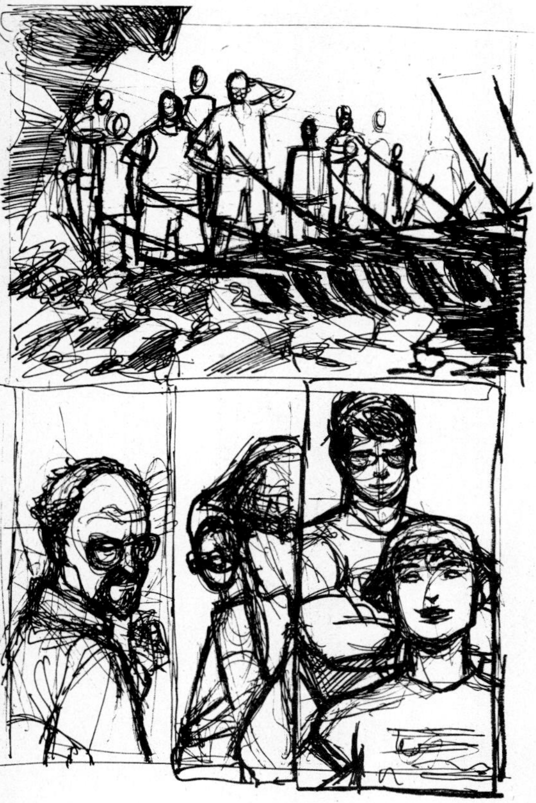

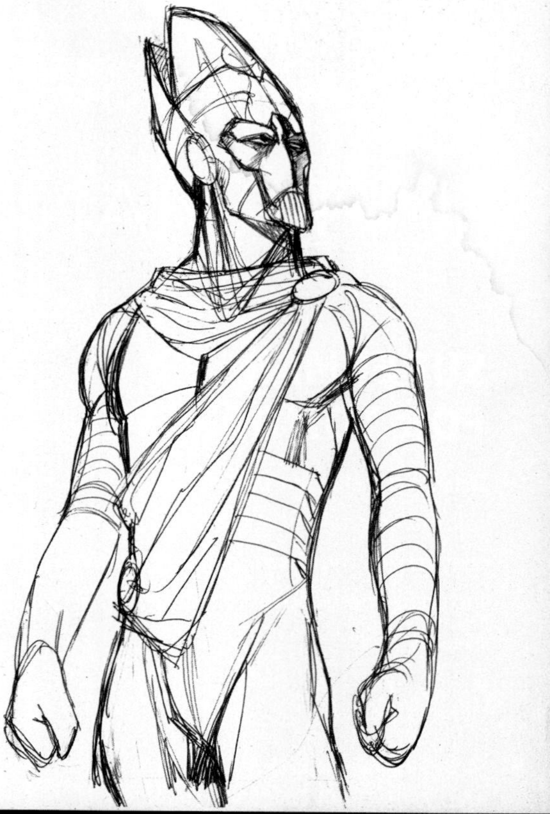

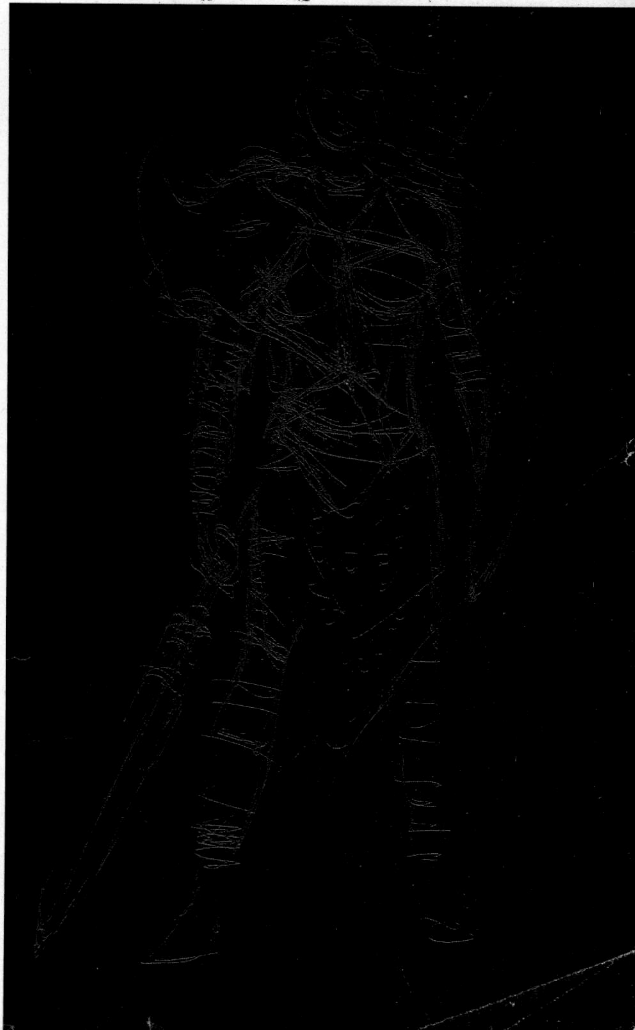

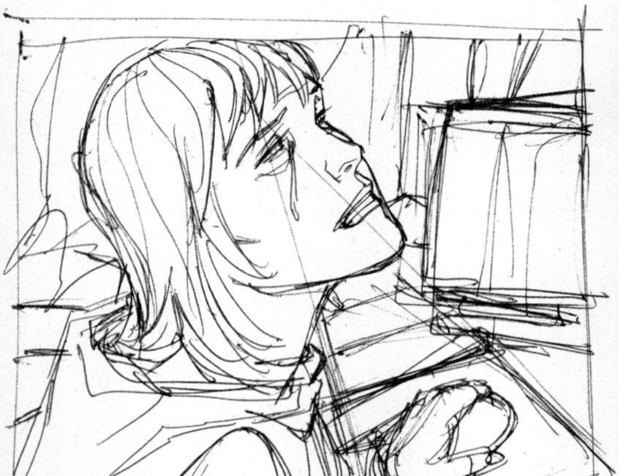

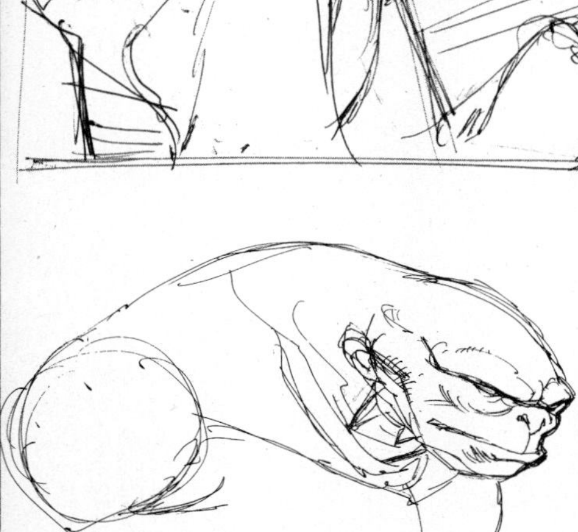

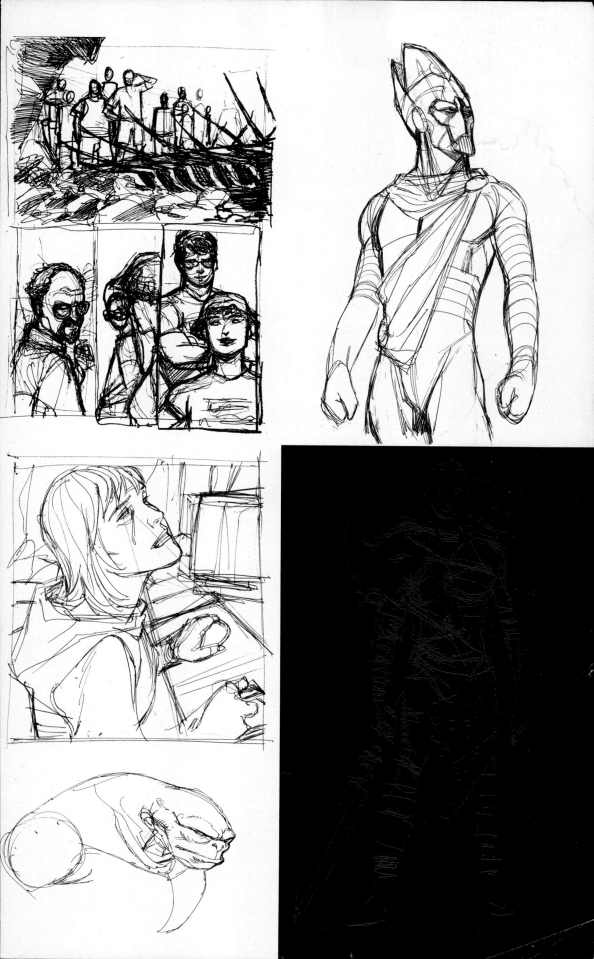

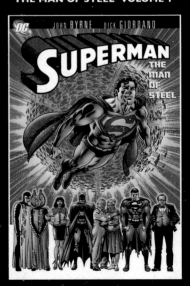
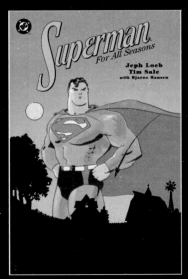